Risk and Uncertainty in Economics

Risk and Uncertainty in Economics

Essays in Honour of James L. Ford

Edited by

David G. Dickinson,
Department of Economics, University of Birmingham

Michael J. Driscoll,
Business School, Middlesex University

Somnath Sen,
Department of Economics, University of Birmingham

Edward Elgar

Published by
Edward Elgar Publishing Limited
Gower House
Croft Road
Aldershot
Hants GU11 3 HR
England

Edward Elgar Publishing Company
Old Post Road
Brookfield
Vermont 05036
USA

British Library Cataloguing in Publication Data
Risk and Uncertainty in Economics : Essays
in Honour of James L. Ford
I. Dickinson, David G.
330

Library of Congress Cataloguing in Publication Data
Risk and uncertainty in economics : essays in honour of James L. Ford
edited by David G. Dickinson, Michael J. Driscoll, Somnath Sen
p. cm.
"Published work of James L. Ford, 1960-1992" : p.
1.Risk. 2. Uncertainty. 3. Decision-making. I. Dickinson,
David G. II. Driscoll, Michael J. III. Sen, S. (Somnath)
IV. Ford, J.L.
HB615.R557 1994
330-dc20 94-15756
CIP

ISBN 1 85278 736 8

Printed and Bound in Great Britain by
Hartnolls Limited, Bodmin, Cornwall.

Contents

Figures

Tables

Contributors

C. Richard Barrett, *Department of Economics, University of Birmingham, Birmingham, UK.*

Atul A. Dar, *St Mary's University, Halifax, Nova Scotia, Canada.*

David G. Dickinson, *Department of Economics, University of Birmingham, Birmingham UK.*

Colin Dodds, *St. Mary's University, Halifax, Nova Scotia, Canada.*

Michael J. Driscoll, *Business School, Middlesex University, Hendon, Middlesex, UK.*

John D. Hey, *Department of Economics, University of York, Heslington, York, UK.*

Marcus Miller, *Department of Economics, University of Warwick, Coventry, UK.*

Andrew W. Mullineux, *Department of Economics, University of Birmingham, Birmingham, UK.*

S. Mansoob Murshed, *Northern Ireland Economic Research Centre, 46–48 University Road, Belfast, Northern Ireland.*

Prasanta K. Pattanaik, *Department of Economics, University of California, Riverside, California, USA.*

David A. Peel, *Department of Economics, University College of Wales, Aberystwyth, UK.*

Peter C.B. Phillips, *Cowles Foundation for Research in Economics, Yale University, New Haven, Connecticut, USA.*

George Shackle, *Emeritus Professor, University of Liverpool*

Somnath Sen, *Department of Economics, University of Birmingham, Birmingham, UK.*

Acknowledgements

The preparation of the manuscript would not have been possible without the financial assistance of the School of Social Sciences at the University of Birmingham.

Many thanks go to Maureen Hyde who showed great patience and understanding in typing the manuscript and dealing with the unreasonable demands of the editors.

Introduction

Professor Jim Ford retired as Mitsui Professor of Economics from the University of Birmingham in 1989. Since then he has been Emeritus Professor of Economics, while continuing with his prolific research output. In an academic life spanning over 30 years and still continuing, Jim Ford seems to have researched almost every aspect of micro- and macroeconomic behaviour. The underlying theme of risk, uncertainty and expectations forms a binding framework for most of the work he has done. The essays in this collection represent a wide diversity of issues and areas – all of which interested him at some time or other in his incredibly fruitful, active and ongoing career.

It is particularly fitting to begin with a paper by George Shackle, who has had such a profound influence on Jim's work. This will represent the final published work of an economist who was always prepared to provide an original and innovative focus to the role of uncertainty in economic life. The focus of 'The Imagined Deemed Possible ...' is essentially a restatement of how individuals, faced with a stochastic environment, form views of what is going to happen and hence determine optimal strategies. As Shackle has explained in the past, this leads him into the concept of possibility and potential surprise. He uses the entrepreneur determining investment as an example of how to apply the concept of potential surprise and argues that it captures the concept of 'animal spirits', which Keynes regarded as a key influence on investment. In so doing Shackle is also reiterating the view that potential surprise, and the analytical framework he built upon it, represents the limits which human minds can go to when forming views of the future to guide decisions.

The theoretical and statistical aspects of choice and decisions under uncertainty are dealt with in a number of contributions to this volume. John Hey has provided a most interesting commentary on Jim's own model of decision-making under uncertainty, perspective theory. He takes the tools developed by Machina to examine expected utility theory and analyses the implications of using them on perspective theory. He finds that the preference curves of the perspective approach have few constraints on their appearance, except that they be downward-sloping. Hey also discusses the explanation for Allais' Paradox provided by perspective theory, and finds it to be very different from the conventional explanation. His analysis is an encouragement to others to explore further the implications of perspective theory.

Richard Barrett and Prasanta Pattanaik present important work on decision-making under complete uncertainty. They argue that such decisions should be analysed within an ordinal utility framework, since Von Neumann and Morgenstern expected utility axioms imply or assume that probabilities can be attached to risky events. One of their main results is to demonstrate that plausible axioms defining behaviour imply that small amounts of optimism or pessimism become universal optimism or pessimism on the part of the economic agent. They evaluate various criteria for ranking actions under complete uncertainty in the light of this insight.

Peter Phillips provides important results on the characteristic function of the Dirichlet and multivariate F distribution. He derives formulae for the characteristic functions of the inverted Dirichlet and hence multivariate F distributions. The analysis involves a new function with multiple arguments that extends the confluent hypergeometric function of the second kind. This function and its properties are studied in the paper, and a simple integral representation is given which is useful for numerical work. A special case connected with the multivariate t distribution is also explored.

Moving into the field of monetary economics, Andrew Mullineux examines the role of bank regulation in an economy with business cycles. He first considers the basic issue of why banks need to be regulated, and provides a comprehensive review of this important policy issue. The actual policy implemented in a number of countries is used to provide a basis for this analysis. The relationship between bank regulation and deposit insurance is next examined, and attention given to the interaction between these two measures for enhancing the stability of the banking system. He then uses the discussion of these key issues to consider whether the current policy stance represented by the Basle Committee is correct, or whether there is a better way forward.

Michael Driscoll analyses the role of monetary policy when macroeconomic relationships are stochastic. He divides his analysis into three parts. First, he considers how the stance of monetary policy can be measured when there is uncertainty about the state of the economy. This is a vital question for policy-makers responsible for setting the monetary policy levers, and one that appears to be so often incorrectly answered. Driscoll suggests ways in which this may be better achieved, essentially by a careful diagnosis of what is the appropriate operational definition of money. He provides a set of criteria for selecting one aggregate rather than another, both on theoretical and empirical grounds. He then considers the problem of using monetary policy when it is not known what influence money actually has on the economy. He reviews the different models used to direct policy and outlines how the issue could be resolved by empirical testing. He concludes that the lessons of past work are that policy-makers need to exercise considerable caution in operating monetary policy, and that the 'look at everything' approach may be the least risky alternative available.

David Dickinson considers the role of two sources of uncertainty in the precautionary demand for reserves. He starts by arguing that the precautionary demand has been developed from both a dynamic and static standpoint. In the dynamic context, the need for reserves results from uncertainty about how long assets will be held before liquidation is required to meet unexpected expenditure. In the static framework, the uncertainty relates to the volume of expenditure. He is interested in exploring a model where both volume and holding period uncertainty exist. By developing such a synthesis model, he is able to investigate the interaction between these two forms of uncertainty and relate it to the type of liquidation cost structure chosen. He is also able to relate the results he presents to discussion of the demand for money and, in particular, to the 'buffer-stock' approach which has received a good deal of attention in the recent literature. He argues that a full recognition of holding period uncertainty could provide one way of explaining the apparent instability in the demand for money and the need for lagged money balances to appear as an explanatory variable before money demand can be successfully explained.

Colin Dodds (with Atul Dar) looks at the demand for policy loans emanating out of the life insurance sector, using a quarterly model with Canadian data. The life insurance sector is an important source of long-term capital. The flow of investible funds from this sector depends primarily on household decisions regarding the purchase of new policies and the continuation of old policies. However, the existence of contracts which permit holders to borrow against surrender of policies implies that the magnitude of policy loans affects the availability of investible funds. The volatility and concomitant uncertainty arising out of policy loans seriously affect the investment activities of life insurers. Yet, there are few studies on the recent behaviour of policy loans in either Canada or the United States. This study by the authors is one of the very few undertaken empirically on this interesting issue. It examines the short-term behaviour of policy loans in Canada during the period of 1977–87, when a significant structural shift seems to have taken place in this market.

Finally, a set of papers deals with issues in applied macroeconomics. David Peel's paper provides new empirical tools which investigate the now well-known issue of efficiency in forward exchange markets and the appropriate empirical methods of testing such efficiency. The forward exchange rate has been found often to be a biased and inefficient predictor of the future spot rate using time-series data. This, of course, also has serious implications for the many theoretical models in open economy macroeconomics which use rational expectations (or perfect myopic foresight) to explain stylized facts regarding policy impact and exchange rate volatility including the presence of bubbles. Peel uses a new and 'high quality' source of survey expectations. This generates survey data on exchange rate expectations which, *a priori*, will not contain any risk premium. Using a new empirical test, he presents evidence that expectations did not possess ex-post properties demanded by the rational expectations hypothesis. On the other hand, there is evidence that a time-varying risk premium might also exist.

Mansoob Murshed analyses the Third World debt crisis in a novel theoretical model which attempts to explain crucial stylized facts in a major area of international finance. The bargaining model between debtor and creditor is characterized by asymmetric information. However, unlike previous principal-agent models in this genre, both debtor and creditor players can improve the probability of the good state of nature by engaging in effort and action, respectively. There is, therefore, double moral hazard since the usual moral hazard arguments apply to both sides. The resultant market failure raises equity problems in addition to the standard efficiency problems. The latter arises since non-cooperative (Nash–Cournot) behaviour leads to second-best outcomes regarding the applications of effort (by debtor) and action (by creditor). The former arises since the creditor can pass on most of the burden of preventive action to debtors, thus raising equity problems. These problems are intensified when insurance is offered asymmetrically to creditors alone.

Standard macroeconomic models rarely emphasize the multiplicity of interest rates that characterize real economies – even when presented in stylized form. That this factor has major consequences for policy decisions is clear from the following quote from Keynes: 'The short term rate of interest is easily controlled by the monetary authority ... but the long term rate may be more recalcitrant when once it has fallen to a level which, on the basis of past experience and present expectations of future monetary policy, is considered unsafe by representative opinion'. In an important paper, Marcus Miller exploits this theme and shows how the impact of monetary and fiscal policy can be studied when future short-term rates of interest differ from the current rate, and thus, the rate on consols tends to differ systematically from the current short rate in the presence of forward-looking behaviour. A large variety of interesting cases are analysed when the short rate is treated as an opportunity cost of holding money while the long rate is taken as the appropriate measure of the cost of borrowing funds for real investment. The cases include unanticipated monetary and fiscal shocks, as well as policy shocks which are known in advance (announcement effects), and those which are believed with probability less than unity.

Somnath Sen contributes a paper which looks at the impact of monetary policy on output in a model with disequilibrium features. The model he uses is classical in the sense that it includes a quantity theory and a theory of loanable funds. Rational expectations are assumed throughout. However, non-neutrality of money arises because of rigidities which exist in the operation of markets. By considering a number of different models with disequilibrium features (in the sense that it is the short side of the market which determines quantity), Sen demonstrates that the existence of disequilibrium is not, on its own, sufficient to generate non-neutrality. It is the underlying behavioural assumptions which determine the structure of the model and hence the neutrality, or otherwise, of monetary policy

The wide range of the papers here complements the range of Jim Ford's own work in economics. This volume is a tribute to Jim's work, but it is not a final celebration. He continues to be prolific in producing research output, to help new students and old practitioners with guidance, as well as to provide us with insights into issues of theory and policy – and long may he continue to do so.

1. The Imagined Deemed Possible: The Germ of the Process of History

George Shackle

Imagination is the gift of mind whose work must precede that of any other. It is this gift, drawing on suggestions from the environing scene and from stored knowledge, which provides the entities that reason and experience can employ to make plans of action and of enterprise. Enterprise indeed is imagination actualized. Enterprise begins with investment, the bringing into being of durable instruments for the sake of the revenues, net of operating expense, that the businessman hopes they will yield in time to come. If he can suppose those revenues, in total, to exceed the construction cost of the instrument, when each instalment of them is discounted to his present moment at the prevailing interest rate, he has in view a profit. But he must reckon, too, with the other possibility: that the revenues will fall short of the construction cost of the instrument, and give him a loss.

In thus describing enterprise, I have used words whose meaning must be examined with critical attention. One group of works especially is of high significance. My title speaks of the 'imagined deemed possible'. If the businessman asks himself what *will* be the outcome of his enterprise, his question can find no justifiable answer. He must ask what, within reason and his understanding of the world, *can* be the outcome at best and at worst. He must consider what is *possible*.

How can possibleness be quantified? Two extreme degrees are evidently perfect possibility and impossibility. The occurrence of something deemed perfectly possible will occasion no surprise. An occurrence which had been deemed impossible will engender the utmost surprise. Between the perfectly possible and the impossible there lies an epistemic interval where adjudged degrees of possibility can in some sense be represented by the intensities of surprise that the businessman thinks various outcomes of his investment would occasion him. My proposal, in short, is to represent degrees of possibleness by degrees of potential surprise. More briefly, we can call the latter 'degrees of disbelief'. To present the adjudged epistemic standing of an hypothesis by degrees of disbelief is to invert the usual procedure with the advantage that the list of hypotheses thus treated can be extended indefinitely without requiring any change in the epistemic standing already assigned to some hypotheses.

In asking himself for each of several feasible investments what is the best and what is the worst result that he shall deem possible for it, the businessman could treat the idea of possibleness as a simple one, not discriminable into degrees. In this case he would be assuming that an hypothetical result is possible or impossible in an absolute sense. However, it is surely unreal to suppose that his conception of the conditions governing the success or failure of his enterprise is always clear enough to allow him to speak unequivocally of a particular result as perfectly possible or perfectly impossible. The interpretation of possibleness as potential surprise gives us at once the range of intensities of potential surprise as a representation of the range of degrees of possibleness.

The businessman's attention and practical engagement of mind will be more or less powerfully attracted by a conceived enterprise or investment according to the possibleness, and to the size, of the gains and losses it seems to offer.

Within a frame of three mutually orthogonal axes, the power of an hypothetical result of an enterprise to claim attention could be represented as a function of its adjudged possibleness shown on one axis and its size of gain or loss represented on another. This power I have called ascendancy. It will be at a maximum where a small increase of gain is exactly balanced by the associated increase of potential surprise. There will be correspondingly a most ascendant hypothesis of loss. These two maxima I have called 'focus outcomes', and in my conception it is such a pair of outcomes that will represent for the businessman the character of a proposed investment in rivalry with other such proposals.

The pair of focus outcomes of an enterprise having the meaning I have suggested, bring to bear on the businessman's choice among rival investments the idea of qualifying his hopes of gain and fears of loss by the degrees of disbelief which he associates with them. Such degrees can be zero or greater than zero. It may be asked how, having shifted the problem of quantification from possibleness to potential surprise, the latter can be graduated. This problem is unreal. As he considers hypotheses of larger and larger gain, the point will come where intuitive doubt or disbelief will call a halt. Such is the point of maximum ascendancy. On the loss side, disbelief will at some point similarly cause rejection of still greater fears. To conceive of an explicit scale of potential surprise or disbelief is needless. In choosing among envisaged investments, the two focus outcomes of each of them must be considered together. The one is the emotional price of the other. The 'animal spirits' which Keynes conceives to motivate the investor have their own principles, administered, as it were, by an intellectual conscience. I am not suggesting that the businessman is a wild gambler. At his best he is one who presses imagination to the limits of the reasoned possible and brings it into actual being.

2. A Wider Perspective

John D. Hey

For many years Jim Ford has been a leading supporter of the rather heretical attempts by G.L.S. Shackle to dislodge the stranglehold of subjective expected utility (SEU) theory on the economics profession. Jim's book, *Choice, Expectation and Uncertainty*, published by Martin Robertson in 1983, was an important attempt to bring Shackle's ideas to the attention of the profession, using language that it could understand, and a methodology that it respected. In many ways, this attempt was successful, though as Graham Loomes remarked in a review in the *Economic Journal* in June 1984, 'Professor Ford faces an uphill task'. I was a witness to this task during the arduous process of bringing the manuscript to publication: Jim laboured long and hard. It is clear that Jim did not regard the task as complete for he almost immediately embarked on the further task of moving from an interpretation of Shackle's ideas to an implementation of that interpretation in the volume *Economic Choice under Uncertainty: A Perspective Theory Approach*, published by Edward Elgar (previously an editor at Martin Robertson) in 1987. I also suspect that Jim was aware that what he was doing was no longer Shacklesque but rather Fordian – though he continued to credit Shackle for the inspiration of his 'Perspective' construction. Jim Ford, like his mentor Shackle, likes to operate outside the cosy circles of convention. So he distanced himself – whether by choice or accident is not clear – from a resurgence of anti-SEU feeling elsewhere in the profession. Ironically, this other resurgence was centred on, and became focused around another great dissenter – the Frenchman Maurice Allais, who was awarded the Nobel Prize in 1988 (though, rather oddly, apparently not for his work on decision-making under uncertainty). As a result of this resurgence, economics now has a huge variety of alternative theories of decision-making under uncertainty: Machina's generalized expected utility theory, Loomes and Sugden's regret theory and disappointment theory, Chew and MacCrimmon's weighted utility theory, Dekel's implicit utility theory and so on and so on. In addition, we have Jim Ford's perspective theory. Ironically this hovers outside the boundaries of conventionality in much the same way as Shackle's ideas did before them. I suspect that Jim gets secret pleasure from this!

But this is unfortunate: the ideas contained in perspective theory need further discussion and a wider airing. This is the purpose of this chapter. First, I propose to analyse perspective theory using the language currently being spoken by the other 'anti-SEU' theorists - hence making it more accessible to the new mainstream. Second, I will explore some of the implications of perspective theory that Jim was unable to examine in his book - perhaps because of an unfortunate (but understandable) desire to see his ideas in print as soon as possible. Finally, I will extend the range of applications of perspective theory beyond those provided by Jim in his book. Ultimately, the intention is to encourage other economists to give perspective theory the attention it deserves.

The essence of perspective theory is contained in the section 'An Application of Perspective Theory in Outline' on pages 38 to 40 of Chapter 3 'On Perspective Theory' in *Economic Choice under Uncertainty*. Figure 3.1 on page 39 illustrates. I reproduce this, with amendments, in Figure 2.1. I will describe this shortly - after describing the scenario under discussion. We are describing individual choice under uncertainty. I shall limit attention in this chapter to situations where the uncertainty concerns a single variable of interest to the decision-maker - which I shall denote by X - and where the uncertainty about X can be described by means of a probability distribution on X - either objective or subjective, discrete or continuous. Let me denote the implied distribution function of X by F(.). Obviously F(.) is bounded below by zero and above by one, and is everywhere non-decreasing. We suppose that the decision-maker has to choose amongst different prospects, that is, different distribution functions, so we need to specify the method by which the decision-maker ranks different distribution functions.

The conventional wisdom (SEU theory) argues that this ranking is done in accordance with expected utility: if the individual obeys the axioms of SEU theory, then the individual has a utility function U(.) (revealed by his or her preferences) and the individual's preference over distributions is indicated by the magnitude of the expectation of this utility. More specifically, if we denote the individual's preference functional (over distributions F) by V(.), then SEU theory concludes that:

$$V(F) = \int_{-\infty}^{\infty} U(X)\ dF(X) \tag{1}$$

Perspective theory has a different conclusion. The simplest way to illustrate this is by use of Figure 2.1, which should be thought of as in two parts: the left-hand part confined to negative values of X (losses) and the right-hand part confined to positive values of X (gains). Figure 2.1 illustrates a distribution for which both gains and losses are possible; later I shall consider prospects with no negative segment.

Figure 2.1 : *Choice under perspective theory I*

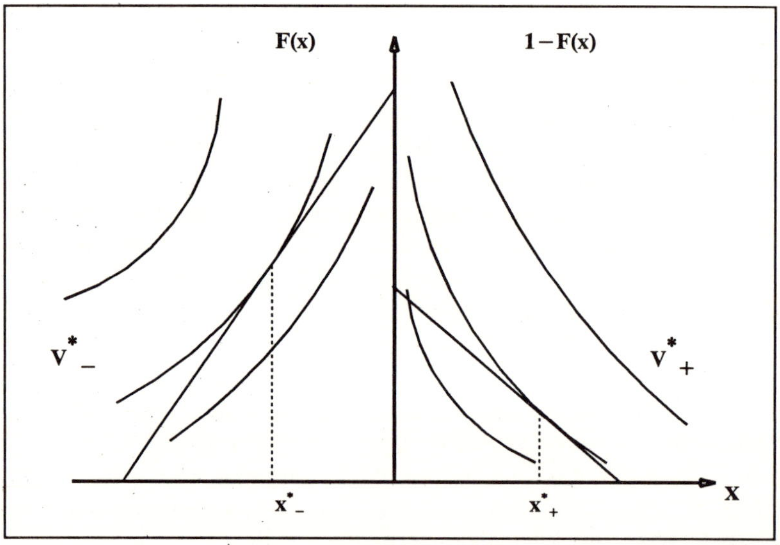

Plotted on the y-axis in the left-hand part of Figure 2.1 is the distribution function, F(x); plotted on the y-axis in the right-hand part is the complement of the distribution function, 1−F(x). These are the bold lines in the figure. Also drawn in the figure are two sets of indifference curves – one in the left-hand part and one in the right-hand part; the former representing locii of indifference between losses (negative values of X) and the probability of the individual receiving a loss at least as large as that amount (F(x)); the latter representing locii of points of indifference between gains (positive values of x) and the probability of the individual receiving a gain at least as large as that $(1-F(x))$. The resemblance between that and diagrams appearing in the various books of Shackle (for instance, his *Expectations in Economics*) and reproduced, for example, by Jim on page 63 of his *Choice, Expectation and Uncertainty*, is not coincidental - despite the fact that the labelling on the axes has undergone a slight metamorphosis. In the Shacklesque version, the bold curves in Figure 2.1 would have been the potential surprise function; here in the Fordian version, they are the distribution function and its complement.

Nevertheless, the next stage is the same. In both the left-hand part and the right-hand part, we have a set of indifference curves. Moreover, in each part, we find the value of X corresponding to the highest attainable indifference curve; these are marked x^*_- and x^*_+ in Figure 2.1, and the highest attainable utility levels. These latter I denote by $V_-(F)$ and $V_+(F)$ in the left-hand part and right-hand part respectively. So $V_-(F)$ is the level of utility corresponding to the highest indifference curve attained in the loss (left-hand) part, and $V_+(F)$ is the level of utility corresponding to the highest indifference curve attained in the gains (right-hand) part. My notation emphasizes that these maximal utilities depend upon the particular prospect (distribution) under consideration.

We are now at the final stage. If we let V(.) denote the Fordian preference functional (over distributions F), then Jim defines it by:

$$V(F) = g(V_-^*(F), V_+^*(F)) \tag{2}$$

where g(.,.) is some bivariate function which is decreasing in its first argument and increasing in its second. Thus, the higher is $V_+^*(F)$ the more preferred is the distribution, but the higher is $V_-^*(F)$ the less preferred is the distribution. Apart from the definition of V_+^* and V_-^* this is all very Shacklesque.

The actual form of the function g does not seem too crucial since V_+^* and V_-^* can be fairly arbitrarily changed. To simplify matters in what follows, I shall usually assume that g takes the particular form:

$$g(u-, u+) = u_+ - ku_- \tag{3}$$

where k is a constant indicating the individual's feelings about the relative importance to be attached to losses as compared with gains.

It is immediately obvious that the Fordian preference functional - or perhaps I should say the perspective theory functional – satisfies dominance: if distribution F stochastically dominates[1] distribution G, then

$$V(F) \geq V(G) \tag{4}$$

that is, F is preferred to G. Figure 2.2 illustrates. The result follows simply because

$$V_-^*(F) \leq V_-^*(G)\ ,\ V_+^*(F) \geq V_+^*(G)$$

as is obvious from Figure 2.2.

Figure 2.2: Choice under perspective theory II

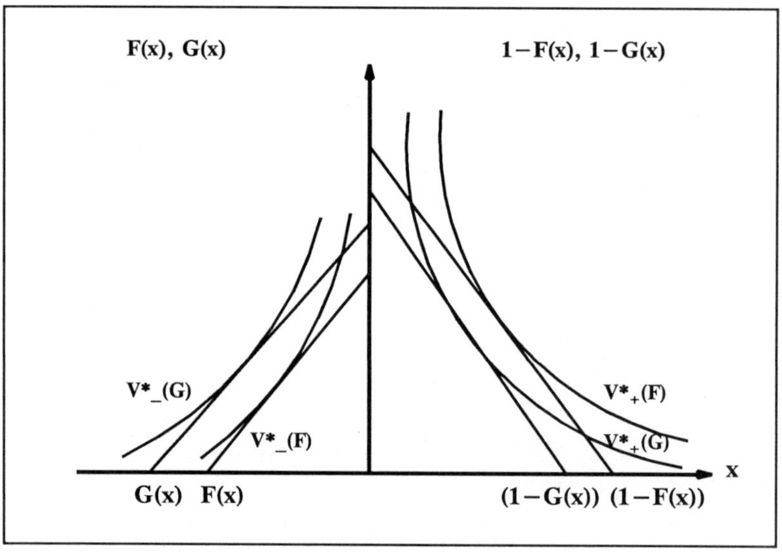

However, unlike SEU theory, perspective theory does not readily lend itself to a characterization of risk aversion. Consider how this is done in SEU theory: we start from the intuitive notion that a risk-averse person is one who would always prefer a certain prospect to a risky prospect with the same expected value; this leads immediately to the result that a risk-averse person has a utility function U(.) that is concave. This, however, does not work so easily with perspective theory. Start with 50–50 gambles and examine Figure 2.3. The 'distribution' marked F is a degenerate distribution which always leads to the certainty of x_0; the distribution G is a 50–50 gamble with the same expected value (x_0). In SEU theory an individual will always prefer F to G – *irrespective of the values of* x_0 *and* δ – if and only if U(.) is concave. In perspective theory, however (assuming that x_0 and δ are such that $x_0-\delta$ remains positive) this would require that the indifference curve passing through point P always lies *above* point Q *whatever are the values of* x *and* δ. A moment's reflection should convince that this is a strong requirement which further requires that any indifference curve that passes above 1.0 should never sink below

Figure 2.3: Risk aversion and perspective theory

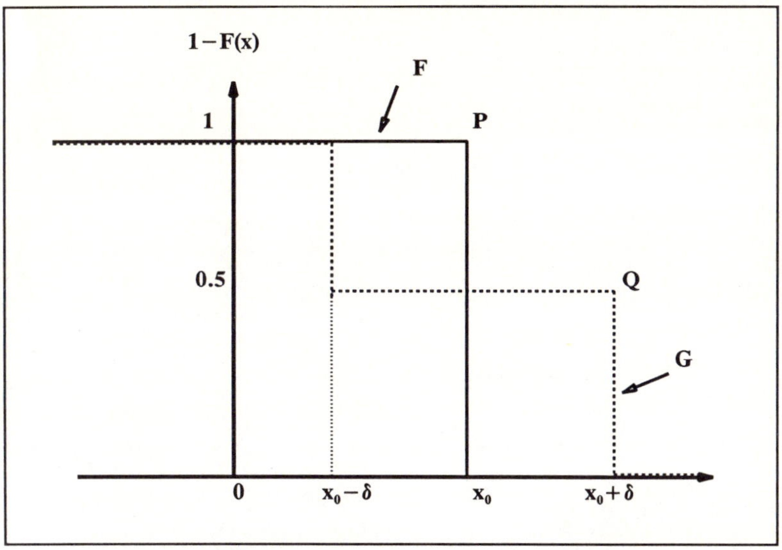

0.5. But if we pursue the argument still further and consider non-50–50 gambles the situation gets worse: we get the implication that for any $\epsilon>0$ any indifference curve that passes through the point (1.0, x) should *never* sink below [(1.0−ε), (x/1−ε)]. Rather a difficult requirement! But perhaps we are expecting too much.

Let me now explore the implications of perspective theory using a diagram that has become very familiar to the followers of the mainstream debate on alternatives to SEU theory: the Marschak-

Machina triangle. This has been put to invaluable expository use by many authors, most notably Mark Machina, one of the leaders of the 'new mainstream', in his splendid paper, 'Choice under Uncertainty: Problems Solved and Unsolved' in the appropriately titled new *Journal of Economic Perspectives*. This triangle is used to illustrate choice among risky prospects involving at most three final outcomes. Without loss of generality we can consider these three final outcomes as being monetary outcomes. I denote them by (x_1, x_2, x_3) where $x_1 < x_2 < x_3$.

Figure 2.4 : The Marschak–Machina triangle

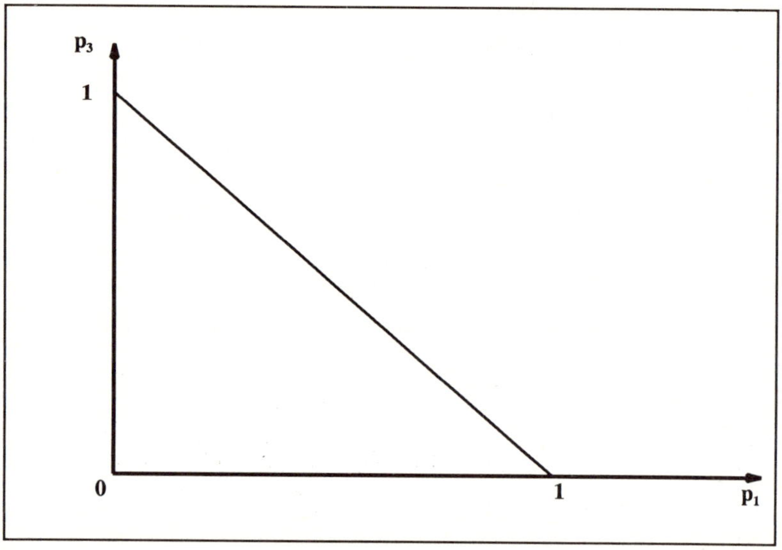

The set of all risky prospects involving just these three final outcomes can be represented by the set of all probability triples of the form $p = (p_1, p_2, p_3)$ where p_i is the probability that the final outcome is x_i ($p_i \geq 0$, of course), and where :

$$p_1 + p_2 + p_3 = 1. \quad (5)$$

Since we can rearrange this restriction to read $p_2 = 1 - p_1 - p_3$, we can geometrically represent these risky prospects in the unit triangle in the (p_1, p_3) plane, as in Figure 2.4.

Any point in this triangle represents a particular prospect: a point properly inside the triangle represents a prospect with all of p_1, p_2 and p_3 strictly positive; a point on the boundary of the triangle (but not at one of the vertices) represents a prospect with one of the p_i zero; while the vertices represent certainties. An individual's preferences over such risky prospects can be expressed in terms of the implied indifference map in the triangle. If the individual obeys the axioms of SEU theory, the indifference map is simply given by 'expected utility = constant', or from (1), by:

$$p_1 U(x_1) + p_2 U(x_2) + p_3 U(x_3) = \text{constant}.$$

Using (5) this can be rearranged to yield:

$$p_3 = \text{constant} - p_1 \{U(x_2) - U(x_1)\} / \{U(x_3) - U(x_1)\}. \quad (6)$$

Thus the indifference map implied by SEU theory consists of parallel straight line indifference curves. (Note that the slope depends on the degree of concavity of the utility function – so that the more risk-averse the individual, the steeper the parallel indifference lines.)

Figure 2.5: Perspective theory indifference curves I

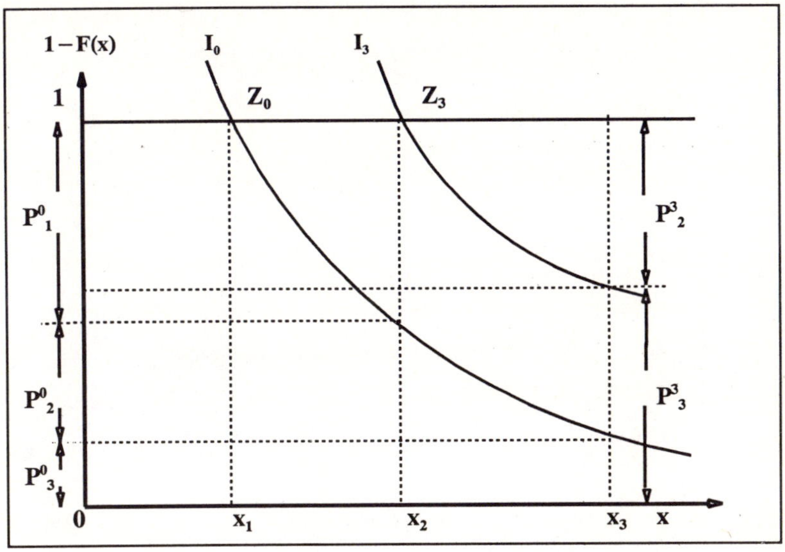

As Machina discusses in some detail in the paper referred to above, different theories of behaviour under uncertainty have different implications for the shape of the indifference map. Regret theory, for example, implies straight line indifference curves fanning out from a point to the south-west of the origin of the triangle; weighted utility theory has a similar prediction; Machina's own generalized expected utility theory also has fanning out indifference curves – but these are not necessarily linear; Implicit utility theory has linear indifference curves – but these do not necessarily fan out, and so on.

It is instructive to derive perspective theory's implied indifference map. This I do in Figure 2.6 with the assistance of Figure 2.5.[2] Without loss of generality, I can take all the x to be positive, so that we are operating in the right-hand (gains) part of Figure 2.5, which illustrates an arbitrary indifference map and the three x values. In Figure 2.5 the indifference curve marked I_0 is the one passing through the point Z_0 (that is $(1, x_1)$); its intersection values with the vertical lines through x_2 and x_3 have special significance as will be seen.

Figure 2.6: Perspective theory indifference curves II

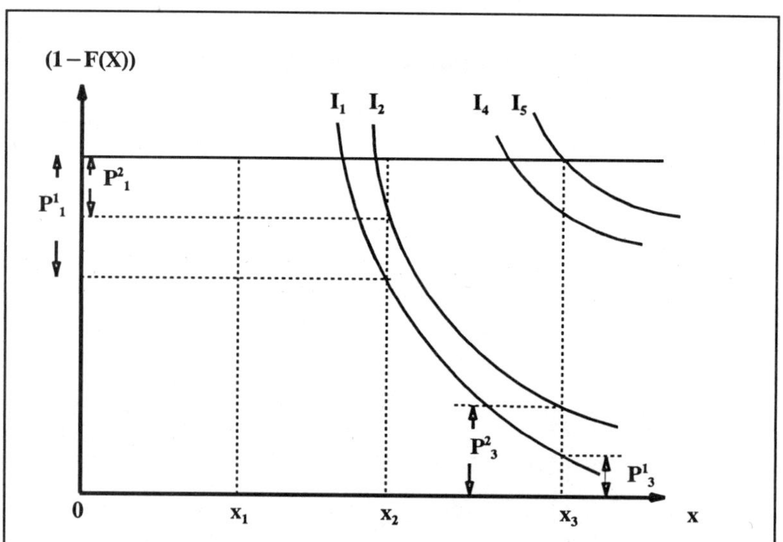

The point A_0 in Figure 2.7 is defined by the (p^0_1, p^0_2, p^0_3) given by these intersection points. It follows from perspective theory that *all points in the shaded area to the south east of A_0* are considered (by the individual obeying the rules of perspective theory) as indifferent to each other. (Consider any prospect within the shaded area: its distribution function hits the highest indifference curve at the point Z_0, in Figure 2.5, and hence is indifferent to all such other prospects.) This is a remarkable result. Clearly the size of the shaded area – this *indifference zone* if you like – depends upon how far to the right is point A_0 which, in turn, depends on how steep are the indifference curves: the steeper they are, the smaller the indifference zone. Point A_3 is also of interest; it is defined in Figure 2.5 by the indifference curve passing through the point Z_3 (that is $(1, x_2)$). It can be shown that the indifference 'curve' passing through point A_3 consists of the horizontal line to the right of A_3 and the vertical line below A_3. Above point A_3 the indifference 'curves' are all horizontal straight lines – such as that passing through point A_4, which comes from the indifference curve I_4 in Figure 2.6. Also shown in Figure 2.7 are two further indifference curves: one coming from I_1 in Figure 2.6 consisting of the horizontal line to the right of the point A_1 and the vertical line below A_1 – and the other coming from I_2 in Figure 2.6 consisting of the horizontal line to the right of the point A_2 and the vertical line below A_2.

Figure 2.7: Perspective theory indifference curves III

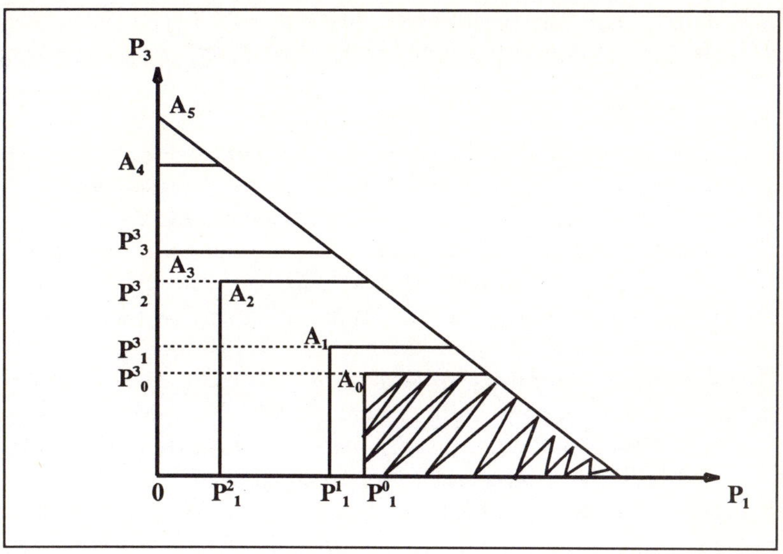

So the perspective theory indifference map in the Marschak-Machina triangle consists of three segments: an indifference zone to the south-east of A_0; a set of upside-down L-shaped indifference curves between A_0 and A_3; and a set of horizontal indifference curves above A_4. The curve joining together the key points $A_0,\ldots,A_1,\ldots,A_2,\ldots$ and A_3 must be downward-sloping, but otherwise there is no restriction on what it does. Fascinating!

The Marschak–Machina triangle has been mainly used as an insightful expository device when discussing violations of SEU-predicted behaviour. Let us begin by discussing possibly the most famous of such violations: the Allais paradox. Here I consider a simplified version, which captures the very essence of the alleged paradox.

Suppose an individual is asked first to choose one or other of two prospects C_1 and C_2 defined as follows: C_1 yields £3000 with certainty; C_2 yields £4000 with probability 0.8 and £0 with probability 0.2. Then the same individual is asked to choose one or other of two prospects D_1 and D_2 defined as follows: D_1 yields £3000 with probability 0.25 and £0 with probability 0.75; D_2 yields £4000 with probability 0.2 and £0 with probability 0.8. Now, according to SEU theory, the individual should choose C_1 in preference to C_2 if and only if he or she chooses D_1 in preference to D_2.[3] This is neatly illustrated in the Marschak–Machina triangle; consider Figure 2.8, where the four points C_1, C_2, D_1 and D_2 represent the four risky prospects discussed above in a triangle with x_1=£0, x_2=£3000 and x_3=£4000. It will be immediately noted that the line joining C_1 to C_2 is parallel to that joining D_1 to D_2. Now recall the discussion above which demonstrated that SEU indifference curves must be parallel straight lines: it is thus clearly impossible for point C_1 to be on a higher SEU indifference curve than C_1 and at the same time for D_2 to be on a higher SEU indifference curve than D_1. But this is the essence of the paradox: the modal pair of choices when real people are asked to make such choices for real (either with or without appropriate monetary incentives) is C_1 and D_2. Rather an embarrassment for SEU theory!

Hence the proliferation of alternative theories. My previous summary of the triangle indifference maps implied by the various alternatives gives insight into the basic alternative explanation – usually they rely on a theoretical structure which implies *fanning out* indifference curves. This is the case with Machina's generalized expected utility theory, with Chew and MacCrimmon's weighted utility theory, and with Loomes and Sugden's regret theory.

Perspective theory gives another alternative explanation. Consider again Figure 2.8, and, in particular the perspective theory indifference curves drawn in that figure. For an individual with such a perspective indifference map (which is a perfectly reasonable one given the framework of perspective theory) it follows that he or she would prefer C_1 to C_2 and D_2 to D_1. Perspective theory can explain the Allais paradox. I leave it to the interested reader to investigate how perspective theory can also explain some of the other violations of SEU behaviour discovered through experimental methods. (These include the common ratio effect and the common consequence effect; see Machina's survey paper for a very lucid discussion.)

Figure 2.8: Perspective theory and the Allais paradox

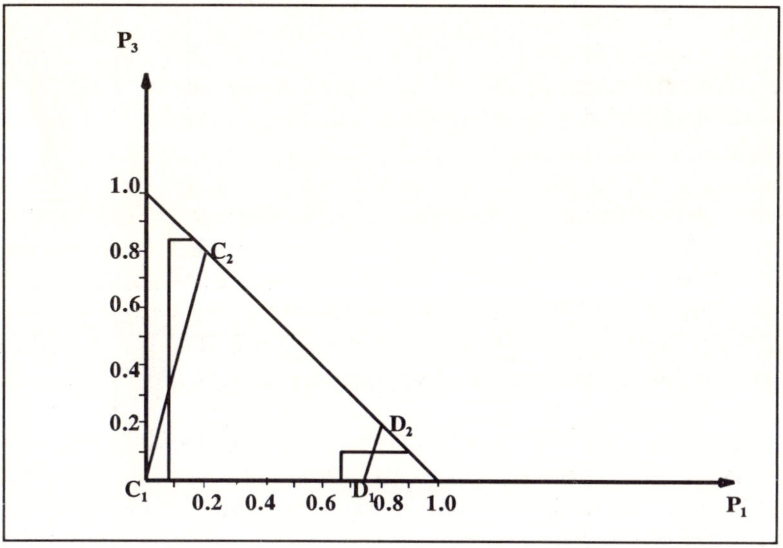

Note that perspective theory's explanation of the Allais paradox differs quite sharply from that given by the other alternatives discussed above. The 'fanning out' explanations effectively (though not necessarily *ab initio*) have risk aversion increasing from right to left in the triangle: individuals have flatter indifference curves (are more risk-loving in the SEU context) in the right-hand side of the triangle, and have steeper indifference curves (are more risk-averse in the SEU context) in the left-hand side. This sort of explanation does not fit easily into the perspective theory context, for reasons, discussed above, connected with the difficulty of defining risk aversion (at least as conventionally understood). One could argue that the perspective theory indifference curves (except in the indifference zone and in the area in the top left-hand corner where the indifference curves are horizontal straight lines) being vertical up to some point, A, and horizontal thereafter, imply perfect risk-aversion up to that point A, and perfect risk-loving thereafter. One could then try to argue that the higher is the point A then the higher is the 'overall' aversion to risk. More generally one could then continue the argument by noting that the closer the locus A_0, A_1, A_2, A_3, A_4, A_5 to the hypotenuse then the more risk–averse is the individual. A glance back at Figures 2.5 and 2.6 indicates that the *flatter* are the original Fordian indifference curves (in Figure 2.5) then the closer will be the locus A_0, A_1, A_2, A_3, A_4, A_5 to the hypotenuse – and the more risk-averse the individual.

Such an interpretation would appear to be plausible: the flatter the Fordian indifference curves, the greater compensation (in terms of gain) the individual requires for a decrease in the probability of getting a particular gain. An alternative way of seeing this is illustrated in Figure 2.9, which portrays a uniform prospect distribution.

Figure 2.9: Choice from a uniform prospect distribution

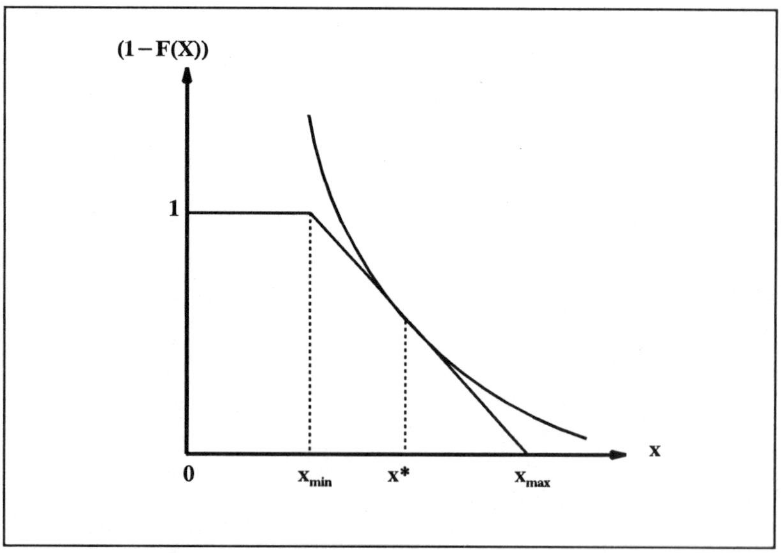

Here X is uniformly distributed between x_{min} and x_{max}. The initial tangency point is x*. Now consider a reduction in x_{min}; ask the question: what increase in x_{max} does the individual require to compensate him or her for this decrease in x_{min}? The answer gives some insight into the 'attitude to risk' of the individual: the bigger the required increase, the greater the risk aversion. Clearly, the flatter are the curves, the greater is the required increase. Consider the following example, based on a uniform distribution and an indifference map defined by the Fordian utility function $U(x,y) = x^{\alpha} y^{\alpha}$. In this example, elementary calculus shows that:

$$dx/dx_{min} = 1 - (x_{max} - x_{min})/(\alpha x_{max})$$

along a Fordian indifference curve. Thus the greater is α the greater is dx_{max} / dx_{min} along a Fordian indifference curve. Once again, the flatness does appear to tell us something about the individual's attitude to risk. Translated into the Marschak–Machina triangle, the closer is the locus A_0, A_1, A_2, A_3, A_4, A_5 to the hypotenuse, the more risk-averse is the individual. Note also that the flatter the Fordian indifference curves, the larger the indifference zone in the Marschak–Machina triangle.

One important feature of perspective theory that will not have escaped the reader's attention is that it is eminently testable – particularly in the context of the triangle. For example, take any individual and any point in the triangle. Then it immediately follows that that individual must be indifferent between that point and *either* all points to the right of it *or* all points below it. I look forward to tests of this simple hypothesis. One interesting possibility that Jim did not explore in his *Economic Choice under Uncertainty* is the existence of multiple points of tangency (in the original Fordian space). While clearly with uniform distributions such multiple solutions cannot exist (at least with conventionally shaped indifference curves), it does not require much ingenuity to give examples of distributions which do. For example, the normal distribution function, which Jim uses extensively, has a point of inflection, which means that, in addition to the point identified in Jim's examples, there is also a further possibility – tangency at some point in the tail (which may dominate the other point). This could happen in either (with the normal distribution) or both (with some other distributions) the negative or the positive segment, and could lead to interesting possibilities, including jump discontinuities in the solution. This would probably appeal to Jim.

This completes my brief exploration of the further properties and implications of perspective theory; limitations on space prevent a more detailed study of particular applications. However, I think it is important that Jim and others explore further the application of perspective theory to the many areas of economics in which SEU theory has already been 'successfully' (in a theoretical not necessarily an empirical sense) applied. But it is not just perspective theory of all the new theories that has not yet been fully applied. Indeed, the absence of applications of regret theory, for example, must be a continuing cause of embarrassment to Graham Loomes and Bob Sugden. True, I have seen some applications, but these have been limited in scope. The problem, of course, with regret theory as presently constituted is that it is a theory of pairwise choice; in contrast, most problems studied by economists usually have a (continuous) spectrum of choice. I understand that Loomes and Sugden (and perhaps others) are working on an extension of regret theory to multiple choice, but formidable problems remain.

In contrast, perspective theory is already a theory of choice among a set of alternatives. It is also clearly a theory which gives rise to *transitive* choice patterns.[4] So, in principle, it can be easily applied to all those problems in which economists are interested. The difficulty, however, is that, at present, there are no general models; moreover, as Jim clearly discovered, particular examples can lead to horrific algebra. I have tried further specific applications – using uniform distributions rather than normal distributions – and although the algebra is somewhat easier (I can give details on request) it is still horrendously messy. One gets nasty expressions to differentiate and solve, quadratic equations to find the roots for, and numerous regimes. Perhaps that is as it should be (I remarked in a review of Jim's *Economic Choice under Uncertainty* that that may simply reflect the messiness of the world), but that is not going to help to increase the appeal of perspective theory to those mainstream economists who like their economics to be nice and tidy and elegant.

What I have tried to do in this chapter is to emphasize that perspective theory can be expressed in terms more familiar to mainstream economists (and in a manner which makes them feel more comfortable) and that perspective theory does address the same concerns as the new alternative mainstream. I hope that I have been successful, as it is important to Jim that his work on this alternative to SEU theory – carrying on the tradition of G.L.S. Shackle before him – should be carried on by others, if not necessarily by Jim himself. There are many good ideas in perspective theory which need to be discussed further. The profession should be grateful to Jim for getting the debate to this stage.

NOTES

1. That is, stochastically dominates to the first degree.
2. If one or more of the x values is negative, while one or more is positive, we need to construct *two* indifference maps – one in the gain space and one in the loss space. This complicates the exposition without significantly altering the conclusions that follow. However, the reader may find it of interest to derive the corresponding triangle indifference map.
3. Let (U(£4000) = 1, U(£3000) = u and U(£0) = 0 (without loss of generality). Then $V(C_1) = u$, $V(C_2) = 0.8$; $V(D_1) = 0.25u$, $V(D_2) = 0.2$; and the result follows.
4. Though whether this is a point in its favour or against it I leave to others to judge!

REFERENCES

Ford, J.L. (1983), *Choice, Expectation and Uncertainty*, Oxford: Martin Robertson.

Ford, J. L. (1987), *Economic Choice under Uncertainty: A Perspective Theory Approach,* Aldershot: Edward Elgar.

Machina, M. J. (1987), 'Choice under Uncertainty: Problems Solved and Unsolved', *Journal of Economic Perspectives*, **1**, pp. 121–54.

Shackle, G.L.S. (1952), *Expectations in Economics,* second edition, Cambridge: Cambridge University Press.

3. Decision-Making Under Complete Uncertainty[1]

C. Richard Barrett and Prasanta K. Pattanaik

1. INTRODUCTION

Consider an agent who is faced with several mutually exclusive actions that he may take. The outcome of each action depends on the specific state of nature that may materialize. The agent knows the set of possible states of nature, but is completely ignorant about the probabilities of these states. How does the agent rank the actions, given his preferences over outcomes? The purpose of this chapter is to discuss this problem of ranking actions under complete uncertainty, in which all information about probabilities is absent.

It is possible to visualize two alternative frameworks for analysing decision-making under complete uncertainty, the distinction between the two depending on the nature of assumptions made about individual preferences over outcomes. First, one can assume that, though the agent does not have any information about the probabilities of the states of nature, his preferences over outcomes are represented by a Neumann–Morgenstern utility function. This cardinal approach has been explicitly adopted by Milnor (1954) and Cohen and Jaffray (1980, 1983) and is, we believe, implicit in Barbera and Jackson (1985).[2] Alternatively, one can assume that an ordering over outcomes summarizes all the available and relevant information about the agent's preferences over outcomes. Essentially, the Arrow-Hurwicz (1972) analysis of the problem can be viewed as following this ordinal approach.[3] Maskin (1979) also explores the ordinal (as well as the cardinal) approach to the problem of decision-making under complete uncertainty.

We believe that the ordinal framework has some inherent attractions in the context of decision-making under complete uncertainty. Since the Neumann–Morgenstern utilities can be derived only from sets of axioms which either assume the existence of probabilities or which, as in Savage (1954), imply the existence of probabilities, if one rules out all probabilistic information in the model, it would seem to be of interest to develop the model without assuming the existence of the Neumann–Morgenstern utility function.[4] For these reasons we have posed the problem of decision-making under complete uncertainty in an ordinal framework. Our discussion of the problem is organized as follows. After introducing in section 2 the basic concepts of actions and preferences, we present in section 3 various axioms (some of which are already familiar from the literature), postulating specific restrictions on the connection between the agent's ordering over outcomes and his ranking of actions. In section 4 we prove one of the basic results of the chapter, which shows how certain plausible axioms drastically constrain the agent's decision-making under uncertainty by imposing on him a severe form of uniformity. In the presence of these axioms, the existence of a minimal, 'local' amount of pessimism or optimism is escalated into universal pessimism or optimism so that the agent cannot even be 'minimally' pessimistic (or optimistic) in comparing some actions in some decision problems without being pessimistic (or optimistic) with respect to all relevant comparisons of actions in all possible decision problems. (This is clearly reminiscent of the Arrow (1963)-type 'neutrality' result in the theory of social choice.) Using this result we provide (in section 5) new axiomatic characterizations of several familiar criteria for ranking actions under complete uncertainty – the maximin, maximax, leximin and leximax criteria, and also the min-based and max-based protective criteria. We conclude in section 6.

2. ACTIONS AND PREFERENCES

Let X be the set of all conceivable *outcomes* for the agent. Let $\succeq$ be the agent's weak preference relation (wpr) 'at least as good as' over X, $\succ$ and $\sim$ being, respectively, the asymmetric and symmetric factors of $\succeq$. $\succeq$ is assumed to be an ordering. Also, we assume that, for some $x,y,z \in X$, $x \succ y \succ z$, that is there are at least three distinct 'indifference classes' in X, defined in terms of $\succeq$. The class of all conceivable finite sets whose elements are (in each case mutually exclusive and exhaustive) possible states of nature is denoted by Z. We assume that, for some $S,S' \in Z$, $|S| = 2$ and $|S'| = 3$. For all $S \in Z$, A(S) denotes the set of all functions $a{:}S \rightarrow X$. The elements of A(S) are called *actions*.

Notation 2.1 Let $S = \{s_1,...,s_n\} \in Z$ and $a \in A(S)$. Suppose for all i, $1 \leq i \leq n$, $a(s_i) = x_i$. Then often, for convenience, we shall represent a as follows:

	s_1	s_2	....	s_n
a	x_1	x_2	....	x_n .

For every $S \in Z$, the agent has a wpr R over A(S). Similarly, the agent has wprs R′ over A(S′), R* over A(S*), and so on. The asymmetric and symmetric factors of R are denoted by P and I, respectively. Similarly, we have P′ and I′ corresponding to R′, P* and I* corresponding to R*, and so on. Our analysis of decision-making under complete uncertainty involves exploration of the relationship between the ordering $\succeq$ over outcomes and the wprs, R, R′, and so on over actions.

3. SOME AXIOMS

In this section we introduce several axioms imposing restrictions on wprs over actions.

Axiom 3.1 Rationality (Ra): For all $S \in Z$, R is an ordering over A(S).

Axiom 3.2 Quasi-rationality (QRa): For all $S \in Z$, R is reflexive and P is transitive over A(S).

Definition 3.3 For all $S \in Z$ and for all $a, b \in A(S)$, a *dominates* b iff for all $s \in S$, $a(s) \succeq b(s)$, and for some $s \in S$, $a(s) \succ b(s)$.

Axiom 3.4 Dominance (D): For all $S \in Z$ and for all $a, b \in A(S)$, if a dominates b, then aPb.

While D is a compelling axiom, some familiar decision criteria (for example, the maximin and maximax criteria) do not satisfy it, though they satisfy the following weaker axiom.

Axiom 3.5 Weak dominance (WD): For all $S \in Z$ and for all $a, b \in A(S)$, if a dominates b, then aRb.

Axiom 3.6 Symmetry (SYM): Let $S,S' \in Z$ ($|S|=|S'|$), and let $a,b \in A(S)$ and $c,d \in A(S')$. Suppose g is a one-to-one function from S to S′ such that for all $s \in S$, $a(s) \sim c(g(s))$ and $b(s) \sim d(g(s))$. Then aRb iff cR′d.

SYM essentially requires that the specific labelling of states of nature, and the specific features which differentiate outcomes in the same indifference class, are of no importance when it comes to ranking two actions.

Axiom 3.7 Independence of the ranking of irrelevant outcomes (IRIO): Let $S \in Z$, and let $a,b,c,d \in A(S)$ be such that, for all $s,s' \in S$ [$a(s) \succeq a(s')$ iff $c(s) \succeq c(s')$]; [$b(s) \succeq b(s')$ iff $d(s) \succeq d(s')$]; [$a(s) \succeq b(s')$ iff $c(s) \succeq d(s')$]; and [$b(s) \succeq a(s')$ iff $d(s) \succeq c(s')$]. Then aRb iff cRd.

IRIO is quite a strong axiom, for it implies that, for a given set of possible states of nature, the ranking of two actions depends just on the ordering of the outcomes of those two actions.

Notation 3.8 Let $T \subset S \subset Z$ and $a \in A(S)$. Then a/T denotes the restriction of a to T.

Notation 3.9 Let $S,S' \in Z$; $s_i,s_j \in S$; $s_k \in S'$; $a,b \in A(S)$; and $c,d \in A(S')$. Then we write $(S;s_i,s_j) \rightarrow (S';s_k)$ iff $S'-S=\{s_k\}$ and $S-S'=\{s_i,s_j\}$. Also we write $(S;s_i,s_j;a,b) \rightarrow (S';s_k;c,d)$ iff [$(S;s_i,s_j) \rightarrow (S';s_k)$ and $a/S \cap S' = c/S \cap S'$ and $b/S \cap S' = d/S \cap S'$ and $a(s_i)=a(s_j)=c(s_k)$ and $b(s_i)=b(s_j)=d(s_k)$]. (See notation 3.8.)

Axiom 3.10 Invariance with respect to merger of states (IMS): Given $S \in Z$ and $s_i,s_j \in S$, there exists $S' \in Z$ and $s_k \in S'$, such that [$(S;s_i,s_j) \rightarrow (S';s_k)$ and, for all $a,b \in A(S)$ and $c,d \in A(S')$, iff $(S;s_i,s_j;a,b) \rightarrow (S';s_k;c,d)$, then (aRb if cR′d)]. (See notation 3.9.)

The intuitive basis of IMS is to be found in the arbitrariness involved in the specification of the states of nature (which, essentially, reflects the way in which the agent chooses to view the problem). An example will help to explain. Suppose the agent starts by considering three possible states of nature: s_1 (less than five inches of rainfall), s_2 (five to seven inches of rainfall) and s_3 (more than seven inches of rainfall); and two actions:

	s_1	s_2	s_3
a	x	y	y
b	x′	y′	y′.

Note that, for the purpose of comparing a and b, the agent could 'merge' s_2 and s_3 into a single state of nature – say s_4. Thus, formally, $a,b \in A(\{s_1,s_2,s_3\})$ may be transformed into $c,d \in A(\{s_1,s_4\})$, defined by:

	s_1	s_4
c	x	y
d	x′	y′ .

As, intuitively, a is the same action as c, and b the same action as d, the ranking of c and d should correspond to the ranking of a and b. (s_k, figuring in the formal statement of IMS, is to be interpreted as the state of nature resulting from the merger of s_i and s_j, figuring in the same statement.) IMS is closely related to Arrow and Hurwicz's (1972) Property C; in fact, it can be checked that SYM and IMS together imply their Property C, if it is assumed that $\varnothing \neq T \subset S \in Z$ implies $T \in Z$.

While IMS is, like dominance, a rather compelling axiom, some familiar decision criteria (for example, the leximin and leximax criteria) do not satisfy it, though they satisfy the weaker axiom 3.12, introduced below.

Definition 3.11 Let $S \in Z$, $s \in S$ and $a,b \in A(S)$. Let $s_1,\ldots,s_{|S|}$ be an arbitrary ordering of the states in S, and denote by L the set of all permutations of $\{1,\ldots,|S|\}$. We say that the *relative positions* of s *under* a *and* b *are similar* iff there exist $\ell,\ell' \in L$ and k, $1 \leq k \leq |S|$, such that $s = s_{\ell(k)} = s_{\ell'(k)}$ and, for $1 \leq i < j \leq |S|$, $a(s_{\ell(j)}) \succeq a(s_{\ell(i)})$ and $b(s_{\ell'(j)}) \succeq b(s_{\ell'(i)})$.

According to definition 3.11, the relative positions of s under a and b are similar, if s can occupy the same numerical position in the order, when the states in S are arranged to give the possible outcomes of first a, and then b, in order of preference.

Axiom 3.12 Weak invariance with respect to merger of states (WIMS): Given $S \in Z$ and $s_i, s_j \in S$, there exists $S' \in Z$ and $s_k \in S'$, such that $[(S;s_i,s_j) \rightarrow (S';s_k)$ and, for all $a,b \in A(S)$ and $c,d \in A(S')$, if $(S;s_i,s_j;a,b) \rightarrow (S';s_k;c,d)$ and the relative positions of both s_i and s_j under a and b are similar, then (aRb iff cR′d)]. (See definition 3.11.)

Axiom 3.13 Independence of common outcomes (ICO): Let $T \subset S \in Z$, and let $a,b,c,d \in A(S)$ be such that $[a/S-T=c/S-T$ and $b/S-T=d/S-T$ and $a/T=b/T$ and $c/T=d/T]$. Then aRb if cRd. (See notation 3.8.)

ICO is in the same spirit as Savage's (1954) well-known independence axiom. It asserts that the ranking of two actions remains the same when a common outcome of the two actions for some state of nature is, for the same state, replaced by another common outcome.

Axiom 3.14 Semi-independence of common outcomes (SICO): Let $T \subset S \in Z$, and let $a,b,c,d \in A(S)$ be such that $[a/S-T=c/S-T$ and $b/S-T=d/S-T$ and $a/T=b/T$ and for all $s \in T$, $c(s) \succ d(s)]$. Then aPb implies cPd. (See notation 3.8.)

Clearly, while SICO is not strictly weaker than ICO, SICO in conjunction with axioms 3.1 (Ra) and 3.5 (WD) is weaker than ICO in conjunction with these two axioms. Our next axiom is very weak.

Axiom 3.15 Ranking of sure outcomes (RSO): Let $S \in Z$ and $x,y \in X$, and let $a,b \in A(S)$ be such that for all $s \in S$, $a(s)=x \succ y=b(s)$. Then aPb.

The axioms so far introduced in this section can be viewed as seeking to explicate various 'rationality' properties of preference over actions under complete uncertainty. The axioms which we introduce below are of a different nature. They may be regarded as 'descriptive' assumptions about the existence or non-existence of different degrees of pessimism and optimism.

Axiom 3.16 Existence of local pessimism (ELP): There exist $S=\{s,s'\} \in Z$, and $a,b \in A(S)$ such that $a(s) \succ b(s) \sim b(s') \succ a(s')$, and bPa.

Axiom 3.17 Existence of local optimism (ELO): There exist $S=\{s,s'\} \in Z$, and $a,b \in A(S)$ such that $a(s) \succ b(s) \sim b(s') \succ a(s)$, and aPb.

Axiom 3.18 Local absence of pessimism and optimism (LAPO): There exist S={s,s′}∈Z, and a,b∈A(S) such that a(s)≻ b(s) ∼ b(s′) ≻ a(s′), and not (bPa or aPb).

It is clear that at least one of the axioms – ELP, ELO or LAPO – must hold.

Notation 3.19 Given S∈Z and a∈A(S), m(a) denotes a specific ≿ – least outcome in a(S), and M(a) denotes a specific ≿ – greatest outcome in a(S).

Axiom 3.20 Existence of local weak pessimism (ELWP): There exist S∈Z, and a,b∈A(S), such that M(a)≻M(b) and bPa.

Axiom 3.21 Existence of local weak optimism (ELWO): There exist S∈Z, and a,b∈A(S), such that m(a)≻m(b) and bPa.

Axioms 3.20 (ELWP) and 3.21 (ELWO) are weaker than axioms 3.16 (ELP) and 3.17 (ELO), respectively. ELWP is due to Maskin (1979).

4. SOME BASIC RESULTS

The main result (see proposition 4.1 and remark 4.3 below) proved in this section shows how, given certain axioms, pessimism (or optimism), if it exists at all even in a very limited local form, spreads everywhere to encompass all comparisons of actions in all possible decision problems.

Proposition 4.1 Suppose S∈Z and a,b∈A(S). Assume that the agent satisfies either:

1. axioms 3.1 (Ra), 3.5 (WD), 3.6 (SYM), 3.7 (IRIO) and 3.12 (WIMS) or

2. axioms 3.2 (QRa), 3.4 (D), 3.6 (SYM), 3.7 (IRIO) and 3.12 (WIMS).

Then:

(4.1.1) under axiom 3.16 (ELP), m(a)≻m(b) implies aPb;

(4.1.2) under axiom 3.17 (ELO), $M(a) \succ M(b)$ implies aPb;

and (4.1.3) under axiom 3.18 (LAPO), $[m(a) \succ m(b)$ and $M(b) \succ M(a)]$ implies not (aPb or bPa).

(See notation 3.19; and note that, if axiom 3.1 (Ra) holds, then not (aPb or bPa) is equivalent to aIb.)

Proof: We give below the proofs only for the case where the agent satisfies the axioms listed under (1); the proofs for the case where the agent satisfies the axioms listed under (2) are exactly analogous and are omitted.

(4.1.1): Let $m(a) \succ m(b)$. We first prove:

If $|S|=2$, then aPb. (4.1)

Let $S=\{s_1,s_2\}$. Consider $x,y,z,w \in X$ such that $x \succ y \succ z$ and $x \succeq w$, and consider *a* , c_1, c_2, $c_3 \in A(S)$, defined by:

	s_1	s_2
a	m(a)	m(a)
c_1	y	y
c_2	x	z
c_3	w	z.

By ELP, IRIO and SYM, c_1Pc_2. Hence, by WD, Ra and SYM, c_1Pc_3. Given IRIO and SYM, it can then be easily checked that *a*Pb. Since either a dominates *a* or $[a(s_1) \sim$ *a*(s_1) and $a(s_2) \sim$ *a*$(s_2)]$, by WD, Ra and SYM we have aPb. This proves (4.1).

Now consider the general case. Let $S=\{s_1,\ldots,s_n\} \in Z$, $S'=\{s_1',s_2'\} \in Z$ and $m(b)=b(s_k)$. Consider $\underline{a},\underline{b} \in A(S)$ and $a',b' \in A(S')$, defined by:

	s_1	...	s_{k-1}	s_k	s_{k+1}	...	s_n
$\underline{a}$	m(a)	...	m(a)	m(a)	m(a)	...	m(a)
$\underline{b}$	M(b)	...	M(b)	m(b)	M(b)	...	M(b)

	s_1'	s_2'
a′	m(a)	m(a)
b′	m(b)	M(b).

By (4.1), given m(a)≻m(b), a′Pb′. Hence, by WIMS and SYM, $\underline{a}$P$\underline{b}$. Since either a dominates $\underline{a}$ or, for all s∈S, a(s)∼ $\underline{a}$(s), by WD, Ra and SYM, we have aP$\underline{b}$. Similarly, aP$\underline{b}$ implies aPb. This completes the proof of proposition 4.1.1.

(4.1.2): The proof here is similar to the proof of proposition 4.1.1.

(4.1.3): Suppose LAPO holds, [m(a)≻m(b) and M(b)≻M(a)], and [aPb or bPa]. We show that aPb leads to a contradiction; the proof that bPa also leads to a contradiction is similar. Suppose aPb. Let $S=\{s_1,\ldots,s_n\}\in Z$, $S'=\{s_1',s_2'\}\in Z$ and $M(b)=b(s_k)$, and consider $\underline{a},\underline{b}\in A(S)$ and $a',b'\in A(S')$, defined by:

	s_1	…	s_{k-1}	s_k	s_{k+1}	…	s_n
$\underline{a}$	M(a)	…	M(a)	M(a)	M(a)	…	M(a)
$\underline{b}$	m(b)	…	m(b)	M(b)	m(b)	…	m(b)

	s_1'	s_2'
a′	M(a)	M(a)
b′	m(b)	M(b).

Since M(b)≻M(a)⪰m(a)≻m(b), by LAPO, IRIO, SYM and Ra, a′Ib′. Hence, by WIMS and SYM $\underline{a}$I$\underline{b}$. Since either b dominates $\underline{b}$ or, for all s∈S, b(s)∼$\underline{b}$(s), by WD, Ra and SYM we have bR$\underline{a}$, Similarly, bR$\underline{a}$ implies bRa, contradicting aPb.

The following proposition shows that given certain other axioms, axioms 3.16 (ELP) and 3.20 (ELWP) are logically equivalent, and so are axioms 3.17 (ELO) and 3.21 (ELWO).

Proposition 4.2 Suppose the agent satisfies either:

1. axioms 3.1 (Ra), 3.5 (WD), 3.6 (SYM), 3.7 (IRIO) and 3.12 (WIMS):

2. axioms 3.2 (QRa), 3.4 (D), 3.6 (SYM), 3.7 (IRIO) and 3.12 (WIMS).

Then:

(4.2.1) axiom 3.16 (ELP) holds iff axiom 3.20 (ELWP) holds; and
(4.2.2) axiom 3.17 (ELO) holds iff axiom 3.21 (ELWO) holds.

Proof: We give the proof only for the case where the agent satisfies Ra, WD, SYM, IRIO and WIMS; the proof for the case where the agent satisfies QRa, D, SYM, IRIO and WIMS, being exactly similar, is omitted.

(4.2.1): Clearly, ELP implies ELWP. Therefore, we only have to show that, given Ra, WD, SYM, IRIO and WIMS, ELWP implies ELP. Suppose ELWP holds. Then there exist $S \in Z$, and $a,b \in A(S)$, such that $M(a) \succ M(b)$ and bPa. If $m(a) \succeq M(b)$, then clearly a dominates b and hence by WD we would have aRb, which contradicts bPa. Hence we must have $M(b) \succ m(a)$. Thus $M(a) \succ M(b) \succ m(a)$. Let $S=\{s_1,\ldots,s_n\}$ and let $a(s_j)=M(a)$. Consider actions $\underline{a},\underline{b} \in A(S)$ such that:

	s_1	...	s_{j-1}	s_j	s_{j+1}	...	s_n
$\underline{a}$	m(a)	...	m(a)	M(a)	m(a)	...	m(a)
$\underline{b}$	M(b)	...	M(b)	M(b)	M(b)	...	M(b).

Either a dominates $\underline{a}$ or for all $s \in S$, $a(s) \sim \underline{a}(s)$. Hence, noting bPa, by WD, Ra and SYM, we have bP$\underline{a}$. Again, either $\underline{b}$ dominates b or for all $s \in S$, $b(s) \sim \underline{b}(s)$. Hence noting bP$\underline{a}$, by WD, Ra and SYM we have $\underline{b}$P$\underline{a}$. Now consider $S'=\{s_1',s_2'\} \in Z$, and $a',b' \in A(S')$, such that:

	s_1'	s_2'
a′	m(a)	M(a)
b′	M(b)	M(b).

Since $\underline{b}$P$\underline{a}$, by WIMS and SYM, b′Pa′. Given $M(a) \succ M(b) \succ m(a)$, it follows that ELP holds.

(4.2.2): The proof is analogous to the proof of proposition 4.2.1.

Remark 4.3 In view of proposition 4.2, one can 'generalize' proposition 4.1 by replacing (in the statement of proposition 4.1) axioms 3.16 (ELP) and 3.17 (ELO) by the weaker axioms 3.20 (ELWP) and 3.21 (ELWO), respectively.

The following proposition, proposition 4.4, is essentially due to Arrow and Hurwicz (1972). However, while Arrow and Hurwicz have proved the result in the framework in which for every feasible set of actions an optimal choice set is specified, we restate their formal result in our framework, in which for every $S \in Z$ the agent has a wpr over A(S).

Proposition 4.4 (Arrow and Hurwicz, 1972) Assume axioms 3.1 (Ra), 3.5 (WD), 3.6 (SYM) and 3.10 (IMS). Then there exists an ordering $\mathfrak{R}$ over $X \times X$ such that, for all $S \in Z$ and for all $a,b \in A(S)$, aRb iff $(m(a),M(a))\mathfrak{R}(m(b),M(b))$.[5]

5. DECISION RULES

In this section we provide new axiomatic characterizations of several familiar criteria for decisions under complete uncertainty. The decision criteria which we consider are: maximin and maximax, the min-based and max-based protective criteria, and leximin and leximax.

Definition 5.1 The agent follows the *maximin* (resp. *maximax*) criterion just in the case that, for all $S \in Z$ and for all $a,b \in A(S)$, aRb iff $m(a) \geq m(b)$ (resp. $M(a) \geq M(b)$).

Proposition 5.2 The agent follows the maximin (resp. maximax) criterion iff he satisfies axioms 3.1 (Ra), 3.5 (WD), 3.6 (SYM), 3.7 (IRIO), 3.10 (IMS), 3.14 (SICO) and 3.16 (ELP) (resp. 3.17 (ELO)).[6]

Proof: We give the proof only for the maximin criterion; the proof for the maximax criterion is exactly similar. As the necessity part of the proof can easily be checked, we only show that the axioms under consideration are sufficient to establish the maximin criterion. Let SϵZ and a,bϵA(S). In view of proposition 4.1.1, we need only consider the case m(a)$\sim$m(b). Suppose m(a)$\sim$m(b) and not aIb, so that by Ra, aPb or bPa. Without loss of generality, assume aPb.

Let $S'=\{s_1',s_2'\}\epsilon Z$ and $S''=\{s_1'',s_2'',s_3''\}\epsilon Z$. Consider x,y,z$\epsilon$X such that x$\succ$y$\succ$z, and consider $c_1,c_2,c_3,c_4,c_5\epsilon A(S')$ and $d_1,d_2,d_3,d_4,d_5,d_6,d_7$ $\epsilon A(S'')$, defined by:

	s_1'	s_2'
c_1	m(a)	M(a)
c_2	m(b)	M(b)
c_3	m(a)	m(a)
c_4	z	x
c_5	z	z

	s_1''	s_2''	s_3''
d_1	z	z	x
d_2	z	z	z
d_3	z	x	x
d_4	z	y	z
d_5	z	y	y
d_6	x	z	x
d_7	y	y	y.

Given aPb, by proposition 4.4 $c_1P'c_2$. Since m(b)$\sim$m(a) and therefore either c_2 dominates c_3 or $[c_2(s_1')\sim c_3(s_1')$ and $c_2(s_2')\sim c_3(s_2')]$, by WD, Ra and SYM we have $c_1P'c_3$. Hence, given SYM, M(a)$\succ$m(a) and, since $c_1P'c_3$ and M(a)$\succ$m(a), by IRIO $c_4P'c_5$. Given $c_4P'c_5$, by proposition 4.4, $d_1P''d_2$ and thus, by SICO, $d_3P''d_4$. Given $d_3P''d_4$, by proposition 4.4 again, $d_1P''d_5$ and then, by SICO again, $d_6P''d_7$. However, since by assumption $m(d_7)=y\succ z=m(d_6)$, $d_6P''d_7$ contradicts proposition 4.1.1. This completes the proof.

Notation 5.3 Let SϵZ and a,bϵA(S). Then a*b denotes the restriction of a to $\{s\epsilon S\,|\,\text{not } a(s)\sim b(s)\}$. m(a*b) and M(a*b) denote, respectively, specific $\succeq$ –least and $\succeq$ –greatest outcomes in the range of a*b.

Definition 5.4 The agent follows the *min-based protective* (resp. *max-based protective*) criterion just in the case that, for all $S \epsilon Z$ and for all $a,b \epsilon A(S)$, a Pb iff $m(a*b) \succ m(b*a)$ (resp. $M(a*b) \succ M(b*a)$).

As far as we know, the term 'protective criterion' was first used by Barbera and Dutta (1982), who used it to denote what we have called the min-based protective criterion. However, the min-based protective criterion can be traced to Cohen and Jaffray (1980). The definition of Barbera and Dutta (1982), which is logically equivalent to our definition of the min-based protective criterion, may be stated as follows: the agent follows the min-based protective criterion iff, for all $S \in Z$ and for all $a,b \epsilon A(S)$, [aPb iff there exists $x \epsilon X$ such that $\{s \epsilon S \mid a(s) \sim x\} \subset \{s \epsilon S \mid b(s) \sim x\}$ and, for all $y \epsilon X$, xPy implies $\{s \epsilon S \mid a(s) \sim y\} = \{s \epsilon S \mid b(s) \sim y\}$].

Proposition 5.5 The agent follows the min-based protective criterion (resp. max-based protective criterion) iff he satisfies axioms 3.2 (QRa), 3.4 (D), 3.6 (SYM), 3.7 (IRIO), 3.10 (IMS), 3.13 (ICO) and 3.16 (ELP) (resp. 3.17 (ELO)).

Proof: We give the proof only for the min-based protective criterion; the case of the max-based protective criterion can be handled similarly. As the necessity part of the proof can be easily checked, we only show that the axioms under consideration are sufficient to establish the min-based protective criterion. Assume that all the axioms under consideration are fulfilled. Let $S \epsilon Z$ and let $a,b \epsilon A(S)$. We shall show that $m(a*b) \succ m(b*a)$ implies aPb, and $m(a*b) \sim m(b*a)$ implies not (aPb or bPa), which will establish the min-based protective criterion.

We first show:

If $m(a) \sim m(b)$ and, for some $s_i,s_j \epsilon S$, $b(s_i) \succ a(s_i) \sim m(a)$ and $a(s_j) \succ b(s_j) \sim m(b)$, then not (aPb or bPa). (5.1)

We show that given the hypothesis of (5.1), aPb leads to a contradiction; the proof that under the same hypothesis bPa also leads to a contradiction is similar. Suppose then the hypothesis of (5.1) holds and aPb. Let $S = \{s_1,\dots,s_n\} \epsilon Z$, $S' = \{s_1',s_2'\} \epsilon Z$, $S'' = \{s_1'',s_2'',s_3''\} \epsilon Z$ and $b(s_i) = x$, and consider $\underline{a},\underline{b} \epsilon A(S)$, $a',b' \epsilon A(S')$ and $c_1,c_2,c_3,c_4,c_5 \epsilon A(S'')$, defined by:

	s_1	...	s_{i-1}	s_i	s_{i+1}	...	s_n
$\underline{a}$	M(a)	...	M(a)	m(a)	M(a)	...	M(a)
$\underline{b}$	m(a)	...	m(a)	x	m(a)	...	m(a)

	s_1'	s_2'
a′	m(a)	M(a)
b′	x	m(a)

	s_1''	s_2''	s_3''
c_1	m(a)	m(a)	M(a)
c_2	x	x	m(a)
c_3	m(a)	x	x
c_4	x	m(a)	M(a)
c_5	x	x	x.

Given aPb, it follows by D, QRa and SYM that $\underline{a}$Pb. Similarly, noting m(a)~m(b), $\underline{a}$Pb implies $\underline{a}$P$\underline{b}$. Hence, by IMS and SYM, a′P′b′ and therefore, again by IMS and SYM, $c_1P''c_2$. By SYM, not $c_3P''c_2$ and hence, noting $c_1P''c_2$, we have by QRa not $c_3P''c_1$. Thus, using ICO, not $c_5P''c_4$. Since $x=b(s_i)\succ m(a)$, not $c_5P''c_4$ contradicts proposition 4.1.1. This completes the proof of (5.1).

Now let $T=\{s\epsilon S \mid \text{not } a(s)\sim b(s)\}$. Consider $a'',b''\epsilon A(S)$ such that:

$$a''|T=a|T \quad \text{and} \quad b''|T=b|T \quad \text{and, for all } s\epsilon S-T, \quad a''(s)=b''(s)=M(a). \tag{5.2}$$

Suppose m(a*b)≻m(b*a). Then, by construction m(a″)≻m(b″), and hence by proposition 4.1.1 a″Pb″. Given a″Pb″ and noting (5.2), we have, by ICO and SYM, aPb. Now suppose m(a*b)~m(b*a). Then, by construction the hypothesis of (5.1) holds, and hence by (5.1) not (a″Pb″ or b″Pa″). It follows by ICO and SYM, again, that not (aPb or bPa). This completes the proof.

Notation 5.6 Let SεZ, xεX and aεA(S). n(x,a) denotes the cardinality of $\{s\epsilon S \mid a(s)\sim x\}$.

Definition 5.7 The agent follows the *leximin* (resp. *leximax*) criterion just in the case that, for all $S\epsilon Z$ and for all $a,b\epsilon A(S)$, [aRb iff there does not exist $x\epsilon X$ such that $n(x,a)>n(x,b)$ (resp. $n(x,a)<n(x,b)$) and, for all $y\epsilon X$, xPy (resp. yPx) implies $n(y,a)=n(y,b)$].

Proposition 5.8 The agent follows the leximin criterion (resp. leximax criterion) iff he satisfies axioms 3.1 (Ra), 3.4 (D), 3.6 (SYM), 3.7 (IRIO), 3.12 (WIMS), 3.13 (ICO) and 3.16 (ELP) (resp. 3.17 (ELO)).[7]

Proof: We give the proof only for the leximin criterion, the case of the leximax criterion being exactly similar. As the necessity part of the proof can easily be checked, we only show that the axioms under consideration are sufficient to establish the leximin criterion.

Let $S=\{s_1,\ldots,s_n\}\epsilon Z$ and let $a,b\epsilon A(S)$. Arrange the outcomes in a(S) in order of preference: $x_n \succsim x_{n-1} \succsim \ldots \succsim x_1$; similarly, arrange the outcomes in b(S) in order of preference: $y_n \succsim y_{n-1} \succsim \ldots \succsim y_1$. (Note that, given $s_i \epsilon S$, x_i need not equal $a(s_i)$, nor y_i equal $b(s_i)$.) Denote by P_{lex} and I_{lex}, respectively, the asymmetric and symmetric factors of the leximin ordering over A(S). If $aI_{lex}b$, it is clear that for $i=1,\ldots,n$, $x_i \sim y_i$. Thus, by SYM and Ra it follows from $aI_{lex}b$ that aIb.

Now, suppose $aP_{lex}b$. Then there exists k, $1\leq k\leq n$, such that $x_k \succ y_k$ and for all j, $1\leq j<k$, $x_j \sim y_j$. Consider $c_1,c_2,c_3,c_4\epsilon A(S)$, defined by:

	s_1	$\ldots$	s_{k-1}	s_k	s_{k+1}	$\ldots$	s_n
c_1	x_1	$\ldots$	x_{k-1}	x_k	x_{k+1}	$\ldots$	x_n
c_2	x_1	$\ldots$	x_{k-1}	y_k	y_{k+1}	$\ldots$	y_n
c_3	x_k	$\ldots$	x_k	x_k	x_{k+1}	$\ldots$	x_n
c_4	x_k	$\ldots$	x_k	y_k	y_{k+1}	$\ldots$	y_n.

Since $m(c_3) \sim x_k \succ y_k \sim m(c_4)$, by proposition 4.1.1 c_3Pc_4. Then, by ICO, c_1Pc_2. Given c_1Pc_2 and noting $x_j \sim y_j$ for $j=1,\ldots,k-1$, by SYM and Ra, we have aPb.

Remark 5.9 In view of proposition 4.2, we can get new valid propositions by replacing axioms 3.16 (ELP) and 3.17 (ELO) by the weaker axioms 3.20 (ELWP) and 3.21 (ELWO), respectively, in the statements of propositions 5.2, 5.5 and 5.8.

We now briefly compare our axiomatic characterization of the different decision criteria with earlier characterizations given by Maskin (1979) and Barbera and Jackson (1985). Maskin gives ordinal (as well as cardinal) characterizations of maximin and leximin criteria, but does not consider the min-based protective criterion. The main difference between Maskin's ordinal characterization of maximin and ours is that while Maskin does not use IRIO, SICO, ELP or ELWP (which we use), he uses the assumption of denseness (for all $x,y \in X$, if $x \succ y$, then, for some $z \in X$, $x \succ z \succ y$), and the assumptions of convexity (defined in an ordinal fashion) and continuity of preferences, none of which are used by us. Note that while denseness is a 'natural' feature when one uses the Neumann–Morgenstern utilities, it is a rather strong structural assumption when the framework is ordinal. Our characterization of leximin is close to Maskin's, though the proofs are different; the main difference in terms of axioms is that, in characterizing the leximin rule, Maskin uses either the structural property of countability (the number of indifference classes generated by $\succeq$ is either one or at least countably infinitely many), or a weaker version of IMS, different from our WIMS.

Barbara and Jackson give characterizations of maximin, leximin and the min-based protective criterion. They consider an action to be a finite dimensional vector of real numbers, the real numbers being interpreted as utilities from the action under alternative states of the world. Every possible finite dimensional vector of real numbers is a permissible action in their framework. This feature builds the structural assumption of denseness, referred to earlier, into all the characterizations of Barbara and Jackson. It also suggests that the utility numbers are perhaps meant to be of the Neumann–Morgenstern variety, though Barbara and Jackson themselves do not explicitly specify the exact ordinal/cardinal status of their utility numbers. The impression that the utilities may be cardinal is further strengthened by their assumption of convexity, which requires that, if each of two actions a and b is better than (resp. at least as good as) action c, then $(a+b)/2$ is better than (resp. at least as good as) c. (Recall that actions are vectors of real numbers, and note that only actions having the same dimension can be compared.) This assumption is unambiguous when the utilities are of the Neumann–Morgenstern variety, but it seems to us that the assumption involves some ambiguities if the utilities are ordinal. (For example, does it hold for some ordinal representation of the underlying ordering over outcomes, or does it hold for all such representations?)

Irrespective of the exact nature of Barbara and Jackson's utilities, denseness, as we have pointed out above, is a basic structural property underlying their characterizations; we do not use this property. There are also other differences. For example, Barbara and Jackson use convexity in all their characterizations, but not IRIO, ELP or ELWP (which we use); for maximin, they use continuity but not SICO; and also, in using axioms similar to, or identical with, Ra, D, SYM and IMS for characterizing maximin and leximin, they restrict the applicability of these axioms to the domain of pairs of actions such that, for every pair, the worst pay-offs of the two actions in the pair are different. (For example, one of the axioms used in characterizing the maximin rule is the dominance axiom restricted to such a domain, though the maximin rule does not satisfy dominance for an unrestricted domain.)

6. CONCLUSION

In this chapter we have considered the implication of various axioms regarding decision-making under complete uncertainty in a framework of ordinal preferences. We have shown that certain sets of assumption impose on the agent a very severe type of uniformity with respect to his possible pessimism or optimism. Using this result we have also provided new ordinal characterizations of several decision criteria, namely the maximin, maximax, leximin and leximax criteria, and the min-based and max-based protective criteria.

It is worth noting that while in this chapter we have concentrated on decision-making under complete uncertainty, the formal structure that we have used bears re-interpretation in terms of welfare rankings of social states (though some of the axioms such as IMS become somewhat implausible under such re-interpretation). The reader who may be interested in such re-interpretation is referred to Maskin (1979) and Barbera and Jackson (1985).[8]

NOTES

1. We are grateful to S. Barbera and M. Jackson for the privilege of reading their unpublished paper. We are also grateful for many helpful comments to F. Hahn, D. Kelsey, M. Salles, R. Sugden and other participants in seminars at Cambridge University, the University of Caen and the University of East Anglia, where an earlier version of this paper was presented.
2. See the discussion at the end of section 5 below.
3. Though Arrow and Hurwitz (1972) use the Neumann–Morgenstern utilities, nothing in their axioms or their proofs depends on the cardinal nature of the utility numbers.
4. Compare with Maskin (1979).
5. Given proposition 4.4, it can easily be shown that axioms 3.1 (Ra), 3.4 (D), 3.6 (SYM) and 3.10 (IMS) are inconsistent, and also axioms 3.1 (Ra), 3.5 (WD), 3.6 (SYM), 3.10 (IMS), 3.13 (ICO) and 3.15 (RSO) are inconsistent.
6. In private correspondence David Kelsey has sent us a result which implies that, if $\succeq$ generates at least four distinct indifference classes, then Ra, IRIO, LAPO and RSO are inconsistent. (Note that throughout the text we have assumed that there are at least three, but not necessarily four or more, indifference classes defined in terms of $\succeq$.) Since the maximin and maximax results both satisfy RSO, and since at least one of the three axioms – ELP, ELO, LAPO – must hold, by proposition 5.2 and Kelsey's result it follows that, if $\succeq$ generates at least four distinct indifference classes, then the only decision rules which satisfy Ra, WD, SYM, IRIO, IMS, SICO and RSO are the maximin and maximax criteria.
7. Following the reasoning in note 5, and using David Kelsey's result together with proposition 5.9, it can be shwon that if $\succeq$ generates at least four indifference classes, then the only decision rules which satisfy Ra, SYM, IRIO, WIMS and ICO are the leximin and leximax criteria.
8. See also d'Aspremont and Gevers (1977) and Deschamps and Gevers (1978).

REFERENCES

Arrow, K.J., (1963), *Social Choice and Individual Values*, second edition New York: Wiley.

Arrow, K.J. and L. Hurwicz, (1972), 'An Optimality Criterion for Decision-Making under Ignorance', in C.F. Carter and J. L. Ford (eds), *Uncertainty and Expectations in Economics*. New Jersey: Augustus M. Kelley.

Barbera, S. and B. Dutta, (1982), 'Implementability via Protective Equilibria', *Journal of Mathematical Economics*, **10**, 49–65.

Barbera, S. and M. Jackson, (1985), 'Maximin, Leximin and the Protective Criterion: Characterizations and Comparisons', mimeograph.

Cohen, M. and J.-Y. Jaffray, (1980), 'Rational Behaviour under Ignorance', *Econometrica*, **48**, 1281–1299.

Cohen, M and J. Y. Jaffray (1983), 'Approximations of Rational Criteria under Complete Ignorance and the Independence Axiom', Journal of Economic Theory, **15**, 121–150.

d'Aspremont, C. and L. Gevers, (1977), 'Equity and the Informational Basis of Collective Choice', *Review of Economic Studies*, **44**, 199–209.

Deschamps, R. and L. Gevers, (1978), 'Leximin and Utilitarian Rules: A Joint Characterization', *Journal of Economic Theory*, **17**, 143–163.

Luce, R.D. and H. Raiffa, (1957), *Games and Decisions*. New York: Wiley.

Maskin, E. (1979), 'Decision-Making under Ignorance with Implications for Social Choice', *Theory and Decision*, **11**, 319–37.

Milnor, J., (1954), 'Games Against Nature', in R.M. Thrall, C.H. Coombe and R.L. Davis (eds), *Decision Processes*, New York: Chapman and Hall.

Savage, L., (1954), *The Foundations of Statistics*. New York: Wiley.

4. The Characteristic Function of the Dirichlet and Multivariate F Distributions

Peter C.B. Phillips

1. INTRODUCTION

Let X_j ($j = 0, 1, \ldots, m$) be independent chi-squared variates with n_j degrees of freedom. The joint density of the ratios $Y_j = X_j/X_0$ ($j = 1, \ldots, m$) is given by:

$$\text{pdf}\,(y_1, \ldots, y_m) = \frac{\Gamma(n/2)}{\prod_{j=0}^{m} \Gamma(n_j/2)} \; \frac{\prod_{j=0}^{m} y_j^{(n_j/2)-1}}{[1 + \sum_{j=1}^{m} y_j]^{n/2}}, \quad n = \sum_{j=0}^{m} n_j, \tag{1}$$

and this is known as an inverted Dirichlet distribution (see Tiao and Guttman, 1965; Johnson and Kotz, 1972, pp. 238–9). The rescaled variates $F_j = (n_0/n_j)Y_j$ ($j = 1, \ldots, m$) are multivariate F and arise in analysis of variance problems with m independent 'effect' sums of squares X_j ($j = 1, \ldots, m$) and an overall residual sum of squares X_0. See Finney (1941) and Johnson and Kotz (1972, pp. 240–43) for a brief review. Other applications occur in econometrics where some simultaneous equations estimators can be written quite simply as ratios of linear combinations of independent χ^2 variates leading to distributions that are of the form (1) in certain cases (see Anderson and Sawa, 1973).

This chapter is concerned with the characteristic function (c.f.) of the multivariate distribution (1). As pointed out by Ifram (1970), the c.f. of the F distribution tends to be avoided in the literature even in the scalar case. This is because correct formulae for the c.f. of the F distribution are not well known and it is often assumed that no simple expression is available. Indeed, until very recently, formulae for the c.f. of the F distribution that have been given in the literature have been incorrect. This was pointed out in independent work by Pestana (1977) and Phillips (1982). Awad (1980) attempted to correct the earlier incorrect formulae by Ifram (1970) and Johnson and Kotz (1972, p. 190). Unfortunately, Awad's expression is also incorrect. In fact, his series representation (equation (2), p. 128 of Awad (1980)) is non-convergent, as is easily verified. Indeed, if his series expression were valid, it would imply that the F distribution had finite moments of all orders which, of course, is not so.

As shown in Phillips (1982) the true c.f. of the (scalar) F distribution has a rather simple expression in terms of a confluent hypergeometric function of the second kind (see equation (6) of Phillips, 1982). When m = 1 above, this result implies that the c.f. of (1) is simply:

$$\text{c.f.}(s) = E(e^{isY_1}) = \frac{\Gamma(n/2)}{\Gamma(n_0/2)} \Psi(n_1/2\ ,\ 1 - n_0/2;\ -is)\ , \tag{2}$$

where Ψ denotes the confluent function of the second kind. The special function Ψ has been extensively studied in the applied mathematics literature; see Erdèlyi (1953, Ch. 6) for a detailed review. Its properties enable us to characterize the behaviour of (2) in the vicinity of the origin, to extract moment formulae and to provide series representations for computation. These and other applications of (2) are discussed in Phillips (1982).

The present paper shows that the joint characteristic function of the inverted Dirichlet distribution (and hence the multivariate F distribution) can be written in terms of a confluent hypergeometric function of the second kind with multiple arguments. The Appendix studies this function in detail and records some of its properties including formulae that are useful in computation. A simple integral representation of the function that arises directly from the multivariate t distribution in a special case is also explored. This representation is extended to apply in the general case.

2. THE CHARACTERISTIC FUNCTION IN THE GENERAL CASE

We shall work with the general inverted Dirichlet distribution whose density function is given by:

$$\text{pdf}\,(y_1, \ldots, y_m) = \frac{\Gamma(\beta)}{\prod_{j=0}^{m} \Gamma(\beta_j)} \; \frac{\prod_{j=1}^{m} y_j^{\beta_j - 1}}{[1 + \sum_{j=1}^{m} y_j]^{\beta}}, \quad \beta = \sum_{j=0}^{m} \beta_j , \tag{3}$$

with $\beta_j > 0$ ($j = 0, \ldots, m$) (see Tiao and Guttman, 1965, equation (2.10)). This is related to the Dirichlet distribution by the transformation:

$$x_j = y_j/(1 + y_1 + \ldots + y_m), \quad j = 1, \ldots, m,$$

leading to the joint density:

$$\text{pdf}\,(x_1, \ldots, x_m) = \left[\prod_{j=0}^{m} \Gamma(\beta_j)\right]^{-1} \Gamma(\beta) \prod_{j=1}^{m} x_j^{\beta_j - 1} \left[1 - \sum_{j=1}^{m} x_j\right]^{\beta_0 - 1} \tag{4}$$

for $x_j > 0, \; \sum_{j=1}^{m} x_j < 1$ (again, see Tiao and Guttman, 1965).

The c.f. of (4) is known to be given by a confluent function of the first kind with many arguments. In fact, as shown by Exton (1976, pp. 232–3), we have:

$$\text{c.f.}(s_1, \ldots, s_m) = E\{e^{i(s_1 x_1 + \ldots + s_m x_m)}\} = \Phi^{[m]}\,(\beta_1, \ldots, \beta_m; \beta; is_1, \ldots, is_m) \tag{5}$$

where:

$$\Phi^{[m]}(b_1, \ldots, b_m; c; z_1, \ldots, z_m) = \sum \frac{(b_1)_{k_1} \cdots (b_m)_{k_m} \cdots z_1^{b_1} \cdots z_m^{b_m}}{(c)_k \, k_1! \ldots k_m!} \tag{6}$$

The summation in (6) is over all integers $k_j = 0, 1, \ldots, \infty$ ($j = 1, \ldots, m$). This series is a confluent form of a Lauricella function (see Exton, 1976, p. 42) and when $m = 1$ it reduces to the well-known confluent hypergeometric function of the first kind with scalar argument. However, (6) is inconvenient for numerical calculation when $m > 2$. Instead a single integral representation is available:

$$\Phi^{[m]} = \frac{\Gamma(c)}{2\pi i} \int_L e^t \, t^{\sum_1^m b_j - c} \prod_{j=1}^{m} (t - z_j)^{-b_j} \, dt , \tag{7}$$

where L denotes any path in the complex t-plane originating at $-\infty$ encircling in the positive direction all finite singularities of the integrand and returning to $-\infty$. Such a contour is illustrated in Figure 4.1. The loop integral (7) was given by Erdèlyi (1939, equation (7)). It may be computed by complex numerical integration along a convenient and appropriate contour in the t-plane.

Figure 4.1: Contour of the Lauricella Function

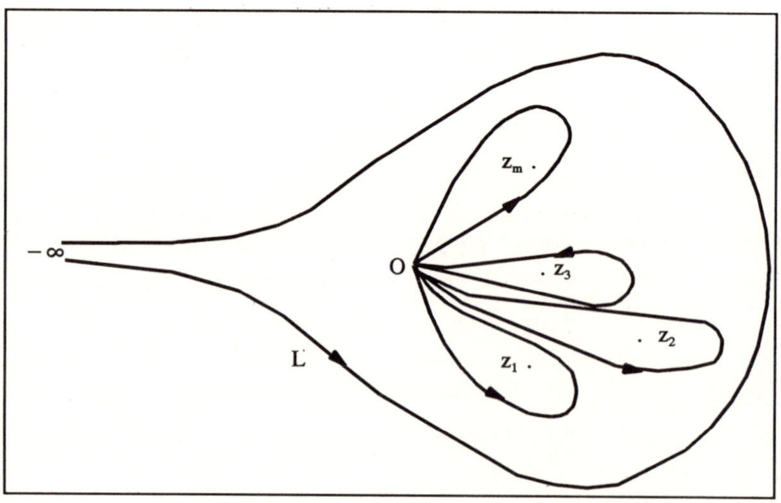

The c.f. of the density (3) is also a confluent function with many arguments. But, as in the scalar case considered in Phillips (1982), the appropriate function is a confluent function of the second kind. To our knowledge this function does not appear in the applied mathematics literature and we have therefore devoted the Appendix to study its properties. We define the function:

$$\Psi^{[m]}(b_1, \ldots, b_m; c; z_1, \ldots, z_m) = K \int_0^\infty \ldots \int_0^\infty \tag{8}$$

$$e^{-u_1 z_1 \ldots -u_m z_m} u_1^{b_1 - 1} \ldots u_m^{b_m - 1} (1 + u_1 + \ldots u_m)^{c - \sum_1^m b_i - 1} du_1 \ldots du_m$$

where:

$$K = \left[\prod_{j=1}^{m} \Gamma(b_j) \right]^{-1}$$

for $\text{Re}(b_j) > 0$ ($j = 1, \ldots, m$) and $\text{Re}(z_j) > 0$ ($j = 1, \ldots, m$). The domain of definition of $\Psi^{[m]}$ can be extended beyond $\text{Re}(z_j) > 0$ ($j = 1, \ldots, m$) and this is useful in determining the required c.f. In fact, if

$$\text{Re}(c) < 1 \tag{9}$$

then the integral representation (8) continues to hold for z_j on the imaginary axis, that is for $\text{Re}(z_j) > 0$ ($j = 1, \ldots, m$).

Setting $z_j = -is_j$ in (8) we deduce that the c.f. of the inverted Dirichlet distribution (3) is:

$$\text{c.f.}(s_1, \ldots, s_m) = \frac{\Gamma(\beta)}{\Gamma(\beta_0)} \Psi^{[m]}(\beta_1, \ldots, \beta_m; 1 - \beta_0; -is_1, \ldots, -is_m), \tag{10}$$

Observe that condition (9) is satisfied in the present case since $c = 1-\beta_0$ and $\beta_j > 0$ ($j = 0, \ldots, m$) in (3).

A simple integral representation of (10) is also available. The following is based on the analysis of $\Psi^{[m]}$ in the Appendix.

Theorem

$$c.f.(s_1, \ldots, s_m) = \{\Gamma(\beta_0)\}^{-1} \int_0^\infty e^{-x} x^{\sum_0^m \beta_j - 1} \prod_{j=1}^m (x - is_j)^{-\beta_j} dx , \tag{11}$$

The integral representation (11) follows directly from (10) and the lemma in the Appendix. It is clearly more convenient for numerical purposes than the multi-dimensional integral based on (8). When $m = 1$ we find from (11) and (A17) that:

$$c.f.(s_1) = \frac{\Gamma(\beta_0 + \beta_1)}{\Gamma(\beta_0)} \Psi(\beta_1, 1-\beta_0; -is_1) , \tag{12}$$

which is the characteristic function of the one dimensional inverted Dirichlet distribution (3). Setting $\beta_0 = n_o/2$, $\beta_1 = n_1/2$ (12) reduces to the earlier formula (2) given in Phillips (1982).

3. CONNECTION WITH THE MULTIVARIATE F DISTRIBUTION

Let $Y = k^{-1/2}t_k$ where t_k is an m-vector multivariate t variate with k degrees of freedom. We may write $y = Y/w$ where $Y = N(0, I_n)$, $w^2 = \chi_k^2$ and Y is independent of w. Here the symbol ' = ' signifies equality in distribution.

We shall consider the transformed vector variate:

$$f = (f_1, f_2, \ldots, f_m) = (y_1^2, y_2^2, \ldots, y_m^2).$$

Clearly, f has the distribution (1) with $n_j = 1$ (j = 1, …, m) and $n_0 = k$. Using the representation $y = Y/w$ it is now easy to obtain the c.f. by iterated expectations:

$$\text{c.f.}(s_1, \ldots, s_m) = E_w\{ E_Y\{ e^{(is_1 Y_1^2 + \ldots + is_m Y_m^2)/w^2} \mid w\} \}$$

$$= E_w\{ \prod_{j=1}^{m} (1 - 2is_j/w^2)^{-1/2} \}$$

$$= \{\Gamma(k/2)\, 2^{k/2}\}^{-1} \int_0^{\infty} e^{-u/2} u^{(k/2)-1} \prod_{j-1}^{m} (1 - 2is_j/u)^{-1/2}\, du$$

$$= \{\Gamma(k/2)\}^{-1} \int_0^{\infty} e^{-v} v^{(k+m)/2-1} \prod_{j=1}^{m} (v - is_j)^{-1/2}\, dv.$$

This expression is, of course, a special case of (11) with $\beta_0 = k/2$ and $\beta_j = 1/2$ (j = 1, …, m).

REFERENCES

Anderson, T.W. and T. Sawa (1973), 'Distributions of Estimates of Coefficients of a Single Equation in a Simultaneous System and their Asymptotic Expansion', *Econometrica*, **41**, 683–714.

Awad, A.M. (1980), 'Remark on the Characteristic Function of the F Distribution', *Sankhya Series A*, **42**, 128–9.

Erdèlyi, A (1939), 'Integration of Certain Systems of Linear Partial Differential Equations of Hypergeometric Type', *Proceedings of the Royal Society of Edinburgh, Section A*, **59**, 224–41.
Erdèlyi, A. (1953), *Higher Transcendental Functions*, New York: McGraw Hill.
Exton, H. (1976), *Multiple Hypergeometric Functions and Applications*, New York: John Wiley.
Finney, D.J. (1941), 'The Joint Distribution of Variance Ratios based on a Common Error Mean Square', *Annals of Eugenics*, **11**, 136–40.
Ifram, A.F. (1970), 'On the Characteristic Function of the F- and t- Distributions', *Sankhya Series A*, **32**, 350–52.
Johnson, N.L. and S. Kotz (1972), *Continuous Multivariate Distributions*, New York: John Wiley.
Pestana, D. (1977), 'Note on a Paper by Ifram', *Sankhya Series A*, **39**, 396–7.
Phillips, P.C.B (1982), 'The True Characteristic Function of the F Distribution', *Biometrika*, **60**, 261-4.
Tiao, G.C. and I. Guttman (1965), 'The Inverted Dirichlet Distribution with Applications', *Journal of the American Statistical Association*, **60**, 793–805.

APPENDIX

The Confluent Hypergeometric Function of the Second Kind With Multiple Arguments

The confluent hypergeometric function:

(A1) $$\Phi(b, c; z) = \sum_{k=0}^{\infty} \frac{(b)_k z^k}{(c)_k k!} = w_1,$$

say, is known to satisfy the linear differential equation:

(A2) $$zw'' + (c\text{-}z)w' - bw = 0, \qquad w = w(z).$$

The function:

$$w_2 = z^{1-c}\,\Phi(1+b-c, 2-c; z)$$

is also a solution of (A2). The confluent hypergeometric function of the second kind is a linear combination of these particular solutions, w_1 and w_2. In fact:

(A3)

$$\Psi(b, c; z) = \frac{\Gamma(1-c)}{\Gamma(1+b-c)}\Phi(b, c; z) + \frac{\Gamma(c-1)}{\Gamma(b)} z^{1-c}\Phi(1+b-c, 2-c; z)$$

$$= [\Gamma(b)]^{-1}\int_0^\infty e^{-zu} u^{b-1}(1+u)^{c-b-1} du$$

with the latter integral representation holding for Re(b) > 0 and Re(z) > 0 (see Erdèlyi, 1953, pp. 255–7).

The confluent function $\Phi^{[m]}$ that is defined in the text by (6) satisfies a system of m partial differential equations that extend (A2) to m variables. Indeed, $\Phi^{[m]}$ satisfies:

(A4) $$\sum_{k=1}^{m} z_k \partial_{kj} w + (c - z_j)\partial_j w - b_j w = 0, \; j = 1, \ldots, m$$

where $\partial_{kj} = \partial^2/\partial z_k \partial z_j$, $\partial_j = \partial/\partial z_j$. The system (A4) was studied by Erdèlyi (1939) and, more recently, by Exton (1976). There are $n+1$ linearly independent (particular) solutions of (A4) and the general solution may be written as a linear combination of these particular integrals. Exton (1976, pp. 173–8) shows that:

$$\int_g^h e^t\, t^{b_1+\ldots b_n-c}(t - z_1)^{-b_1} \ldots (t - z_n)^{-b_n}\, dt$$

is a solution of (A4) provided the contour of integration is a closed path on the Riemann surface of the integrand or a simple path in the t-plane connecting any two zeroes of the integrand. Let $z_1, \ldots, z_m$ be distinct points and suppose $z_j \neq 0$ for all j. Then $m+1$ linearly independent solutions of (A4) are given by the contour integrals:

(A5)
$$w_i = \int_0^{(z_i+)} e^t \, t^{\sum_1^m b_j - c} \prod_{j=1}^m (t - z_j)^{-b_j} \, dt, \quad i = 1, \ldots, m$$

(A6)
$$w_0 = \Phi^{[m]} = \frac{\Gamma(c)}{2\pi i} \int_L e^t \, t^{\sum_1^m (b_j - c)} \prod_{j=1}^m (t - z_j)^{-b_j} dt.$$

The contour in (A5) is a loop that starts and ends at $t = 0$ and encircles the point z_i once in the positive sense. In (A6) L is a loop that starts and ends at $-\infty$ and encircles all finite singularities of the integrand in the positive direction. These contours are illustrated in Figure 4.1.

The confluent function of the second kind $\Psi^{[m]}$ defined by (8) is also a solution of (A4). To see this we write $\Psi^{[m]}$ in the alternative form:

(A7)
$$\Psi^{[m]}(b_1, \ldots, b_m; c; z_1, \ldots, z_m)$$

$$= [\Gamma(b_m)]^{-1} \int_0^\infty e^{-u_m z_m} u_m^{b_m - 1} (1 + u_m)^{c - b_m - 1}$$

$$\Psi^{[m-1]}(b_1, \ldots, b_{m-1}; c - b_m; (1 + u_m) z_1, \ldots, (1 + u_m) z_{m-1}) \, du_m.$$

Substituting $w = \Psi^{[m]}$ in (A4) and writing partial derivatives of $\Psi^{[m-1]}$ as $\partial_k \Psi^{[m-1]} = \Psi_k^{[m-1]}$, we find that the left side of the m'th equation of (A4) is proportional to :

$$\int_0^\infty \{- \sum_{k=1}^{m-1} e^{-u_m z_m} u_m^{b_m} (1 + u_m)^{c - b_m} \Psi_k^{[m-1]} + z_m e^{-u_m z_m} u_m^{b_m - 1} (1 + u_m)^{c - b_m - 1} \Psi^{[m-1]}$$

$$-(c-z_m)\, e^{-u_m z_m}\, u_m^{b_m}(1+u_m)^{c-b_m-1}\Psi^{[m-1]} - b_m e^{-u_m z_m}\, u_m^{b_m-1}(1+u_m)^{c-b_m-1}\Psi^{[m-1]}\big\}du_m$$

$$= -\int_0^\infty \frac{d}{du_m}\Big[\, e^{-u_m z_m}\, u_m^{b_m}\,(1+u_m)^{(c-b_m)}$$

$$\Psi^{[m-1]}(b_1,\ldots,b_{m-1};\, c;\, (1+u_m)z_1,\ldots,(1+u_m)\, z_{m-1}\,\Big]\, du_m$$

$$= \quad 0$$

To verify that $\Psi^{[m]}$ is a solution of the j'th equation of (A4) we write:

$$\Psi_m = [\Gamma(b_j)]^{-1}\int_0^\infty\{e^{-u_j z_j}\, u_j^{b_j-1}(1+u_j)^{c-b_j-1}\,\Psi^{[m-1]}(b_1,\ldots,b_{j-1},b_{j+1},\ldots,b_m;$$

$$c-b_j;\,(1+u_j)z_1,\,\ldots,\,(1+u_j)z_{j-1},\,(1+u_j)z_{j+1},\,\ldots,\,(1+u_j)z_m\}\, du_j$$

and, in an analogous way, $\Psi^{[m]}$ satisfies the j'th equation of (A4) by substitution.

Since $\Psi^{[m]}$ is a particular integral of (A4) it may be written as a linear combination of the solutions w_j ($j = 0, \ldots, m$). Let:

$$\text{(A8)} \qquad \Psi^{[m]} = \sum_{j=0}^{m} A_j w_j$$

The constants A_j ($j = 0, \ldots, m$) in this expression may be found by taking certain limits as $z_j \to 0$. From the definition of $\Psi^{[m]}$ in (A8) and in view of the intended application to (3) we require $\mathrm{Re}(b_j) > 0$ ($j = 1, \ldots, m$). It is also convenient to assume temporarily that $0 < \mathrm{Re}(c) < 1$ and that $z_j \neq 0$ for all j. Then, by allowing $z_j \to 0$ so that $\mathrm{Re}(z_j) \to 0+$ for all j, we obtain:

(A9)
$$A_0 = \lim_{z_1,\dots,z_m \to 0+} K \int_0^\infty \dots \int_0^\infty e^{-u_1 z_1 + \dots - u_m z_m} u_1^{b_1 - 1} \dots u_m^{b_m - 1}$$

$$(1 + u_1 + \dots + u_m)^{c - \sum_1^m b_i - 1} du_1 \dots du_m$$

$$= K \int_0^\infty \dots \int_0^\infty u_1^{b_1 - 1} \dots u_m^{b_m - 1} (1 + u_1 + \dots u_m)^{c - \sum_1^m b_i - 1} du_1 \dots du_m$$

$$= \frac{K \prod_1^m \Gamma(b_i)\, \Gamma(1-c)}{\Gamma(\sum_1^m b_i + 1 - c)}$$

$$= \frac{\Gamma(1-c)}{\Gamma(\sum_1^m b_i + 1 - c)} .$$

Next, to find A_1 we let $z_j \to 0$ with $\mathrm{Re}(z_j) \to 0+$ for $j = 2, \dots, m$ giving:

(A10)
$$K_1 \int_0^\infty e^{-u_1 z_1} u_1^{b_1 - 1} (1 + u_1)^{c - b_1 - 1} du_1$$

$$= A_0 w_0(z_1, 0, \dots, 0) + A_1 \int_0^{(z_1+)} e^t t^{b_1 - c} (t - z_1)^{-b_1} dt ,$$

where:

$$K_1 = [\Gamma(b_1)]^{-1}\ \Psi^{[m-1]}(b_2, \ldots, b_m;\ c - b_1;\ 0, \ldots, 0)$$

$$= \frac{\Gamma(1 + b_1 - c)}{\Gamma(b_1)\ \Gamma\left(\sum_1^m b_j + 1 - c\right)} .$$

The second term on the right side of (A10) can be written:

$$A_1 z_1^{1-c} \int_0^{(1+)} e^{z_1 r}\ r^{b_1 - c}(r-1)^{-b_1} dr$$

$$= \quad A_1 z_1^{1-c}\ \frac{2\pi i\ \Gamma(b_1 - c + 1)}{\Gamma(2-c)\ \Gamma(b_1)}\ \Phi(b_1 - c + 1,\ 2-c;\ z_1)$$

(see Erdèlyi, 1953, p. 272, equation (2)).

We now differentiate (A10) with respect to z_1, multiply the equation through by z_1^c and allow $z_1 \rightarrow 0$ with $\mathrm{Re}(z_1) \rightarrow 0+$. The left side is:

$$-K \lim_{z_1 \to 0}\ z_1^c \int_0^\infty e^{-u_1 z_1}\ u_1^{b_1}(1 + u_1)^{c - b_1 - 1} du_1$$

$$= -\ K_1 \lim_{z_1 \to 0} \int_0^\infty e^{-v}\ v^{b_1}(v + z_1)^{c - b_1 - 1}\ dv$$

$$= -K_1 \int_0^\infty e^{-v}\ v^{c-1}\ dv$$

$$= -K_1 \Gamma(c).$$

The first term on the right side of (A10) tends to zero with these operations. The second term tends to:

$$\frac{(1-c)\ 2\pi i\ A_1\ \Gamma(b_1 - c + 1)}{\Gamma(2-c)\ \Gamma(b_1)}.$$

We deduce that:

$$A_1 = -\frac{K_1\ \Gamma(c)\ \Gamma(2-c)\ \Gamma(b_1)}{(1-c)\ 2\pi i\ \Gamma(b_1 - c + 1)}$$

$$= \frac{\Gamma(c-1)\ \Gamma(2-c)}{2\pi i\ \Gamma(\sum_1^m b_j + 1 - c)}.$$

In a similar way we find:

$$\text{(A11)} \qquad A_j = \frac{\Gamma(c-1)\ \Gamma(2-c)}{2\pi i\ \Gamma(\sum_1^m b_j + 1 - c)}, \quad j = 2, \ldots, m.$$

From (A8)–(A11) it follows that

$$\text{(A12)} \qquad \Psi^{[m]} = \frac{\Gamma(1-c)}{\Gamma(\sum_1^m b_j + 1 - c)}\ \Phi^{[m]}(b_1, \ldots, b_m; c; z_1, \ldots, z_m)$$

$$+ \frac{\Gamma(c-1)\,\Gamma(2-c)}{2\pi i\,\Gamma(\sum_{i}^{m} b_j + 1 - c)} \sum_{k=1}^{m} \int_0^{(z_k+)} e^t\, t^{\sum_1^m b_j - c} \prod_{j=1}^{m} (t - z_j)^{-b_j}\, dt\,.$$

and since:

$$\Gamma(c)\,\Gamma(1-c) = -\Gamma(c-1)\,\Gamma(2-c),$$

we deduce from (A6) and (A12) that:

(A13) $$\Psi^{[m]}(b_1, \ldots, b_m;\, c;\, z_1, \ldots, z_m)$$

$$= \frac{\Gamma(c)\,\Gamma(1-c)}{2\pi i\,\Gamma(\sum_1^m b_j + 1 - c)} \{\int_L - \sum_{k=1}^{m} \int_0^{(z_k+)}\} [e^t\, t^{\sum_1^m b_j - c} \prod_{j=1}^{m} (t-z_j)^{-b_j}]dt$$

It is now convenient to take L as the path displayed in Figure 4.2 with branch cuts from $-\infty$ to the origin and from the origin to each of the points z_k $(k = 1, \ldots, m)$. Let $C = C_1 + C_2 + \ldots + C_m$ be the part of this contour which is the curve centred at the origin in the Figure. Upon shrinking C to the origin we obtain:

(A14) $$\int_L - \sum_{k=1}^{m} \int_0^{(z_k+)} = \int_{-\infty}^{0} + \int_0^{-\infty}.$$

To evaluate the right side of (A14) we note that in passing from L_1 to L_2 in the Figure we have, in effect, encircled each of the branch points $0, z_1, \ldots, z_m$.

We make the multivalued functions in the integrand of (A13) definite by writing $t = xe^{-\pi i}$ on L_1 and choosing the branches:

$$t^{\sum_1^m b_j - c} = x^{\sum_1^m b_j - c} e^{-i\pi(\sum_1^m b_j - c)}$$

$$(t - z_j)^{-b_j} = (-x - z_j)^{-b_j}$$

on L_1 with $0 < x < \infty$. Then on L_2 we have:

$$t^{\sum_1^m b_j - c} = x^{\sum_1^m b_j - c} e^{i\pi(\sum_1^m b_j - c)}$$

$$(t - z_j)^{-b_j} = (-x - z_j)^{-b_j} e^{-2\pi i b_j}$$

again with $0 < x < \infty$.

Figure 4.2 : Contour map for L

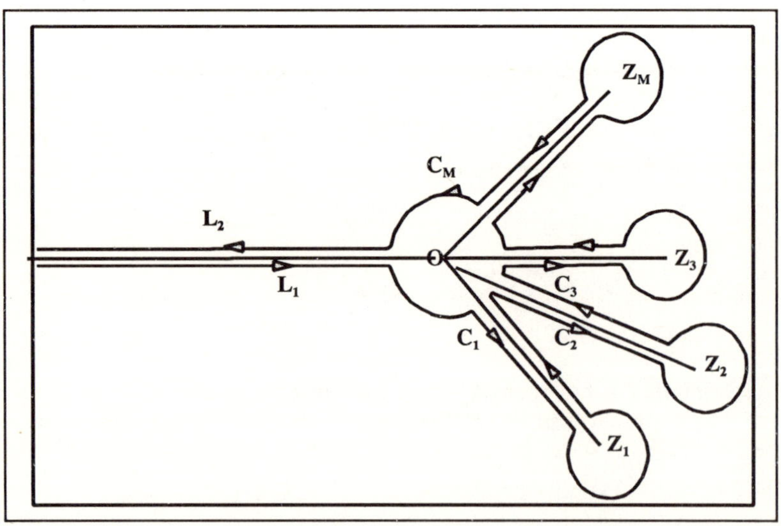

It follows that the integrals on the right side of (A14) have the form:

$$e^{-i\pi(\sum_1^m b_j - c + 1)} \int_0^\infty e^{-x} x^{\sum_1^m b_j - c} \prod_{j=1}^m (-x - z_j)^{-b_j} dx$$

$$+ e^{-i\pi(\sum_1^m b_j + c - 1)} \int_0^\infty e^{-x} x^{\sum_1^m b_j - c} \prod_{j=1}^m (-x - z_j)^{-b_j} dx$$

$$= \{e^{i\pi(1-c)} - c^{-i\pi(1-c)}\} \int_0^\infty e^{-x} x^{\sum_1^m b_j - c} \prod_{j=1}^m (x + z_j)^{-b_j} dx$$

$$= 2i \sin\{\pi(1-c)\} \int_0^\infty e^{-x} x^{\sum_i^m b_j - c} \prod_{j=1}^m (x + z_j)^{-b_j} dx.$$

Noting that:

$$\Gamma(c)\Gamma(1-c) = \pi/\sin\{\pi(1-c)\}$$

we deduce the following result from (A13) and the above:

Lemma

If $\mathrm{Re}(b_j) > 0$ $(j = 1, \ldots, m)$ *and* $\mathrm{Re}(c) < 1$ *then*:

(A15) $$\Psi^{[m]}(b_1, \ldots, b_m; c; z_1, \ldots, z_m)$$

$$= \{\Gamma(\sum_1^m b_j + 1 - c)\}^{-1} \int_0^\infty e^{-x} x^{\sum_1^m b_j - c} \prod_{j=0}^m (x + z_j)^{-b_j} dx$$

The integral representation (A15) is much simpler than (8) and is also more convenient for numerical computation.

Now consider the case $m = 1$. Writing $z_1 = re^{i\varphi}$ we find that (A15) becomes upon transforming $x \to x/z_1 = y$

$$\text{(A16)} \qquad \{\Gamma(b_1 + 1 - c)\}^{-1} \int_0^\infty e^{-x}\, x^{b_1-c} (x + z_1)^{-b_1}\, dx$$

$$= \{\Gamma(b_1 + 1 - c)\}^{-1}\, z_1^{1-c} \int_0^\infty e^{-i\varphi}\, e^{-yz_1}\, y^{b_1-c}\, (1+y)^{-b_1}\, dy$$

$$= \{\Gamma(b_1 + 1 - c)\}^{-1}\, \Gamma(b_1 + 1 - c)\, z_1^{1-c}\, \Psi(b_1 - c + 1,\ 2-c;\ z_1)$$

$$\text{(A17)} \qquad = \Psi(b_1,\ c;\ z_1)$$

Line (A16) follows from the integral representation of the Ψ function with scalar argument (see Erdèlyi, 1953, equation (3), p. 256). Line (A17) follows from equation (6), p. 257 of the same reference.

5. Bank Regulation, Uncertainty and Business Cycles

Andrew W. Mullineux

I first met Jim Ford in 1980, when I was appointed as a Research Associate in the Department of Economics at the University of Birmingham. We subsequently worked closely, with a number of our colleagues, on Divisia monetary aggregates and the testing of the rational expectations and structural neutrality hypotheses. Jim has generously devoted a considerable amount of time to advising me on the development of my career, and I am extremely grateful to him for this. I am sure that members of the Departments of Economics at the Universities of Sheffield and Birmingham, which Jim has headed, will echo this sentiment.

As an example of his influence, in the summer of 1987 Jim restimulated my interest in business cycle theory by drawing my attention to Shackle's *Expectations, Investment and Income*, which was originally published in 1938. I soon realized that I had not fully appreciated the significance of Shackle's contribution when I was writing my thesis on business cycles. The reason for this was that, despite the fact that, like Jim, I graduated from the University of Liverpool, I was too late to benefit from Shackle's tuition in the way that Jim clearly has. We have both remained besotted by the accent and the humour of the people of Liverpool, and have spent many happy hours in the staff-house bar discussing whether our time might not have been better served managing the 'men in red'. They have of course done very well without us, and the last thing they probably need is the advice of a couple of economists!

My previous studies of business cycle theory had convinced me of the need to consider the roles of non-linearity and the banking sector; in business cycle generation and as part of a more comprehensive theory of dynamic economic development. Shackle had clearly come to a similar conclusion whilst re-writing his doctorial thesis in response to exposure to Keynesian and Wicksellian ideas in the mid-

1930s. Shackle's business cycle model consisted of: a bunching of innovations; multiplier–accelerator interaction, under uncertainty of course; an antecedent of Duesenberry's (1949) consumption ratchet, introducing non-linearity; and a banking sector which contributed to asymmetry by facilitating over-expansion in the boom and adopting a cautious approach to lending in the recession. Not surprisingly, certain aspects of the model remained underdeveloped. This applied particularly to the explanation of the bunching and diffusion of innovations and Jim and I were about to embark on a research project involving extensions to Shackle's work in this area when Jim fell prey to illness. In Jim's absence, my interest was drawn to the implications for bank regulation of linkages between the business cycle and the banking system.

1. INTRODUCTION

If the banking system plays a key role in the cyclical motion of dynamic economic development, then it is important to know whether it: imparts instability, by generating monetary shocks and speculative bubbles, for example; acts as a medium or conduit through which the effects of real shocks are spread from one market to another, and perhaps amplified; or serves as a shock absorber or buffer (Eichengreen and Portes, 1987). Such knowledge would guide policy decisions concerning the appropriate supervision and regulation of banks.

The debate regarding the relative stability or instability of the real and monetary sectors of the economy is a longstanding and complex one and shall not be entered into here. Instead, commonly cited explanations of the need for bank regulation and supervision will be examined, and principles that should guide the choice of an efficient regulatory regime will be considered. The discussion relates to the banking, rather than the wider financial, system but the banks under consideration are regarded as highly diversified financial conglomerates, rather than narrowly defined commercial banks. To the extent that the banking system plays a key role in the generation of business cycles, and deep depressions in particular, bank regulation can be regarded as a key component of anticyclical policy.

It should be stressed, however, that a key role of the banking system is to assume risks that would otherwise be borne by economic agents themselves (Rybczynski, 1985). By pooling risks and developing appropriately diversified portfolios, using their specialist credit risk appraisal skills, banks should be able to reduce risk, but they can never eliminate it entirely. Further, it should be acknowledged that risk management takes place under uncertainty, in the sense of Knight (1921) and Keynes (1936), and so risk management decisions must rely, to some extent, on hunches based on past experience, rather than purely statistical techniques. If banks' managers act prudently, they may be able to enhance the stability of the economy and the banking system could perhaps perform a buffer function. If they act imprudently, however, and take excessive risks, the effectiveness of the buffer will be impaired or, worse still, the banking system may start to amplify shocks, rather than dampen them.

Recent work applying agency theory to the analysis of the role of banks (for example, Gorton and Haubrich, 1987) suggests that banks should be regarded as performing a monitoring function in a world where ownership and control of capital is separated. The investor–owners employ agents to run their businesses and can control their behaviour only indirectly, whilst banks are capable of exerting direct control. In their monitoring role, banks have access to information that is not publicly available. Their willingness to lend can be taken as a certification of the credit worthiness of the borrowing firm, giving it access to other forms of debt finance, such as debentures, and assuring the continued confidence of equity investors. Because bank loan portfolios are built up using information to form risk assessments which is not publicly available, however, their loans are not generally marketable and it is often difficult for depositors to decide whether one bank's loan portfolio is more risky than another's. This raises the question of who is capable of monitoring the monitors and has created the possibility that 'flights to cash', or 'banking panics', can occur, since the inadequacy of bank-specific information means that depositor uncertainty about a small number of banks may soon infect the system as a whole.

In the absence of a monitor, agency theory would suggest that bank managements will be tempted to pursue their own interests, and that this may not lead to the prudent running of the banking system which plays such a crucial monitoring role in the economy. If depositors, shareholders and other creditors, such as debenture holders, along with credit rating agencies and securities firms, cannot monitor banks adequately, then in the public interest, it is incumbent on the government to ensure that the banking system is efficiently regulated and supervised, so that it can perform its essential monitoring role effectively. The key advantage which banks have (over securities firms and credit rating agencies) in assessing credit risks, appears to be their access to confidential information. To the extent that borrowers from the capital markets are willing to volunteer similar information to securities firms and credit rating agencies, the banks' advantage is diminished. As long as disclosure is less than complete, the risk of 'bank runs' remains and there is a role for a public sector regulator which can demand information not revealed to the public. The agency perspective suggests that excessive risk-taking means either taking risks in excess of those that depositors as a group would sanction; or taking risks that would threaten the stability of the banking system, which may amount to the same thing. In what follows, the need for bank regulation will be examined more closely in order to form a view on the essential ingredients of an efficient bank regulatory and supervisory system.

2. CONVENTIONAL WISDOM CONCERNING BANKS AND THEIR REGULATION

A cursory review of the burgeoning literature on bank regulation[1] reveals the following widely accepted propositions, *inter alia*:

1) The banking market suffers from information deficiencies which make it necessary to intervene to protect depositors and prevent 'banking panics'.

2) Large banks cannot be allowed to fail because their failure would lead to a systemic crisis and cause a widespread breakdown of credit relationships and significant real economic damage.

3) The provision of lender of last resort (LOLR) cover, particularly to large banks, encourages excessive risk-taking and the formation of oligopolies in banking markets.

4) The introduction of 100 per cent deposit insurance (DI), *with flat rate premia*, can counter the tendency for deposits to gravitate to the large banks (which are assured of LOLR support), and also reduce calls for LOLR support, but creates an additional moral hazard problem. This is because depositors have no incentive to try to assess the riskiness of the banks in which they place their money, and market discipline is weakened.

5) When combined with deregulated interest rates, as in the USA in the 1980s, the moral hazard problems become acute because risk-prone banks can bid deposits away from more prudent banks by offering depositors a higher return on equally protected deposits.

6) Deregulation led to increased competition among commercial banks, 'thrifts' and investment banks in the USA in the late 1970s. This encouraged commercial banks to economize on capital and loan loss provisions and to attach inadequate risk premia to lending rates.

7) Securitization has resulted in a loss of prime business and banks have had to seek lower quality, more risky, assets to maintain their profitability.

* BANKS SEEKING LOWER QUALITY, MORE RISKY ASSETS

The broad picture in the 1980s has been one of a move away from prohibitive regulations, designed to inhibit risk-taking, towards a more permissive regime in which competition is increased and banks appear to have become more risk-prone. Some regulatory authorities have taken deregulatory initiatives, others have reacted to *de facto* deregulation and financial innovation, and the rest have had to respond to such developments in order to avoid handicapping their own banks in increasingly internationalized banking markets. The desire to create a 'level playing-field' in international banking has encouraged international regulatory and supervisory coordination in the form of a series of agreements under the aegis of the Basle Committee.[2]

BASLE

The need for bank regulation will be considered in more detail in the next section. Following this we will examine the roles of the LOLR and DI, and will outline the Basle Committee's approach, which involves introducing risk-related capital adequacy requirements. The concluding section will argue that this approach is broadly correct, but suggestions will be made concerning its further development.

3. WHY DO BANKS NEED TO BE REGULATED?

There are three basic approaches to explaining the need for the prudential regulation and supervision of banks. One is motivated by depositor protection. It starts from a microeconomic perspective and stresses market failure. Another starts from a macroeconomic perspective and emphasizes the damage to the economy that a widespread interruption of credit relationships would cause. The source of the instability that might give rise to systemic banking crises or panics is the dependence of fractional reserve banking systems on depositor confidence and is, therefore, microeconomic. A third justification for regulation, again a result of market failure, follows from the observation that, in many countries, banking systems resemble oligopolies with a competitive fringe. This means that banking systems need to be regulated to ensure that restrictive practices are not enforced; to the disadvantage of the fringe banks and consumers. Recent history suggests that the oligopolistic structure in banking markets has resulted in the development of a 'herd instinct', which leads banks into over-exposure to certain risks (Plender, 1989). This provides a further justification for the prudential regulation and supervision of banks.

It has been persuasively argued (Tobin, 1963; Black, 1970; Fama, 1980) that differences between commercial banks and non-bank financial intermediaries are largely the result of differential regulatory regimes. Deregulation in the 1970s and 1980s would seem to confirm this. It has also been noted that the regulatory regime may influence the banking market structure (Hirsch, 1977). The basic choice is between preventive, risk-inhibiting, regulation, and competition. To the extent that there is self-regulation or the regulators are 'captured' by practitioners, the former route tends to lead to club-like or cartelistic arrangements (enforced by regulations); in which larger established banks come to dominate and potential rivals are forced to compete on the fringe (Goodhart, 1985; Llewellyn, 1986). Under the competitive alternative, however, some banks may take advantage of economies of scale and grow to a size where they are viewed as being too large to be allowed to fail. Their depositors will, therefore, effectively enjoy 100 per cent insurance cover whilst depositors in smaller banks, which cannot rely on automatic assistance from the LOLR, will not. The larger banks are consequently likely to attract an increasing share of total deposits and grow yet larger. Thus both approaches appear to indicate a tendency towards oligopoly if there are significant economies of scale in banking, a matter hotly debated in the literature. DI can be used to break this tendency by providing 100 per cent cover to depositors in large and small banks alike. Less than 100 per cent insurance leaves an incentive to place funds with the larger banks enjoying automatic LOLR cover, especially when confidence in the banking system is impaired. It should be noted that the tendency of deposits to gravitate to larger banks appears to owe little to their ability to reduce risks through pooling similar assets and holding more diversified portfolios. Empirical evidence (see Lewis and Davis, 1987, Chapter 7 for a review) suggests that relatively small banks can capture the bulk of the benefits from pooling and diversification.

READ The various arguments supporting bank regulation have hitherto proved sufficient to convince governments in most countries to impose more stringent regulations on banks than most other financial institutions and other sectors of the economy. In response to accelerating inflation, more volatile exchange rates and higher and more variable interest rates in the 1970s, there was an acceleration of financial innovation. Technological innovation clearly aided and abetted in this process and also made the rapid internationalization of banking in the 1970s, and the globalization of capital markets in the 1980s, possible. In the 1980s, financial innovation manifested itself through securitization, which undermined traditional banking intermediation functions and encouraged banks to enter capital market-related business. In countries where universal banking has long been established, such as Germany and Switzerland, relatively little has changed. In other countries there has been major transformation of the financial system and the role of the banking system within it. This has made regulatory reform necessary. The extent of the reform required has depended on the flexibility of the regulatory and supervisory system. The UK has traditionally relied on a flexible self-regulatory approach, but found it necessary to introduce statutory backing in the 1980s. The USA, in contrast, was forced to adopt a statutory approach following the banking crisis in the early 1930s and, despite the fact that the US banking supervisors have been seeking increased flexibility and regulatory reform throughout the 1980s and into the 1990s, Congress has found it difficult to agree on a change to the regime in the face of intensive lobbying by special interest groups. Flexibility is clearly desirable in times of rapid change, but statutory backing has become necessary in the UK as the 'banking clubs' have been thrown open to international membership. Because domestic and international financial innovation has made regulatory reform necessary in many countries, particularly the USA and Japan, it is helpful to examine the reasons for regulating banks more closely so that we can be clear about what is required of new regulatory regimes.

The objective should be to devise a regulatory and supervisory system that eliminates systemic crises and yet is sufficiently flexible to adapt, in times of rapid financial innovation, whilst encouraging competition, to promote efficiency. Previous regimes have usually been distortionary. They have put banks at a competitive disadvantage in respect to other financial institutions and have encouraged circumventory innovation (Kane, 1987). This tendency has been enhanced by the fact that, because of the general acceptability of some bank liabilities as a means of payment and the belief that an excessive growth in the supply of bank money is inflationary, banks are encumbered by restraints designed to facilitate monetary control, as well as prudential constraints. It is often not clear whether the liquidity requirements are imposed for prudential or monetary control purposes. Whilst it should be possible to clarify such issues, and there has been a tendency to do so in a number of countries, it should be recognized that there are fundamental links between prudential and monetary control policies. LOLR intervention, for example, increases the money supply but need not be inflationary if the rise is just sufficient to satisfy the abnormal increase in the demand for cash in times of heightened uncertainty. The art is to prevent a leakage into the banking system as the abnormal demand subsides. Further, the monetary brakes can be put on more effectively if the banking system is not exposed to excessive interest rate and credit risks.

An efficient regulatory regime would have to recognize the tensions between competition and prudence (Barclay, 1978; Revell, 1978, 1986) and should ensure that banks make realistic assessments of, and adequate provisions for, risks taken in an uncertain world. The widespread adoption of 'best practices' should, therefore, be encouraged, and supervisors should vigorously discourage fraud and malfeasance.

The microeconomic approach to justifying bank regulation rests on identifying the source of the failure in the market for banking services. The market failure is particularly important if it creates instability in the banking system and the possibility of systemic banking crises. Because a significant proportion of bank deposits can be withdrawn on demand and their nominal value is guaranteed, whilst the majority of assets cannot be liquidated at short notice without loss, banking systems are subject to flights to quality or to cash. 'Flights to quality' can be dealt with by recycling: as in the 'lifeboat operation' launched by the Bank of England and the major UK banks in response to the secondary banking crisis of the early 1970s (Reid, 1982). Opinions differ about the degree of macroeconomic damage done by 'flights to quality'.[3] Adverse effects will result from disruption to credit relationships. There is little dispute over the damage caused by 'flights to cash' or 'banking panics', although there is disagreement over the frequency with which they have occurred (Kaufman, 1986). When they do occur, there is much more serious and widespread interruption of credit relationships and a multiple credit contraction. LOLR and DI cover are, therefore, necessary to reinforce depositors' confidence in fractional reserve systems. DI alone is unlikely to be sufficient to prevent panics, but may discourage flights to quality when comprehensive cover is available. This is because, even if it were possible, it would be inefficient to build up a fund large enough to cover all deposits in the system. Consequently, the fund must ultimately rely on LOLR support as a result. This suggests that private insurance schemes, which do not enjoy implicit or explicit LOLR cover, cannot be relied upon alone.[4] Most countries in fact rely on the LOLR rather than comprehensive DI schemes. The reason for this will be discussed further below.

LOLR + DI COVER IN A FRACTIONAL SYSTEM

The source of the market failure is usually attributed to the asymmetry of information (between a bank's management and its depositors) concerning the risks associated with bank assets. Because of their superior information, managers may be tempted to take risks that are excessive, in the sense that they would not be acceptable to depositors, who expect the nominal value of their deposits to be protected and to be able to make withdrawals on demand. As noted above, banks may gain access to confidential information in the course of carrying out a monitoring role. Like other financial intermediaries, banks contribute to economic efficiency by absorbing and redistributing risks so that the diverse needs of depositors and borrowers can be matched as closely as possible (Tobin, 1984; Rybczynski, 1985). They do this by creating liquidity (Diamond and Dybvig, 1983; Niehans 1978, Chapter 9) and guaranteeing the nominal value of deposits. Fractional reserve banking is a necessary corollary of their liquidity production role and is not inconsistent with their insurance function, when banks enjoy the confidence of their depositors. The insurance is not available in the market because information about individuals' liquidity needs is private and uncertain (Diamond and Dybvig, 1983). As financial intermediaries, banks do not just lend money at call in multiple amounts. They also take risks through mismatching or transformation. Fractional reserve banking without mismatching exposes banks to liquidity risk. These are enhanced by mismatching, which also exposes them to interest rate risk. Banks also face credit risk by virtue of their lending activities.[5] If exposure to such risks reduces the confidence of depositors, then runs on particular banks can occur and there is a risk of contagion. Because depositors have inadequate information about the liquidity and solvency of other banks, they may withdraw deposits from them too and there will be knock-on effects if these banks are unable to liquidate assets without incurring 'fire sale' losses.

The fact that banking relationships are built on trust increases the probability of crises because a loss of confidence will ensure that the banking system fails to achieve its potential. The viability of the system will be threatened as a consequence. Over-confidence will, however, produce unrealistically high expectations.Bank managements must therefore achieve a balance between mistrust and over confidence (Hicks, 1967) and, if they can't do so, the instability must be dealt with by regulation.

On the face of it the solution is simple. The information asymmetry should be removed by a regulatory requirement that banks disclose all information about their balance sheets to the public. This is tantamount to requiring full disclosure by all companies since otherwise banks would be unable to respect confidentiality. Depositors would be able to assess bank-specific risks if the information was of sufficient quality; widespread banking panics would be eliminated, but the possibility of individual bank runs, and perhaps flights to quality, would remain. Market value reporting would be appropriate because it would force management to publish their own estimates of the values and risks incorporated in their portfolios. It would also discourage discourage excessive risk-taking by making riskier banks pay more for wholesale funds, subordinate debt and equity capital, whilst encouraging more comprehensive provisioning against risks. The job of supervisors and auditors would then be to attempt to verify the published information. Strict disclosure rules would, however, prove costly to comply with and depositors would need to incur costs of processing the information unless they felt that they could rely on others, such as share and debenture holders and wholesale depositors (including other banks), or credit rating agencies, to discipline the behaviour of bank management. If, as seems likely, these costs are high and they are duplicated, then there would remain a rationale for a regulatory authority to collect and appraise information on the public's behalf, because the information is a public good and there are likely to be significant economies of scale in collecting and processing it.

Greater disclosure can only be a solution, however, if the information provided is of sufficient quality. If it is not, greater disclosure could potentially be destabilizing because it may increase depositors' uncertainty and make runs on basically solvent banks facing temporary liquidity difficulties more likely. It appears unlikely that the information provided would be of sufficient quality. It is more likely that, because both managers and depositors are in fact dealing with uncertainties, rather than risks, bank managers have a greater understanding of the 'risks' in their asset portfolios and depositors have a greater understanding of their own liquidity requirements. Further, because of lack of standardization, banking assets, particularly corporate and personal loans, are not widely traded in secondary markets, despite the significant developments in securitization that took place in the 1980s. Thus assessment of their value is subjective. There is the additional problem that modern asset and liability management techniques[6] make it possible to transform balance sheets rapidly following the publication of a report, and so reported data are unlikely to be a reliable guide to the risks contained in a bank's portfolio.

The instability resulting from the market failure has probably been compounded by the price structure imposed by oligopolistic banks and often reinforced by regulators. The widespread practice of not paying explicit interest on current accounts,[7] for example, engendered the belief that demand deposits are riskless, since normally a return is paid to compensate for risks of illiquidity and loss of nominal value. This arrangement was highly profitable for banks, which enjoyed an 'endowment effect' from borrowing at zero rates and lending at positive rates. As competition increased in the 1980s,[8] however, banks adjusted their price structure and began to offer both explicit and implicit interest on current account balances in order to attract customers. A better arrangement would be to eliminate cross-subsidization by charging fully for usage of money transmission services (MTS) and to pay interest commensurate with risk and illiquidity. The risk-averse might still want the nominal value and liquidity of their deposits to be guaranteed; in which case segregated, non-interest bearing, accounts, with 100 per cent liquid reserve backing and services charged for in full, could be provided. Depositors could, however, be given the choice between such accounts and accounts related to money market mutual funds (MMMFs), which would pay interest, charge for MTS and adjust the value of the deposit/investment to the market value of the portfolio of liquid assets held. If all depositors proved willing to accept MMMF accounts, banks would be protected against runs because the value of deposit withdrawals would be matched to the value of assets (Karaken, 1986; Goodhart, 1987). The risk of 'fire sale' insolvency would, therefore, be eliminated. If there is widespread risk aversion concerning the value of deposits, then MMMFs would not be widely accepted as an alternative to traditional MTS accounts. The imposition of a 100 per cent reserve requirement would prevent banks from reaping the benefits of pooling liquid reserves and exploiting the law of large numbers to create credit, and from creating liquidity and absorbing risks, which are their essential contributions to economic efficiency as financial institutions. By performing these functions banks contribute to growth and wealth creation (Bencivenga and Smith, 1991). Elimination of all risk-taking would remove the basis of their profitability and their *raison d'être*. It is only excessive risk-taking that needs to be discouraged. One hundred per cent reserve backing for segregated current accounts is, therefore, a Draconian solution and should only be imposed in the absence of viable alternatives.

If the public remains sufficiently risk-averse that there remains a significant demand for current accounts, rather than MMMFs, and full disclosure is not a realistic solution, then the market failure, which is in fact a failure of a market in bank loans to develop due to information deficiencies, still needs to be tackled. The presence of market failure requires: preventive regulation, to ensure that bank management does not take excessive risks; and regulation to protect depositors, especially the small ones, and the banking system from the consequences of excessive risk-taking, should it occur. Thus, some combination of preventive and protective regulation appears to be required. The policy problem is to determine the optimal mix or to find some way of combining protective regulation with a disincentive to excessive risk-taking.

It should be noted that, if the key problem is the lack of transparency of bank asset values caused by the non-marketability of bank loans, then standardization of loans might allow markets to develop and the problem would disappear. In the 1980s, as part of the securitization process, there has been a trend towards increased marketability of bank assets, but the process has some way to go before full transparency is achieved. Few loans are sufficiently standardized to be packaged and sold as securities, and secondary markets remain thin, so that the prices set in them are unlikely to provide realistic valuations of banking assets.

It has been argued (Rybczynski, 1984, 1985) that financial systems gradually evolve from banking-oriented systems towards market-oriented systems. If this is true and the process is accelerated by deregulation, then, as the proportion of bank assets that are marketable increases, the need for official regulation may decline. Ultimately all bank assets may be traded on exchanges overseen by self-regulatory organizations which will have an incentive to set their own rules to prevent abuses (Grossman, 1986). Gorton and Haubrich (1987) argue that branching restrictions and the 1933 Glass–Steagall Act[9] have prevented optimal diversification and that the current US regulations are anachronistic and create conditions under which banking panics can occur. Complete deregulation would consequently remove the need for regulation or non-market supervision. There must, however, be considerable doubt that optimal diversification can eliminate all 'risk', especially under uncertainty and, consequently, the probability of a banking panic occurring may be reduced by diversification but not eliminated, especially since changes in depositors' perceptions of the 'risks' are the source of instability under uncertainty. As noted above, empirical evidence indicates that gains from diversification do not increase proportionality with scale, so that removal of restrictions on US banks may allow a relatively rapid adjustment of their portfolios, but this may not require them to increase their scale markedly. Further, diversification may not lead automatically to a reduction in portfolio risk. In the short term, sub-optimal diversification may well take place as there is bound to be a learning process following a move into unfamiliar business. The experience of the US savings and loan associations in the 1980s appears to indicate that heightened supervisory vigilance may be required following deregulation.

The actions of the supervisors in the USA reveal that large (money centre) banks are already regarded as being too large to be allowed to fail. The easing of branching restrictions in the USA in the 1980s has already resulted in the creation of super-regional banks, which may also be deemed 'too big to fail'. If increased scale is indeed required to achieve adequate diversification and risk is thereby reduced but not eliminated, then LOLR cover will be required to protect the big banks from failure. Further, if increased concentration results in an oligopolistic structure, then there is an additional rationale for continued regulation. Even if diversification did allow reliance on market discipline and an oligopoly did not develop, an LOLR may still be needed to underwrite market liquidity. The existence of an LOLR, however, creates a moral hazard problem by encouraging excessive risk-taking. This can be curbed if the LOLR imposes regulations to prevent abuse of its cover. Thus, if there remains a need for an LOLR, then regulation is required.

The problem may be caused by asymmetry of information, but it is

ASYMMETRY OF INFO

compounded by inadequacy of information. This is highlighted by fears expressed by the Bank for International Settlements (BIS, 1986a,b) and the banks themselves: that bank management is not fully cognisant of the risks being undertaken in the development of off-balance sheet business. It is to be noted that, in developing off-balance sheet contingent liabilities, banks are again adopting an insurance role (Lewis, 1988; Artis and Lewis, 1991, Chapter 9).

Faced with market failure, depositors will seek protection against uncompensated risks. In an oligopolistic environment, practitioners are likely to form a club to prevent free-riders from damaging their reputation and trustworthiness. Such clubs are likely to prefer a public sector central bank (CB) or banking commission (Goodhart, 1985) to regulate them because private sector CBs face conflicts of interest. A public CB will also possess the power to exclude free riders, who wish to trade in the light of the credibility established by the club, without the need for entry deterring pricing strategies. CBs may emerge naturally from the bank chosen as government's banker. The implicit government backing enjoyed by the chosen bank allows it to develop into a monopolistic supplier of base money and the natural LOLR, and it will probably also be adopted as the bankers' bank. Such a process of evolution has been observed in Europe (Congdon, 1981; Goodhart, 1985) and accounts for the existence of some of the older CBs, which were brought into the public sector relatively recently.[10]

Given that oligopoly with a competitive fringe is the closest model of most banking systems, with the notable exception of the US system, demands for regulation are likely to come from practitioners seeking an official stamp of approval for their attempts to build up trustworthiness. Even in cases where regulations are imposed upon banks, in the name of consumer or systemic protection, 'capture theory' would suggest that the regulations may eventually be adapted to serve the needs of the regulated (Goodhart, 1985; Llewellyn, 1986). There is a clear danger of 'capture' in regulatory systems that rely heavily on self-regulation. To counteract this tendency, there is a need to ensure that lay members or consumer representatives are adequately represented on the executive boards of the self-regulatory organizations. The presence of the practitioners is, however, justified by the fact that they are more likely to detect fraud and bad practices quickly and have an incentive to exclude free-riders. Practitioners are also likely to understand new developments and will be able to respond quickly to them. The lay members and consumer representatives should attempt to ensure that preclusion is not used to protect or build an oligopolistic cartel, and that flexibility is not used to adapt rules to the practitioners' sole benefit.

4. LIQUIDITY AND CAPITAL ADEQUACY, DEPOSIT INSURANCE AND THE LOLR

If greater disclosure and 100 per cent reserve backing are rejected as solutions to the market failure, and diversification is likely to be beneficial (at least in the long run), but cannot eliminate the need for regulation, then the solution would appear to lie in providing insurance (to protect depositors and to eliminate systemic crises) whilst regulating banks to prevent abuse of the insurer(s). Insurance may be discretionary (LOLR cover) or contractual (DI) but once it is in place moral hazard is created because banks have the incentive to take excessive risks, with the costs falling on the insurer(s) and, ultimately, on taxpayers. Given this bias towards uncompensated risk-taking, the insurers will seek to regulate the insured banks by restricting their ability to take risks unless adequate checks and balances can be built into the insurance schemes themselves. Providers of insurance to the banking system have long been aware of this problem. In order to discourage exploitation of LOLR support, the Bank of England, along with other CBs, has aimed to provide assistance to banks unstintingly but at penal rates.[11]

The moral hazard problem arises because the insurance cover provided to banks does not vary in line with risk-taking and is, therefore, mispriced. LOLR cover is usually provided in return for flat rate premia implicit in non-interest bearing deposits held by banks with the CB. DI contributions are normally also levied at a flat rate, related to the size of a bank's deposits. If large banks cannot be allowed to fail because of large negative externalities, then they may enjoy *de facto* insurance beyond that bought through contributions to the LOLR or DI schemes. CBs are generally abstruse about the conditions under which LOLR cover will be made available. The deliberate creation of uncertainty about LOLR intervention reflects their desire to discourage exploitation of the insurance cover provided. The residual uncertainty about the availability and extent of cover, however, prevents a total elimination of banking panics. Depositors and taxpayers would be better protected by a system that forced banks to contribute directly, in relation to risk taken, to the insurance of the banking system.

Despite the deliberate obfuscation about the conditions under which

LOLR support will be provided, most CBs in the major Western industrialized economies have established sufficient credibility to assure depositor confidence in the banking systems they serve. In these countries DI plays a relatively minor role. In many cases no fund exists and a mutual help agreement is in place instead. Further, the DI provided is normally less than 100 per cent and the schemes have commonly been introduced relatively recently, often in response to pressure from consumer groups. The situation in the USA is markedly different. The Federal Deposit Insurance Corporation (FDIC) provides 100 per cent insurance of deposits up to the relatively large maximum amount of $100,000. The USA was probably forced to introduce a DI scheme in the early 1930s because the CB, the Federal Reserve (Fed) had failed to establish credibility as an LOLR. In contrast, in the UK and other countries, CBs established credibility long ago (Gilbert and Wood, 1986). To prevent panics, it is probably more efficient to have high profile insurance cover in the form of a DI fund, to which banks are forced to contribute. The existence of a comprehensive DI fund should underwrite consumer confidence and reduce the risk of bank runs and the likelihood of LOLR intervention being required and taxpayers being called upon.

Because, even in the presence of a DI, the LOLR is still required to insure the banking system against large bank failures and systemic crises, it is not surprising that CBs usually have some role in overseeing DI schemes. In the USA, however, the FDIC has assumed a major supervisory role independent of the Fed. As a result, the USA probably has the most complex regulatory system of all the OECD countries (see for example, Mullineux, 1987a, Chapter 3). There have been a series of proposals for its rationalization (Benston, 1986, Chapter 11), but none has generated significant legislation to date. Opinions differ over whether the existence of numerous regulators leads to a slackening of regulation in response to banks engaging in regulatory arbitrage, or to improvements in regulatory efficiency (Benston, 1986; Kane, 1987). However, if it is accepted, as argued below, that regulation is best pursued through risk-related insurance of the banking system, then it is essential that the regulators responsible for providing the various forms of insurance coordinate their activities effectively. Once this is achieved, the policy problem boils down to choosing the optimal weight to be attached to the various components of the insurance package (DI, LOLR and liquidity and capital adequacy requirements) whilst finding a way to deal with the moral hazard problem.

The existence of DI implies that small banks have no automatic access to the LOLR and can be allowed to fail. Under flat rate premia, however, these banks may still be tempted to take excessive risks in the knowledge that depositors expect to be bailed out by the DI fund if anything goes wrong and are, therefore, unconcerned about their activities. Thus the moral hazard problem that results because bank management cannot be adequately monitored by depositors is complemented by a second moral hazard problem. This stems from introducing 100 per cent DI cover to deal with the consequences of the original moral hazard problem. Because the introduction of 100 per cent DI reduces the risk of flights to quality, and perhaps to cash, there is no incentive for depositors to impose market discipline. There is no point in them wasting time and effort on finding the safest repository for their money, if all banks are equally safe as far as they are concerned. Market discipline is left to the shareholders and bondholders, who are no more able than depositors to assess the riskiness of bank portfolios on the basis of published accounts. It is also likely that banks covered by DI will be tempted to reduce their in-house insurance fund by running down their capital ratios (Peltzeman, 1970; Benston, 1986). The efficient solution would appear to be to introduce insurance premia related to the risk inherent in banks' portfolios. Risk-prone banks would be forced to consider the costs of increasing the riskiness in their portfolios. Flights to quality would be eliminated completely if there was credible 100 per cent DI cover. Private DI schemes are unlikely to command the confidence of explicitly (or implicitly) state-backed schemes, but big banks are likely to prefer private schemes because they will expect to have greater access to the LOLR under them. Regulators are more likely to favour statutory schemes, since they force banks to participate in co-insurance of the banking system and give central banks greater discretion over the use of LOLR.

The moral hazard problems associated with flat rate premia are compounded when interest rates are deregulated because adverse selection can occur as risk-prone banks are able to bid actively for deposits. There is clear evidence of this in the USA. Interest rate ceilings were lifted in the early 1980s at about the same time as savings and loan associations (SLAs) were permitted to diversify away from their traditional home loans business following the difficulties they had faced in the 1970s. The hope was that diversification would allow them to improve their profitability. The more risk-prone SLAs chose to bid aggressively for deposits to fund investments in non-residential real estate, which had previously been prohibited. Falling property prices in states such as Texas following the 1986 oil price slump, led these SLAs into further difficulties and made the 1989 Bush rescue plan necessary.

Given that bank lending involves uncertainty, rather than strictly quantifiable risk, it should be acknowledged that it would be impossible to introduce a perfectly discriminatory set of risk-related DI premia. Further, if this were to be attempted, there might be adverse announcement effects to deal with, unless the premia were set by the regulators confidentially. Not all announcement effects need be negative, however, and it would be more consistent with the supervisors' monitoring role for the information to be made public. To be equitable, the risk-related DI premia should include a levy on big banks, to force them to contribute to the supplementary cover they implicity receive from the LOLR, which must underwrite the DI fund.

One hundred per cent DI also has the merit that it maintains competition in the system by reducing the tendency to oligopoly. This is perhaps another reason why 100 per cent DI for deposits up to a fairly large maximum limit was introduced in the USA, where there is a well-documented (Karaken, 1986) fear of 'bigness' in banking. One hundred per cent DI with a maximum limit is a reasonable compromise because it gives potentially large depositors an incentive to break up deposits into smaller amounts and spread them around the system to gain full cover. Electronic banking and brokerage facilities make it possible to do this cheaply, but the incentive to do so is reduced if big banks are not to be allowed to fail, since large depositors may receive benefits from placing large deposits with large banks. The maximum limit may, therefore, achieve little in the end, although it may be necessary to increase the credibility of the fund and to reduce reliance on the LOLR to supplement the fund. If 100 per cent DI, with flat rate premia and with or without a maximum deposit limit, is maintained, and residual LOLR cover is required to assure its credibility, then market discipline will be weakened. The moral hazard problems will have to be dealt with and regulations will still be required.

In addition to introducing risk-related DI premia, to discourage bank management from taking advantage of the information asymmetry, a number of suggestions have been made which involve either imposing costs on depositors, to strengthen market discipline, or exposing management to the consequences of their actions (Benston, 1986; Karakan, 1986; Baltensperger and Dermine, 1987). In order to expose depositors to some losses and eliminate one of the moral hazard problems, there have been frequent calls in the US for DI cover to be reduced below 100 per cent. In the light of the information asymmetry, this appears to be unfair and can only increase the risk of bank panics and the need for LOLR intervention, and thereby enhance the other moral hazard problem. In January 1989, Beryl Sprinkel, the outgoing Chief Economic Adviser of the Reagan administration, recommended the removal of 100 per cent DI cover, but the proposal was swiftly rejected by Nicholas Brady, the US Treasury Secretary. Brady evidently felt that the mere suggestion that 100 per cent cover might not be available could cause a run on the SLAs, whose difficulties were receiving high media coverage because the newly elected President Bush had attached a high priority to launching an initiative to resolve the problem. To further reduce the risk of a run on deposits, the Fed declared itself ready to stand behind the SLAs as LOLR.

Others have suggested that large depositors who 'cut and run' and spark panics should be singled out for special punishment. One proposal (Baltensperger and Dermine, 1987) is to impose an ex-post penalty on those who cut and run. The problem is to decide when the crisis started, so that it can be determined who actually did the cutting and running and who withdrew deposits for other, perfectly legitimate, reasons. Such a proposal might encourage hoarding and would anyway fail to punish the management and shareholders, who must bear ultimate responsibility for the banks' problems. Acknowledging this, it has been proposed, given their fiduciary responsibility and their crucial monitoring role, that bank managements should be exposed to unlimited liability. This is clearly a Draconian suggestion and is unlikely to encourage potentially able managers to choose a career in banking.

Another proposal is the 'dual deposit scheme' (Dale, 1985, Chapter 5), under which banks are required to hold both insured and uninsured deposits. The uninsured quota would be set low enough to prevent withdrawals threatening solvency, but high enough to create a market in uninsured deposits. The underinsured deposits would attract risk premia and could be used to calculate risk-related premia for insured deposits. Such a scheme would be likely to encourage concentration in banking because uninsured deposits would tend to be attracted to large banks. Minimum subordinated debt requirements could similarly give guidance to appropriate risk-related DI premia and capital adequacy requirements (Benston, 1986). Such proposals, however, rely on the market to make an accurate risk assessment in the absence of information that only bank managers may be privy to.

Risk-related capital adequacy requirements provide an alternative to risk-related DI premia, and were adopted in the UK in the early 1980s (Bank of England, 1980). These requirements were later extended to cover some off-balance sheet, contingent, liabilities (Bank of England, 1986). In January 1987, the monetary authorities in the US and the UK introduced a joint proposal for imposing risk-related capital adequacy requirements to cover both on- and off-balance sheet risks (Bank of England, 1987). This accord was extended to other OECD countries in August 1988 under the aegis of the Basle Committee (BIS, 1987). Agreement was reached on a common definition of capital and minimum risk-related capital adequacy requirements for on- and off-balance sheet risks. These were to be phased in by the end of 1992 and interim targets were to be hit by 1990. Supplementary capital requirements are to be established on a case-by-case basis, in accordance with the risks in a bank's portfolio. Capital adequacy requirements were initially based primarily on credit risk weights applied to various groups of bank assets. Such an approach avoids announcement effects and allows flexibility in the light of the rapidly changing banking environment. The introduction of risk-related capital adequacy requirements effectively puts a price on the supplementary discretionary insurance provided by the LOLR to banks. Existing DI schemes meanwhile provide a basic level of insurance that is visible and helps to maintain confidence. The proposals give purpose and direction to bank examination procedures by making the adequacy of capitalization dependent on portfolio risks. Capital should be deemed adequate if it reduces the risk of insolvency to a socially acceptable level. The minimum capital requirement also has the effect of building depositor confidence and can perhaps be viewed as a reservoir to deal with uncertain events, whilst the supplementary capital requirements and 'bad and doubtful' debt provisions, agreed with supervisors on the basis of inspections and prudential interviews, cover more tangible and identifiable risks.

The Basle Committee proposals included provisions to allow a preset proportion of subordinate debt to qualify as secondary capital. It is likely that, in order to hit minimum capital ratio targets, weaker banks will be forced to take on as much subordinated debt as they are allowed and may be subjected to greater market discipline as a result. Stronger banks, with greater access to equity markets and a larger flow of retained profits, will find it easier to hit the minimum capital targets and may choose to take on less subordinated debt. The provision of flat rate DI probably necessitates capital adequacy regulation to prevent banks from running down their capital ratios and relying on DI and LOLR cover. As with risk-related insurance premia, risk-related capital adequacy requirements cannot be expected to be perfectly discriminatory. They are, however, likely to be improved with experience and to be better than flat rate arrangements. In future, the number of risk classes taken into account is to be increased and weights will be adjusted to take more account of non-credit risks such as market-related 'position' (interest and exchange rate) risks.

It is often argued that large depositors do not need DI protection because they have the ability and the resources to assess risks themselves. But if information is of insufficient quality to allow risks to be gauged accurately, large depositors are likely to be particularly responsive to rumours and will tend to 'cut and run' and consequently increase instability. There was some evidence of this in the 1984 Continental Illinois crisis, and new technology and financial innovation has made it much easier for large depositors to move money around the financial system at short notice. It may be appropriate to consider introducing a separate insurance scheme for wholesale deposits and setting a limit on the maximum size of insurable deposit for the retail DI scheme accordingly.

Some economists advocate not only the introduction of a wholesale deposit protection scheme but also an asset insurance scheme (Revell, 1975). The development of hedging devices (such as futures, options and swaps) may have made such a development unnecessary but the rapid growth of the financial derivatives markets has in turn compounded the problem of assessing banks' risk exposure.

5. HAS THE BASLE COMMITTEE GOT IT RIGHT?

Deregulatory pressure in the 1980s has led to a removal of preventive restrictions on risk-taking by banks, and to an enhancement of regulation designed to protect depositors and investors. Greater attention has been paid by supervisors to capital adequacy, with the effect that banks taking on extra on- and off-balance sheet risks are forced to increase the capital backing for their activities. This approach has been rubber-stamped by the Basle Committee, which has also aimed to create a 'level playing-field' for international banks. The effect of these developments has been to transfer some of the costs of insuring the banking system against panics from the taxpayer to the individual banks and their depositors whilst promoting competition and increased efficiency.

The role of a DI fund in the overall banking system insurance package is to allow banks to pool insurance cover and to underwrite depositor confidence, which is crucial to banking stability. To use both risk-related insurance and risk-related capital adequacy requirements would appear to be an overkill. The aim should be to achieve an optimal mix between LOLR, DI and in-house liquid reserve and capital holdings. Such a mix would eliminate the potential for crisis whilst allowing genuinely insolvent banks to fail, and thus counteract the moral hazard. As long as the overall insurance package carries risk-related premia, the moral hazard problem should be containable.

The capital adequacy route has the advantage of placing greater onus on banks to insure themselves, rather than to rely on LOLR cover or the DI fund. This protects the LOLR and the DI fund from abuse at the cost of requiring more capital in aggregate to be held by the banks than may be strictly necessary to protect the system. Principles of insurance imply that if some sort of pooling of capital were allowed, the aggregate capital holdings could be reduced. Funded DI schemes in fact provide for such pooling. The policy problem is to find the balance, between LOLR, DI and in-house liquid reserve and capital requirements, that maximizes the benefits of pooling subject to the constraint that moral hazard problems must be kept in check so that the DI and LOLR cover is not abused.

The countries party to the Basle Agreement on capital adequacy were forced to opt for risk-related capital adequacy requirements because only the USA had a comprehensive, funded DI scheme. The disadvantage of the current approach is that it does not take advantage of principles of insurance to reduce aggregate capital holdings. It would be more efficient to move to a funded, risk-related, DI scheme with minimum capital requirements to cover for uninsurable, uncertain outcomes. Banks should, therefore, be required to make risk-related contributions to a public, LOLR-backed, DI fund. This would require comprehensive DI schemes to be introduced in countries outside the USA[12] which, along with minimum capital requirements, will provide a basic underpinning for the banking system. In addition, banks should be encouraged to take out private sector insurance cover for a variety of risks affecting their assets and liabilities. In the transitional period, capital adequacy requirements could be reduced as insurance cover is increased. This is consistent with the provision in the Basle Agreement for estimated risk exposure to be reduced if loans are collateralized. Growing competition between banks and securities houses, which are commonly subject to more liberal capital adequacy requirements, may encourage bank regulators to adjust their agreement. A shift from reliance on risk-related capital adequacy requirements to risk-related asset and liability insurance would be consistent with the overall approach of the Basle Committee, allow a reduction in aggregate bank capital holdings, and help promote competitive equality between banks and securities houses.

NOTES

1. *Journal of Business* (1986, No. 1), Goodhart (1985, 1987), Gardener (1986), Goodhart *et al.* (1987), Benston (1986), Baltensperger and Dermine (1987), Dale (1985), *National Westminster Bank Quarterly Review* (1987, August), Lewis and Davis (1987, Chapter 5), *inter alia*.
2. The Committee on Bank Regulation and Supervisory Practices which meets at the Bank of International Settlements in Basle. See Mullineux (1987a, Chapter 4) for further discussion. See also Dale (1985) and Kane (1987) on competition between regulators and its implications.
3. See Kaufman (1986) and Goodhart (1985) for conflicting views.
4. As illustrated by the runs on privately insured savings and loan associations in Maryland and Ohio in 1986.
5. See Vojta (1973) or Cooper (1984) for a fuller discussion of banking risks.
6. See Harrington (1987) for a detailed discussion.
7. Interest is implicitly paid when full charges are not made for money transmission services supplied.
8. See Mullineux (1987b, Chapters 2 and 3) for discussion of the UK case.
9. Which separates banking from private sector securities' underwriting.
10. At the end of World War II in the cases of the Banks of France and England.
11. In line with principles laid down by Bagehot (1927), which was originally published in 1873.
12. The proposed EC directive on deposit insurance, which is expected to be issued in 1992, aims to ensure that DI schemes are introduced in all EC member states but 100 per cent DI is not to be required and the limit of cover is to be considerably lower than $100,000.

REFERENCES

Artis, M.J. and M.K. Lewis (1991), *Money in Britain: Monetary Policy, Innovation and Europe*, London: Philip Allan.

Bagehot, W. (1927), *Lombard Street*, London: John Murray.

Baltensperger, E. and J. Dermine (1987), 'Banking Deregulation in Europe', *Economic Policy*, **4** (April), 63–109.

Bank of International Settlements (BIS) (1986a), *Recent Innovations in International Banking*, Basle.

Bank for International Settlements (BIS) (1986b), Committee on Bank Regulation and Supervisory Practices, *The Management of Banks' Off-Balance Sheet Exposures: A Supervisory Perspective*, March, Basle.

Bank for International Settlements (BIS) (1987), Committee on Bank Regulations and Supervisory Practices, *Proposals for International Convergence of Capital Measurement and Capital Standards*, Consultative Paper, December, Basle.

Bank of England (1980), 'The Measurement of Capital', *Bank of England Quarterly Bulletin*, **20** (3), 324–29, London.

Bank of England (1986), 'Consolidated supervision of institutions authorised under the Banking Act 1979', *Bank of England Quarterly Bulletin*, **26**(1), 85–9.

Bank of England (1987), 'Convergence of capital adequacy in the UK and US', *Bank of England Quarterly Bulletin*, **27**(1), 87–93, London.

Barclay, C. (1978), 'Competition and financial crises – past and present', in J. Revell, (ed), *Competition and Regulation of Banks, Bangor Occasional Papers in Economics*, No. 14, Cardiff: University of Wales Press.

Bencivenga, V.R. and B.D. Smith (1991), 'Financial Intermediation and Economic Growth', *Review of Economic Studies*, **58**, 159–209.

Benston, G.J. (ed), (1986), *Perspectives in Safe and Sound Banking: Past, Present and Future*, Cambridge, Mass.: MIT Press.

Black, F. (1970), 'Banking and Interest in a World Without Money', *Journal of Bank Research*, Autumn, 9–20. Reprinted in Black (1987).

Black, F. (1987), *Business Cycles and Equilibrium*, Oxford: Basil Blackwell.

Congdon, T. (1981), 'Is the Provision of Sound Currency a Necessary Function of the State?', *National Westminster Bank Quarterly Review*, August, 2–21.

Cooper, J. (1984), *The Management and Regulation of Banks*, London: Macmillan.

Dale, R.S. (1985), *The Regulation of International Banking*, London: Woodhead-Faulkner.

Diamond, D. and P. Dybvig (1983), 'Bank Runs, Deposit Insurance and Liquidity', *Journal of Political Economy*, **91**, 401–19.

Diamond, D. and P. Dybvig (1986), 'Banking Theory, Deposit Insurance and Bank Regulation', *Journal of Business*, **59**, 55–68.

Duesenberry, J. (1949), *Income, Saving and the Theory of Consumer Behaviour*, Cambridge, Mass.: Harvard University Press.

Eichengreen, B. and R. Portes (1987), 'The Anatomy of Financial Crises', 10–58 (Chapter 1) in R. Portes and A.K. Svoboda (eds), *Threats to International Financial Stability*, International Centre for Monetary and Banking Studies and Centre for Economic Policy Research, Cambridge: Cambridge University Press.

Fama, E.F. (1980), 'Banking in the Theory of Finance', *Journal of Monetary Economics*, **6**, 39–57.

Gardener, E.P.M. (ed.) (1986), *UK Banking Supervision: Evolution, Practice and Issues*, London: George Allen and Unwin.

Gilbert, R.A. and G.E. Wood (1986), 'Coping with Bank Failures: Some Lessons from the United States and the United Kingdom', *Federal Reserve Bank of St Louis Review*, **68**(10), 5–14.

Goodhart, C.A.E. (1985), *The Evolution of Central Banks: A Natural Development?*, STICERD Occasional Paper No. 8, London: London School of Economics and Political Science.

Goodhart, C.A.E. (1987), 'Why do Banks Need a Central Bank?', *Oxford Economic Papers*, **39**, 750–89.

Goodhart, C.A.E., D. Currie, and D.T. Llewellyn (eds) (1987), *The Operation and Regulation of Financial Markets*, Basingstoke: Macmillan.

Gorton, G.B. and J.G. Haubrich (1987), 'Bank Deregulation, Credit Markets and the Control of Capital, pp. 289–334 in K. Brunner and A.H. Meltzer (eds), *Bubbles and Other Essays, Carnegie–Richester Conference Series on Public Policy*, **26**,

Amsterdam: North Holland.

Grossman, S.J. (1986), 'An Analysis of the Role of "Insider Trading" on Futures Markets', *Journal of Business*, **57**, 129–146.

Harrington, R. (1987), *Asset and Liability Management by Banks*, Trends in Banking Structure and Regulation in OECD Countries Series, Paris: OECD.

Hicks, J.R. (1967), *Critical Essays in Monetary Theory*, Oxford: Clarendon Press.

Hirsch, F. (1977), 'The Bagehot Problem', *The Manchester School*, **45** (3), 241–55.

Kane, E.J. (1987), 'Competitive Financial Regulation: An International Perspective', pp. 111–47 (Chapter 4) in R. Portes and A.K. Swoboda (eds), *Threats to International Financial Stability*, International Centre for Monetary and Banking Studies and Centre for Economic Policy Research, Cambridge: Cambridge University Press.

Karaken, J.H. (1986), 'Federal Reserve Bank Regulatory Policy, a Description and Some Observations', *Journal of Business*, **59** (1), 48.

Kaufman, G. (1986), 'Consequences of Bank Failures', Chapter 2 in Benston, G.J. (ed.) (1986).

Keynes, J.M. (1936), *The General Theory of Employment Interest and Money*, London: Macmillan.

Knight, F.H. (1921), *Risk, Uncertainty and Profit*, New Edition 1971, Chicago: University of Chicago Press.

Lewis, M.K. (1988), 'Off-Balance Sheet Activities and Financial Innovation in Banking, *Banca Nazionale de Lavoro Quarterly Review*, **167**, 387–410.

Lewis, M.K. and K.T. Davis (1987), *Domestic and International Banking*, Oxford: Philip Allan.

Llewellyn, D.T. (1986), *The Regulation and Supervision of Financial Institutions*, London: Institute of Bankers.

Luckett, D.G. (1984), *Money and Banking*, third edition, New York: McGraw Hill.

Mullineaux, A.W. (1987a), *International Money and Banking: The Creation of a New Order*, Brighton: Wheatsheaf; New Jersey: Barnes and Noble.

Mullineux, A.W. (1987b), *UK Banking After Deregulation*, London: Croom Helm.

National Westminster Bank Quarterly Review (1987), Issue on Financial Regulation and Supervision, August.

Niehans, J. (1978), *The Theory of Money*, Baltimore and London: Johns Hopkins.

Peltzeman, S. (1970), 'Capital Investment in Commercial Banking and its Relationship to Portfolio Regulation', *Journal of Political Economy*, **78** (Jan./Feb.), 1–26.

Plender, J. (1989), 'Mad, Mad World of Banking', *Financial Times*, Weekend FT January 28/9, 1.

Reid, M. (1982), *The Secondary Banking Crisis: 1973–5*, London: Macmillan.

Revell, J. (1975), 'Solvency and the Regulation of Banks: Theoretical and Practical Implications', *Bangor Occasional Papers in Economics No. 5*, Cardiff: University of Wales Press.

Revell, J (ed.) (1978), 'Competition and the Regulation of Banks', *Bangor Occasional Papers in Economics No. 24*, Bangor: University of Wales Press.

Revell, J. (1986), 'The Complementary Nature of Competition and Regulation in the Financial Sector', Chapter 10 in E.P.M. Gardener (ed.), *UK Banking Supervision: Evolution, Practice and Issues*, London: George Allen and Unwin.

Rybczynski, T.M. (1984), 'The UK Financial System in Transition', *National Westminster Bank Quarterly Review*, Nov., 26–42.

Rybczynski, T.M. (1985), 'Financial Systems, Risk and Public Policy', *Royal Bank of Scotland Review*, **148** (Dec.), 35–45.

Shackle, G.L.S. (1938), *Expectations, Investment and Income*, new edition 1968, Oxford: Oxford University Press.

Tobin, J. (1963), 'Commercial Banks as Creators of Money', in D. Carlson (ed.), *Banking and Monetary Studies*, Homeward, Illinois: Irwin.
Tobin, J. (1984), 'On the Efficiency of the Financial System', *Lloyds Bank Review*, **153** (July), 1–15.
Vojta, G.J. (1973), *Bank Capital Adequacy*, Chicago: First National City Bank.

6. Monetary Policy Under Uncertainty

Michael J. Driscoll

1. INTRODUCTION

In taking action to adjust the stance of monetary policy, monetary authorities face considerable risks. Policy which moves to reduce inflation or support recovery risks being too little, too late or too much, too early. The failure to calibrate policy correctly or to aim it at appropriate targets risks giving rise not only to adverse outcomes for inflation and employment in the short run but risks making policy implementation more difficult in the longer term if the credibility of the monetary authority is damaged. These policy risks would not be present in a world of full information where the monetary authority was able to measure the stance of monetary policy accurately, and knew what the outcomes of policy actions would be and the shape of the time profile of these outcomes.

Unfortunately monetary authorities do not have accurate information about the stance and effects of monetary policy and must therefore operate in an environment characterized by uncertainty. In this chapter the nature and sources of uncertainty faced by monetary authorities are explored. In section 2 ideas on the appropriate measurement of monetary policy are reviewed. Section 3 contains a discussion of the range of views on the relevant framework for the analysis of the scope and effects of monetary policy. Recent experience with attempts to measure the effects of monetary policy is discussed in section 4. Section 5 contains a short conclusion.

2. UNCERTAINTY IN THE MEASUREMENT OF MONETARY POLICY

Ideally the starting point for any assessment of the effects of monetary policy should be a clear statement about what is meant by the term 'monetary policy' and how the stance of monetary policy is to be measured. On the face of it this should be a straightforward task. The term 'monetary policy' is used widely and frequently in the media and in the economics literature with rarely any acknowledged need to elaborate on what the term means or to give a clear definition of what policy actions it encompasses. The equally frequent and widespread use of terms describing the stance of monetary policy, such as 'tight' or 'easy', 'contractionary' or 'expansionary', gives the impression of an established view of how the stance of monetary policy can be measured and that there is a reliable index available which is consistent with this view. An examination of the official publications of many central banks over the last few years should, however, dispel any impression that might have been gained from other sources that any consensus exists about the best index of monetary policy. In what follows, the main issues involved in the measurement of monetary policy are discussed.

What is Monetary Policy?

At present there is no agreed definition of the term 'monetary policy'. A broad definition could encompass any deliberate action taken by the authorities to affect the quantities of assets and liabilities in financial markets and the cost of borrowing and lending. At this level of generality 'monetary policy' could include policy actions which might typically be included under the headings of fiscal policy and industrial policy as well as those actions more commonly associated with monetary policy. For example, taxation of interest income will affect the cost of borrowing or the return on lending or both, and thereby affect the size of the loan market and the banking industry. But such effects would usually be thought of as being the results of fiscal policy, as they follow from the use of a fiscal instrument. Similarly, changes in the regulations governing the conduct of business in financial markets may have price and quantity implications for financial markets; but these developments, like tax changes, are of a discrete structural variety and have more to do with the pursuit of microeconomic allocative and efficiency objectives in individual markets than with the more global stability considerations normally associated with monetary policy. This should not be taken as suggesting that it is possible to separate completely microeconomic developments in financial markets and macroeconomic effects of monetary policy; it is likely that there will be interdependence between them.

A narrow definition of monetary policy which is more common in discussions of stabilization policy, is that it is an aspect of macroeconomic policy aimed, in the first instance, at achieving a particular level for the money stock, the credit stock, the rate of interest and the exchange rate. This is the meaning of monetary policy that is used here. The specific monetary policy actions aimed at achieving a particular value for one or more of the monetary variables in the above list involve the direct adjustment of such monetary policy instruments as: open market purchases or sales of bonds; the discount rate; ceilings on interest rates; ceilings on bank lending or borrowing; reserve requirements; hire-purchase controls; moral suasion, and so on. In an operational sense monetary policy is conducted through the direct control of these instruments.

Principles of Measurement

At the instrument level, monetary policy is clearly multidimensional. This feature of the operation of monetary policy makes it difficult to gauge the ex-ante stance of monetary policy. If the only influences on financial markets and the real economy were the settings of monetary policy instruments it would, in principle, be possible to construct an index of monetary policy by measuring the effects of each instrument on the goal variables of interest, using the measured independent influences as the weights for the construction of the index. In practice, there are two main obstacles to this approach. In the first place, even if policy instruments are an important source of variation in financial and real variables, they are not likely to be the only source of such variation; other policy and non-policy factors may have an important role to play. This raises what may be a serious and possibly intractable problem of identification. It is, however, a problem faced in all empirical work which seeks to isolate the effects of a particular factor. Secondly and perhaps more seriously, any attempt to isolate the effects of particular policy instruments is likely to be thwarted by the lack of variability in the statistical data on some instruments, such as reserve ratios, or by the limited number of observations on other instruments, such as moral suasion. There are no well-determined econometric models which can answer such questions as: what will the effect be upon the money supply, the level of credit, short- and long-term interest rates and the exchange rate of a request by the central bank for commercial banks to 'moderate their lending'? At present the construction of an instrument-based index of monetary policy is not feasible.

A less ideal, but more practical at present, approach to the measurement of the ex ante stance of monetary policy is to make a qualitative assessment further along the chain of causation at a point where conditions reflect the changes made at the initial instrument level. The measurement of policy at this intermediate level can, however, only be exact to the extent that there exist some variables which fully reflect the overall change in the stance of monetary policy brought about by adjustments in various policy instruments and that are, at the same time, free from the influence of other policy and non-policy factors. It is unlikely that any variable exists at the intermediate level which is totally free of contamination from non-monetary policy influences. Intermediate measures of monetary policy such as the money stock, credit, interest rates and the exchange rate may all change independently of the ex-ante stance of monetary policy as described by the settings of directly controlled policy instruments. The money stock will generally depend on the portfolio behaviour of the banks and the non-bank private sector, as well as the activities of the public sector. There is no evidence to suggest that non-public sector portfolio behaviour is being determined exclusively by the policy of the monetary authorities. The level of credit, where this is not being controlled directly, will be subject to the same non-policy influences as the money stock. Interest rates that are not pegged may be influenced by productivity shifts and expectations, neither of which can plausibly be closely manipulated by the monetary authorities. The exchange rate, when not completely fixed, is also likely to depend upon factors beyond the direct control of the monetary authorities, not least of which might be the monetary developments in the rest of the world, or speculative capital flows which can only be tenuously linked to changes in the relative stance of monetary policy.

Where intermediate variables are not free from non-monetary policy influences, which will generally be the case, the question then arises as to which of these variables best reflects the stance of monetary policy. The answer depends, in part, on the types of monetary policy regime being pursued. Under fixed exchange rates, the exchange rate itself provides no information about the stance of monetary policy. Furthermore, the money stock will, in the absence of effective sterilization, depend on foreign monetary influences. Under these circumstances, interest rates and domestic credit would seem to be the best indicators of the direction of domestic monetary policy, though if the fixed exchange rate is to be maintained, domestic interest rates and credit expansion will only be able to depart temporarily from the levels prevailing without serious current disequilibrium and exchange rate pressure developing.

Under floating exchange rates the choice of monetary policy measure becomes more complicated. In these circumstances all intermediate variables are likely to reflect the adjustments made to the instruments of monetary policy. But the extent to which movements in intermediate variables can be explained by changes in the instruments of monetary policy may not be the same. The ranking of intermediate monetary variables in terms of the amount of their variation that can be explained by the variation in the stance of monetary policy may not be stable even if the links with the ultimate instruments of monetary policy and each of the intermediate monetary variables are stable. The reason for this is perhaps obvious. If individual instruments affect individual intermediate variables differently, then different mixes of instruments which correspond to the same monetary policy stance may bring about a corresponding different mix of movement in intermediate variables. The greater the scope for independent variation in observed intermediate monetary variables, the more difficult it is likely to be to interpret their movements. In the absence of a single intermediate variable giving consistent and unambiguous signals of the stance of monetary policy, each intermediate indicator will need to be 'interpreted' in the light of observed movements in other indicators. For operational purposes the current 'look at everything' approach of many central banks must ultimately be reduced to a single index of the stance of policy. The process by which even the most qualitative of assessments of the stance of monetary policy is arrived at is not formalized and may differ considerably from one monetary authority to another.

Much of the ambiguity in the movement of intermediate policy variables could be eliminated by moving from indirect and imperfect control of these variables to direct control. In principle any, but not all simultaneously, of the intermediate policy variables could be brought under direct control in the short run; the exchange rate can be fixed, restrictions can be placed on the quantity advanced of certain types of credit, the rate of interest can be pegged and institutional arrangements can be created to bring the money supply under tight control. The non-policy contamination could be eliminated from any of the intermediate variables that were chosen to play the role of policy instruments. The question remains, though, whether or not these variables would retain their indicator value once controlled. In the case of the exchange rate and the rate of interest it is clear that they would not, and there is also doubt about the relevance of financial quantities which are subject to controls.

The choice of measure of the stance of monetary policy as presented above, although complicated enough, is a simplification of the situation faced in practice. Even if it were possible to decide *a priori* which intermediate variables, or combinations thereof, were the best indicators of monetary policy it would still be necessary to know, for example, which interest rate, exchange rate, credit aggregate or monetary aggregate is the most relevant. If the stance of monetary policy is thought on *a priori* grounds to be best measured by the money supply, what is the appropriate empirical counterpart of this concept? Should a narrow or broad monetary aggregate be selected? Should the aggregate be a simple sum aggregate, implying that the components are perfect substitutes, or should it be a weighted sum where the weights are meant to capture the degree of moneyness of the assets? The selection of credit aggregates encounters similar problems to those faced in choosing a monetary aggregate. These complications are not confined to money and credit aggregates. Choices have to be made between the short rate of interest and the long rate of interest and, for countries other than the United States, the exchange rate in terms of the US dollar and a trade-weighted index of exchange rates. The most problematic indicators, from the point of view of selecting an appropriate measure, are the monetary and credit aggregates.

Choosing between Monetary Aggregates

As the trend, at least until recently, has been for monetary authorities to rely more and more on monetary aggregates as indicators of the stance of monetary policy, it would seem appropriate here to examine the methods that have been advanced for selecting monetary aggregates. Approaches to the selection of monetary aggregates fall into two broad categories: (a) those that rely on a mainly theoretical approach supported by causal empiricism; and (b) those which employ statistical criteria and in which theory has a subordinate role.

Theoretical criteria

Of the purely theoretical approaches two have been dominant in their influence. The first of these emphasizes the medium of exchange function as the essential property and distinguishing feature of money.[1] The second view holds that it is the liquidity or asset function of money which makes it an important potential determinant of economic activity.[2] Both of these views have been influential in guiding monetary authorities in the selection of monetary aggregates.

The idea that money should be defined exclusively as the 'means of payment' was widely held in the 1950s. One advantage of this approach to the measurement of money is that, allowing for minor qualifications, there is general agreement that in modern economies, domestic currency and sight deposits constitute the bulk of the means of payment. But with the rapid development in the post-war period of highly liquid claims which provide an alternative temporary abode of purchasing power to the means of payment already included in the traditional narrow measure of money, the emphasis shifted away from the notion that the medium of exchange was the essential property of money. One alternative view that developed was that the link between the means of payment and economic activity was likely to become increasingly tenuous and unstable as the financial system became more developed, and that a more useful monetary aggregate would be one that measured the overall liquidity of the economy.[3] The idea that money should include more than the medium of exchange became influential in the 1960s at the time that many central banks began to publish statistics for the money supply.[4] It is not surprising, therefore, that broad measures of money tended to be the ones favoured. As well as being a major consideration in the construction of official monetary aggregates, the relative liquidity of assets has also been an important guiding principle in the work of thinkers who have stressed the role of money in the determination of aggregate demand.

Empirical criteria

The asset approach to measuring money raises serious difficulties. No clear and unambiguous definition of liquidity has been produced to guide the choice of liquidity-based monetary aggregate.[5] The response to this problem has either been to deny the possibility of arriving at a useful measure of money[6] or to employ statistical criteria to resolve the issue of which assets to include in the measure of money.[7] Several alternative empirical methods for approaching the selection of monetary aggregates have been used.

Substitutability in demand One way of measuring money that has proved popular is to measure the substitutability in demand of the medium of exchange and alternative financial assets.[8] Those assets that appear to be close substitutes for the medium of exchange are classed as money and aggregated into a broad measure of money. The rationale for the substitutability criterion is that if money can be defined in a way that internalizes asset substitution in the aggregate then such an aggregate will be a substitute for goods alone, to the exclusion of other financial assets. The obvious problem with this criterion is the arbitrary nature of the degree of substitutability used as the cut-off point for including assets in the monetary aggregate. What is a 'high' or 'low' degree of substitutability? Strictly speaking, only if the elasticity of substitution is infinite can aggregation be justified.

Stability of demand What is of more importance than the degree of substitutability is the stability of the substitution relationship. If the substitution relationship between the medium of exchange and other assets is known, the degree of substitutability presents no problem for monetary policy (it merely affects the size of the multiplier) but unstable and unpredictable relationships do. Recognition of this fact led to the suggestion that the measure of money chosen for policy purposes should be the one that exhibits the most stable demand for money function.[9] This idea is based on an assertion that stability in the demand for money is a necessary requirement for there to be stability in the relationship between money and income.[10] The voluminous amount of empirical research on the demand for money function has been motivated above all by belief in the necessity of a stable demand for money function for monetary policy, based on the control of the money supply, to be effective.[11]

There is, however, a basic problem in trying to select a monetary aggregate on the basis of its stability in demand that has been overlooked in much of the literature.[12] The importance attached to the stability of the demand for money and the motivation for its use in ranking monetary aggregates may not be well founded. Stability in the demand for money may only be 'necessary' for a stable money–income multiplier if the demand for goods and services is stable. If there is instability in the real sector, then it will be necessary for the demand for money to exhibit sufficient instability to absorb real sector instability for the relationship between money and economic activity to remain stable. If disturbances to money demand are combined with disturbances to expenditure, instability in money demand can be consistent with stability in the money–nominal income relationship. If disturbances to expenditure and money demand are independent, the ranking of monetary aggregates according to their stability in demand would seem a perfectly reasonable approach to adopt. The demand for money function is only one among many structural relationships in the economic system. Information about this function cannot be used properly without reference to the properties of other structural equations. This observation throws doubt on the inferences that have been drawn so freely from empirical studies of the demand for alternative monetary aggregates.

Direct measures of association Rather than trying to choose a monetary aggregate in terms of the size of the interest rate elasticity or stability of a demand for money function, other researchers have used more direct methods based on the measurement of the association between monetary aggregates and the policy goals to which they are relevant – nominal income and the price level. These methods include: simple correlation, St Louis Equations, causality tests and information content.

1. *Simple correlation:* This method typically involves the ranking of alternative aggregates in terms of the size of their simple contemporaneous correlation with nominal income.[13] Despite its naivety, this method, or variations of it, has been used widely.[14] The use of simple correlation as a criterion does not imply anything about causation although most studies assume that money determines income.

2. *St Louis Equations:* These early studies gave way to the selection of monetary aggregates in terms of their explanatory power in equations purporting to be reduced forms of larger, unspecified structural models. The St Louis Equation, so named because it was devised at the Federal Reserve Bank of St Louis, is the most well-known example of such a 'reduced form' model. St Louis Equations were meant to be an improvement on the *ad hoc* regressions that were used previously, but they have also been criticized for being arbitrary and *ad hoc.*[15] Nevertheless St. Louis Equations have proved to be a popular device for comparing alternative monetary aggregates.[16]

3. *Causality test:* There has been a growing tendency recently to avoid prejudging the causal relationships that exist between variables such as money, income and the price level and to avoid the use in models of identifying assumptions that cannot reasonably be justified.[17] This has given rise to the use of statistical methods that are meant to determine model structure and causal ordering from the data rather than *a priori,* or merely as data description and non-economic forecasting devices.[18] The usual aim of these studies has been to find a monetary aggregate

which does not exhibit feedback from income and prices, that is one that can be taken to be exogenous and amenable to control. The use of autoregressive models to make these sort of economic inferences has come in for criticism on the grounds that atheoretical models of this type cannot be used to make statements about structural relationships between economic variables.[19]

4. *Information content:* Where it is thought prudent to avoid making strong prior assumptions about causality and model structure there would seem to be little left but to use the established time-series methods for data description and forecasting. This is a perfectly reasonable approach to take, if all that is required is an assessment of what the knowledge of current and past values of alternative monetary aggregates can tell us about the current (but unknown) and future values of income and the price level. Of course, much more needs to be known or assumed about the properties of monetary aggregates than their indicator properties to say anything about their macroeconomic effects. But if the main aim is to measure the indicator value or information content of monetary aggregates, the use of economic theory-neutral statistical methods is one solution.[20]

In addition to the limitations that apply to each of the above empirical approaches to measuring money, there are potentially serious drawbacks to using these procedures. They all involve the implicit use of a maintained hypothesis that money is a close substitute for goods but not non-money financial assets, that money is stable in demand, that money is highly correlated with nominal income, that money is exogenous and causes nominal income, or that money is a good leading indicator of nominal income. Though there is nothing inherently wrong with basing the search for a measure of money on any of these empirical criteria (leaving aside the questionable relevance of some of them for the stability and predictability of the money–nominal income relationship), the subsequent use of such measures of money to assess the validity of the maintained hypothesis is questionable. There is an obvious circularity in the reasoning underlying this procedure.

3. UNCERTAINTY ABOUT THE CONCEPTUAL FRAMEWORK[21]

Even if monetary authorities were able to decide on the 'best' indicator or monetary policy, the risks that monetary policy will be aimed at inappropriate targets and that changes in the direction of monetary policy will be mistimed remain. These risks arise from the lack of understanding about how monetary policy works and the short-run and long-run effects it has on real and nominal economic activity. This lack of understanding extends even to the choice of an appropriate framework for the analysis of monetary policy effects. The two main approaches to macroeconomic analysis are the traditional short-run non-clearing markets approach to macroeconomic analysis, which derives its inspiration from the widely accepted 'stylised fact' of inertia in the adjustment of wages and prices, and the more recent radical market-clearing approach. The problem facing monetary authorities is that these approaches are divergent in the predictions that they make about the scope and effects of monetary policy.

Market-Clearing Models

Within the non-clearing markets approach Keynesianism and monetarism share the two main features of what is frequently referred to as the 'neoclassical synthesis' (short-run disequilibrium and long-run market clearing). However, there are differences in crucial aspects of these frameworks which lead to radically different predictions about the effects of monetary policy. Keynesian thinking on the role of monetary policy is often taken to be epitomized by the standard Hicksian ISLM model. In the simplest versions of this model, prices are taken to be given. Expenditure functions and the money demand function are interest rate-sensitive and are well determined with identifiable parameters. Output is perfectly elastic. In this set-up, monetary policy-induced changes in aggregate demand affect output and have no effect on prices. In practice, elements of the perceived real world economy have been grafted onto this analysis. Generally, prices are not assumed to be constant but instead to adjust gradually. Output is assumed to depend upon the productive potential of the economy. The nearer to the capacity limit of the economy, the more that aggregate demand raises prices and the less it affects output. This trade-off between output and prices, known as the Phillips curve in its original labour market price–quantity formulation, is assumed to be sufficiently stable for it to be exploited for stabilizing employment and output. This framework indicates the existence of substantial scope for active discretionary stabilization policy.

Another striking feature of the neo-Keynesian approach is the assumed mechanism by which inflation is generated. Prices are viewed as being determined by a simple mark-up on costs. One implication of this is that aggregate demand pressure will have little or no direct impact on prices and will have more powerful effects on supply. Another implication is that inflation is largely determined by the attempts of labour to alter the distribution of income in its favour. With a full employment goal, monetary policy will have to accommodate any change in wage rates and prices. Within this framework, monetary policy has no role in containing inflation. Policy towards inflation has instead to be based on measures to stem inflationary wage demands. Such measures include incomes policies, wage indexation, wage–price guideposts and 'social contracts'. Inflation in the Keynesian world is largely a social phenomenon. Failure to recognize this, and instead to try to achieve rapid disinflation via monetary deflation, would accordingly result in high real costs for little or no short-run gain, especially if wage settlements are not sensitive to rising unemployment. In open economies operating a floating exchange rate regime, monetary policy could be expected to influence inflation via the response of the exchange rate and, hence, import prices. In general, floating exchange rates would be expected to worsen the output–inflation trade-off and, thereby, reduce the potential gains to the discretionary stabilization policy.

Monetarist thought has diverged from neo-Keynesian ideas on a number of issues. Perhaps the most important point of divergence concerns the confidence with which a well-determined model of the economy can be identified. While generally rejecting the possibility of generating such a model and, therefore, discounting completely the simulation results of large-scale Keynesian models, monetarists have placed substantial emphasis on the power of the same econometric techniques to identify a well-determined structural money demand function and a well-determined 'reduced-form' relationship between money and nominal income. At the same time they have been noted for maintaining that the relationship between money and nominal income suffers from 'long and variable lags', which prevent the efficient use of active monetary stabilization policy. The main message of the monetarist approach is that active discretionary monetary policy is likely to be destabilizing. It would not be too much of an exaggeration to characterize monetarist thought on the business cycle as viewing this feature of non-market-clearing economies not only as a disequilibrium phenomenon, but also as a largely monetary phenomenon. According to this view, the excessive swings that have been experienced in economic activity could be avoided by formulating monetary policy in terms of a simple, non-reactive rule for the growth of an appropriate monetary aggregate.

A second important point of divergence in monetarist thought from that of Keynesians concerns the existence of a stable long-run trade-off between inflation and output implied by the Keynesian Phillips curve. Such a long-run trade-off is rejected on the grounds that it seems to imply an implausible degree of money illusion. While monetarists are prepared to accept that inflation might not be fully anticipated in the short run, they cannot countenance the idea that such errors will remain persistently large in the long run. Indeed, the idea of a long-run equilibrium seems, to monetarists, to be at odds with the existence of expectational errors. The monetarists' alternative view of the Phillips curve is that it is a short-run phenomenon caused by expectational errors. So if inflation suddenly increased, this may lead to an increase in output and employment because labour costs (real wages) decline given temporarily fixed nominal wages. This situation of increased activity will only last as long, however, as it takes to adjust nominal wages to the new level of expected inflation. Output and employment will then return to its former level. In these circumstances the only way in which higher output and employment can be maintained will be to accelerate the rate of increase in inflation in order to stay ahead of expectations. This implies an ever deteriorating trade-off; a given level of 'excess employment' requires more and more inflation. In the long run 'excess employment' is not sustainable. Actual inflation will coincide with expected inflation and the economy will revert to its natural long-run equilibrium output growth and employment rate. This monetarist analysis offers a considerably more pessimistic prognosis of the scope for trading output against inflation; it depends on the speed with which wage rates respond to inflation and is at best temporary. It also offers a bleak outlook for attempts to achieve rapid disinflation via monetary deflation. If nominal wage rates do not adjust quickly, disinflation will be accompanied by high output and employment costs. Monetarist awareness of the potential costs of rapid disinflation have led them to advocate a gradualist approach in which the money supply growth (though which 'money supply' is not always clearly identified) rate is decelerated very slowly in the hope of reducing the adverse output and employment consequences.

A temporary trade-off will exist, with consequential real costs of disinflation, as long as expectations formation is confined to an adaptive process that uses past values of inflation alone. If inflation is accelerating, this will give rise to systematically biased forecasts of inflation. If the resulting positive prediction errors are interpreted as involving a favourable change in relative prices (real wages appear higher than expected), this may cause a positive supply response. If expectations formation is, on the other hand, forward-looking and is based on all relevant available information, including aspects of the process by which inflation is generated, no exploitable trade-off will exist. For example, if monetary policy was the sole determinant of the price level, and such a policy could be observed, then the price level would be known also. No errors will occur in expectations, and movements in nominal wage rate will not be mistaken for movements in real wages. Perfect foresight is not a requirement for the elimination of an exploitable trade-off based on expectations error. In general all that is required is that price forecasts be based on the efficient use of all available information – that is be rational – and that there be an absence of asymmetries of information. The monetary authorities, for example, should not have superior information to the private sector about the inflation process.

The closed economy tone that characterized much of the early monetarist and Keynesian analysis has given way increasingly to an analysis which recognizes explicitly the openness of economies to external influences, including foreign monetary influences. The possible existence of significant interdependence between countries has raised questions about the scope and benefits of international coordination of monetary policy. In the seminal Mundell–Fleming model, which is usually taken as the benchmark model for the analysis of macroeconomic policy in a multicountry setting, monetary policy is a 'beggar-thy-neighbour' policy; expansionary domestic policy lowers foreign output. Within this framework there is an obvious conflict of interest which a cooperative approach to monetary policy may be able to eliminate. However, the negative spillovers upon which the potential gains from cooperation depend may not occur in practice. Even from an *a priori* standpoint, the direction of any spillover effects of monetary policy are not clear-cut; it will depend upon, among other things, the way that expectations are formed, the role of domestic and foreign producer prices in the demand for domestic goods and financial assets, and the differences between countries in the degree of indexation of wages to prices. Under some circumstances monetary policy will have positive spillovers. As things stand there is no consensus about the correct specification of the macroeconomic framework within which to analyse monetary interdependence and cooperation. But even in models which allow for large negative spillovers, potential gains from cooperation seem to be small. One thing does appear to be clear, however, and that is that domestic economies cannot usefully be analysed as if they exhibited full monetary independence under floating exchange rates. Whether the extent of monetary interdependence is such that it is the world money supply, rather than the national money supply, which matters more for the domestic economy is unclear.[22]

Keynesian and modern quantity theory approaches to macroeconomic policy analysis are predicated on the assumption that in the short run the economy may be driven into disequilibrium, and that such disequilibrium states are undesirable and should be avoided or corrected if possible. In the early 1970s a radical alternative to this view emerged. This new approach goes under the title of 'new classical economics', reflecting the fact that it appears to draw much of its inspiration from classical equilibrium analysis. The key proposition of new classical economics is that prices always adjust sufficiently to maintain continuous market clearing. This proposition alone implies a 'root and branch' rejection of the Keynesian/monetarist theory of the business cycle, which is based mainly on non-clearing markets. The new classical approach does not, however, reject the idea of a business cycle. In a continuous market-clearing framework the cycle is an equilibrium phenomenon which may not be undesirable and, even if it were undesirable, may not be correctable. The new classical approach to macroeconomic analysis has far-reaching implications for the effects of monetary policy and its potential as a tool of stabilization policy.

Non-Market-Clearing Models

New classical economists have typically dismissed the idea of using monetary policy to stabilize output and employment. In the new classical analytical framework, real variables can only deviate from their full information values because of random (non-systematic) variations in the price level induced by random monetary policy. The full information equilibrium, or 'natural' values of variables, is taken to be the 'best' (Pareto-optimal) values that can be achieved. The essential prediction of the new classical framework is that only the unanticipated component of domestic monetary policy will have any real effects and that these effects will be only temporary. The price level, on the other hand, will depend upon both the unanticipated and anticipated components. Given that the full information equilibrium is the 'best' position for the economy, unanticipated policy is undesirable. Viewed in this way the new classical framework provides, from a different perspective, an alternative rationalization for simple, credible announced monetary targets to that offered by modern quantity theory monetarists. As far as disinflation is concerned, new classical economics gives the comfortable prediction that monetary policy can achieve a rapid and costless reduction in inflation if the policy is well understood and is believed.

There are reasons for believing that monetary policy surprises may play no more than a minor role in explaining variations in real economic activity and may not be able to account for the strength of the correlation between money and real activity. From an *a priori* point of view, the assumption that significant informational gaps would persist and not be eliminated by information gathering, motivated by maximizing behaviour, seems as arbitrary and *ad hoc* as the assumption that prices do not adjust instantaneously because of unspecified costs of adjustment. In practice there exists a good deal of information that might help to avoid confusion between relative price and absolute price level changes. Many goods are traded throughout the economy, and the prices at which they are sold in different localities is easily established. Also there is readily available information on such global price variables as the exchange rate and interest rates. Moreover, in some countries preliminary monetary statistics are available with a very short lag.

If monetary surprises are rejected as a source of the business cycle, two questions remain to be answered. First: why are the money supply and real activity correlated? Secondly: if variations in real activity are not caused by monetary disturbances, what is their cause? One explanation, which also ironically is advanced by Keynesians, for the existence of a significant correlation between money and real activity is that reverse causation is responsible and that the money supply is responding positively to money demand which is determined by changes in the level of real activity. If the observed correlation has indeed been derived from data in which money is endogenous, it leaves open the question of what would happen if monetary policy ceased to accommodate output changes; would output be affected or would the effects be confined to prices? One approach to macroeconomic analysis, known as the real theory of the business cycle, posits that exogenous monetary policy would have no real effects and that the business cycle is an exclusively real phenomenon. In this framework, monetary policy could not even be destabilizing; random monetary policy has no real consequences. In this world it does not matter whether monetary policy announcements are credible or not. The source of the serial correlation observed in output and employment is real shocks. These real shocks are translated, through a propagation mechanism implied by production-smoothing behaviour, into serially correlated output and employment. If, in addition, the observed values of output and employment at any point in the business cycle reflect rational maximizing behaviour and market clearing then such observations will correspond to a Pareto-optimal equilibrium. The business cycle, viewed in this light, as well as being independent of nominal monetary policy, is a desirable response of the economy to supply shocks. This framework describes a true Panglossian world where, '*Tout est pour le mieux dans le meilleur des mondes*'.

4. UNCERTAINTY IN EMPIRICAL TESTS

Progress on arriving at a definite view of which macro/monetary model is most relevant for the analysis of monetary policy is hampered by data limitations, a lack of agreement about the appropriate econometric methodology and the limitations of statistical tests to discriminate between alternative models. The result is that policy-makers are deluged with competing and often quite divergent estimates of the effects of monetary policy and have no sound basis on which to choose among alternative estimates.

Views on what constitutes appropriate empirical methodology and how formal econometric estimates should be interpreted, appeared fairly fixed in the early 1970s. That time, in some sense, marked a high point in the confidence that the economics profession had about what could be achieved by applying classical statistical theory to the measurement and testing of economic relationships. Econometric model-building proceeded on the assumption that the parameters of major structural relationships could be estimated and, once estimated, could be relied upon for the evaluation of economic policy. The major limitations to the programme of econometric modelling were in the area of data availability in long series, and the refinement of techniques to cope with departures from the classical properties of the error term (autocorrelation; heteroscedasticity; multicollinearity; and so on) and the simultaneity of relationships. These limitations were not thought, however, to be a serious impediment to obtaining useful estimates. However, there was some scepticism, especially among monetarists, about the possibility of being able to identify correctly the true detailed structure of the economy in the way attempted by the builders of large-scale Keynesian models. Nevertheless, even this more circumspect group was confident that some of the key macroeconomic relationships, such as the aggregate demand for money function, could be reliably identified, enabling classical hypothesis testing to be undertaken.

The Emergence of Instability in Econometric Relationships

In support of their case for stable money growth rules, monetarists reported evidence of a reliable relationship between money and nominal income and the existence of a stable, aggregate demand for money relationship. Given a stable money supply, this latter finding implied a stable LM-schedule which was taken as pointing to the money stock rather than the interest rate as the best instrument of monetary policy. Work by central banks at first provided support for monetarist empirical findings. But evidence began to emerge from the early 1970s onwards that money demand and money multiplier relationships had become unstable. Money demand equations began to predict badly out of sample, and measures of income velocity were subject to unexpected shifts. In addition, different measures of money moved in divergent ways, often at crucial times.

A number of reasons have been advanced for the breakdown in these key economic relationships. One popular explanation has been that financial innovation and financial market deregulation distorted the monetary aggregates. The implication of this argument is that some underlying, not yet identified, monetary aggregate is stable in demand and has a stable velocity, or that stability in existing relationships will re-emerge once adjustment to new market conditions has been completed. Another account of this development, which is more an observation than an explanation, is known as Goodhart's Law. According to Goodhart's Law, formerly well-determined and stable relationships disintegrate when any attempt is made to exploit them for policy purposes. The shift towards a quantitative objective for the money supply in the 1970s is responsible for the deterioration in money demand and velocity behaviour. A closely related argument, which also emphasizes the importance of changes in policy regime, arises from the Lucas critique of macroeconometric policy analysis. The basis for the Lucas critique is the view that the parameters in aggregate macroeconomic relationships are the outcome of individual maximizing behaviour. If individuals are rational they will typically take into account all factors that are likely to impinge upon their own activity. If government policy, including monetary policy, is of importance in determining individual behaviour, then changes in policy regime of the sort connected with the move to floating exchange rates, monetary targets and financial deregulation, are likely to change parameter values. Though the Lucas critique, unlike Goodhart's Law, implies that parameter values will change in a systematic way, it may take a considerable amount of time before the new values emerge from the data.

Whatever the reason for the instability that has been a feature of important macroeconomic relationships since the early 1970s, it has left its mark on the trust that policy-makers place in statistical evidence, whether this is of a descriptive or sophisticatedly estimated character. This new scepticism is well illustrated in the following recent statement by the Governor of the Bank of England:

> shifts in previously established statistical regularities have provided a challenge to economists to come up with new and better relationships. Battles have been fought over whether or not meaningful econometric relationships can be found. For myself I take all their offerings, their regressions, coefficients and simulations with a liberal dose of salt, (Governor of the Bank of England, 1984, p. 476).

The Crisis in Methodology

In addition to the emergence of instability, another striking feature of empirical estimates of macroeconomic relationships has been the diversity of results that are reported on any particular relationship. Differences in results, which is one aspect of the instability issue, have arisen because of such factors as the time period covered, the country in question, the frequency of observation, the measurement of variables, the method of estimation and model builder discretion. The marriage of classical statistical theory and economic theory, known as econometrics, has not proved to be a very fruitful one in the area of macroeconomics. Few, if any, reliable and robust parameter estimates have been produced. Possible reasons for this include inadequate and inappropriate data and the lack of sufficiently well-developed theory.

The procedures used in most econometric work are more appropriate to the 'hard' sciences where controlled experiments are feasible. The data used in econometrics are, by and large, a by-product of the administrative process. As such econometrics embodies a large number of influences, only a few of which are measured or could be measured. Furthermore, there is no consensus on how key variables such as the money stock should be measured in practice. These data and definitional problems come on top of the, perhaps, more serious limitations of existing theoretical frameworks. Theory generally offers little guidance to the model-builder as to the appropriate functional forms for econometric relationships. Beyond suggesting the variables that are likely to be of importance and whether the relationships will be dynamic or not, theory has little further to say. In this situation a substantial amount of discretion is left to the econometrician. Typically, the modelling process involves a good deal of 'off-the-cuff' *ad hoc* hypothesizing, data-sifting and data-mining. The theoretical lacunae have given rise to the development of informal model-building strategies designed to 'discover from the data', among other things: the direction of causation in relationships; the relevant variables to include in models; and the most appropriate dynamic structure. One methodological stream, which developed in the 1970s and is still influential, moved towards less and less reliance on *a priori* ideas, justified by the poor state of economic theory and the increasing lack of any consensus on basic aspects of macroeconomic structure, and more and more towards dependence on purely atheoretical statistical methods (Box–Jenkins time-series methods and vector autoregressions) of data description. The use of such methods for the evaluation and analysis of policy have recently been the subject of substantial criticism. However, the only alternative that more conventional econometricians can offer at present is the greater use of a wide range of techniques to assess the robustness of estimates and the adoption of a more humble stance in the reporting of econometric results.

Though neo-Keynesian views have by no means been completely abandoned, monetarism and new classical economics in particular have become important forces in framing monetary policy. Of these two latter frameworks monetarism has been by far the more dominant alternative to neo-Keynesian analysis in policy-making circles, possibly because it is more familiar and less radical. At one stage, from the mid-1970s to the beginning of the 1980s, it appeared possible that monetarism might completely eclipse Keynesianism. In the 1980s the down-grading of short-run employment goals in favour of inflation control and the emphasis on stable medium-term growth of the money supply, underlined by the widespread adoption of monetary targets in the 1970s, reflected monetarist thinking. However, the stubbornly high unemployment rates experienced in many industrial countries in more recent times, coupled with disappointments in the conduct and performance of a money aggregate-oriented monetary policy, have revived interest in Keynesian demand management, even if of a coarser variety than previously practised. The use of rules has come to play an important role in the formulation of monetary policy, but the exercise of discretion is far from having been abandoned.

5. CONCLUSION

The current monetary policy environment is characterized by a high degree of risk and uncertainty. There exists scepticism and mistrust about the reliability of any single measure of the stance of monetary policy. Theoretical developments and empirical evidence have highlighted the flaws in such monetary indicators as monetary aggregates, interest rates and exchange rates. The current tendency of central banks is to 'look at everything' when assessing the stance of monetary policy. This 'pragmatism' is a clear reflection of the lack of any agreed guiding principles on which to base monetary policy and the resulting eclecticism in policy formulation. The existence of competing conceptual frameworks is an additional source of uncertainty faced by policy-makers. Given current data and statistical limitations, which seem to offer little immediate prospect of settling outstanding issues over model choice, monetary authorities will have to continue to pursue policy with considerable caution.

NOTES

1. See Yeager (1968).
2. See Keynes (1936) and Friedman (1956).
3. See Gurley and Shaw (1960).
4. Milton Friedman (1956), for example, has always been in favour of including more than the medium of exchange in his own measure of the money stock (see Friedman and Schwartz (1983)) on the grounds that money is a 'temporary abode of purchasing power' and that assets other than the medium of exchange are sufficiently liquid to possess this property.
5. Despite the efforts of Hicks (1962).
6. This view is shared, among others, by the Radcliffe Committee and Tobin (1963).
7. This is the approach adopted by Friedman and Meiselman (1963).
8. See Feige and Pearce (1977) for a comprehensive survey of the evidence using this approach.
9. This approach was suggested by Laidler (1969).
10. The original statement of the significance of the demand for money in these terms is contained in Friedman (1956).

11. See Judd and Scadding (1982) and the works cited therein.
12. See Driscoll and Ford (1980) for a critique of this view.
13. This approach was first used by Friedman and Meiselman (1963).
14. See Hulett (1971) and Jonung (1981).
15. See Goldfeld and Blinder (1973), Gramlich (1971), Modigliano and Ando (1976) and Sargent (1976).
16. Among the studies that have used this approach are those by Cagan (1982), Carlson and Hein (1980), Dennis (1983), Friedman (1983), Hafer (1981), Islam (1982) and Batten and Thornton (1983).
17. For an exposition of this viewpoint, see Simms (1980).
18. Methods used to determine causal orderings, such as vector autoregressions, have been used recently as a means of ranking monetary aggregates by Friedman (1983), Pautler and Richard (1979), Hafer (1981), McMillin and Fackler (1983) and Selody (1978).
19. See Cooley and LeRoy (1983).
20. This approach has been used by Barnett *et al.* (1981), Bailey *et al.* (1982a, 1982b) and Bordes *et al.* (1984).
21. For a more detailed review of the material covered here, including references to relevant publications, see Chouraqui *et al.* (1989).
22. Even if the law of one price held in commodity and asset markets so that the real exchange rate remained constant and the real interest rate was fixed by the world real rate, the insulation of the domestic economy from foreign monetary developments would depend upon the absence of significant currency substitution. If rational investors indulge in significant amounts of switching between currencies, domestic money demand will be sensitive to changes in foreign, as well as domestic, influences. The domestic economy will, via this channel, be exposed to foreign monetary developments. In the limit, a high degree of currency substitution could render the relationship between domestic money demand and purely domestic factors highly erratic. Under these circumstances, it would be the world's money supply, as in the case of a fixed exchange rate regime with non-sterilized intervention, that would be relevant to the determination of domestic aggregate demand.

REFERENCES

Bailey, R.W., M.J. Driscoll, J.L. Ford and A.W. Mullineux (1982a), 'The Information Content of Monetary Aggregates in the UK', *Economics Letters*, **9**, 61–7.

Bailey, R.W., M.J. Driscoll, J.L. Ford and A.W. Mullineux (1982b), 'The Aggregation Error in Divisia Monetary Aggregates: Some Findings for the UK, 1963–1980', Economics Letters, **10**, 123–8.

Bank of England, *Quarterly Bulletin*, 1984.

Barnett, W.A., P.A. Spindt and E.K. Offenbacher (1981), 'Empirical Comparisons of Divisia and Simple Sum Monetary Aggregates', Conference Paper no. 122, National Bureau of Economic Research, Cambridge, Mass.

Batten, D.S. and D.L. Thornton (1983), 'M1 or M2: Which is the Better Monetary Target', *Quarterly Review – Federal Reserve Bank of St Louis*, **65**, 36–42.

Bordes, C., M.J. Driscoll, J.L. Ford and A.W. Mullineux (1984), 'Tests Économétriques de l'Hypothèse de Rationalité et de l'Hypothèse de Neutralité Structurelle: Le Cas de la France: 1963–1980', miméo, Centre de Recherche en Macro-économie Monétaire, Faculté de Droit et des Sciences Économiques de Limoges.

Cagan, P. (1982), 'The Choice among Monetary Aggregates as Targets and Guides for Monetary Policy', *Journal of Money, Credit and Banking*, **14**, 661–2.

Carlson, K.M. and S.E. Hein (1980), 'Monetary Aggregates as Monetary Indicators', *Quarterly Review – Federal Reserve Bank of St Louis*, **62**, 12–21.

Chouraqui, J.C., M.J. Driscoll and M.O. Strauss-Kahn (1989), 'The Effects of Monetary Policy on the Real Sector: An Overview of Evidence for Selected OECD Countries', *Banca Nationale del Lavoro Review*, March, 3–49.

Cooley, T.F. and S.R. LeRoy (1983), 'Atheoretical Macroeconometrics: A Critique', miméo, Santa Barbara, University of California.

Dennis, G.E.J. (1983), 'Monetary Aggregates and Economic Activity: Evidence from Five Industrial Countries', Bank for International Settlements, *International Papers*, 7.

Driscoll, M.J. and J.L. Ford (1980), 'The Stability of the Demand for Money Function and the Predictability of the Effects of Monetary Policy', *Economic Journal*, **90**, 867–84.

Feige, E.L. and D.K. Pearce (1977), 'The Substitutability of Money and Near-Monies', *Journal of Economic Literature*, **28**, 302–56.

Friedman, B.M. (1983), 'The Roles of Money and Credit in Macroeconomic Analysis', in J. Tobin ed., *Macroeconomics, Prices and Quantities: Essays in Memory of Arthur M Okun*, Washington: Brookings Institute.

Friedman, M. (1956), 'The Quantity Theory of Money: A Restatement', in M.Friedman ed., *Studies in the Quantity Theory of Money*, Chicago: Chicago University Press, 3–21.

Friedman, M. and D. Meiselman (1963), 'The Relative Stability of Monetary Velocity and the Investment Multiplier in the United States, 1897–1958', in *Commission on Money and Credit Stabilization Policies*, Englewood Cliffs.

Friedman, M, and A.J. Schwartz (1983), *Monetary Trends in the United States and the United Kingdom*, New York: National Bureau of Economic Research.

Goldfeld, S.M. and A. Blinder (1973), 'Some Implications of Endogenous Stabilization Policy', *Brookings Papers on Economic Activity*, **3**, 585–644.

Gramlich, E.M. (1971), 'The Usefulness of Monetary and Fiscal Policy as Discretionary Policy Tools', *Journal of Money, Credit and Banking*, **3**, 506–60.

Gurley, J.G. and E.S. Shaw (1960), *Money in a Theory of Finance*, Washington: Brookings Institute.

Hafer, R.W. (1981), 'Selecting a Monetary Indicator: A Test of the New Monetary Aggregates', *Quarterly Review – Federal Reserve Bank of St Louis*, **63**, 12–18.

Hicks, J.R. (1962), 'Liquidity', *Economic Journal*, **82**, 787–802.

Hulett, D.T. (1971), 'More on an Empirical Definition of Money: Note', *American Economic Review*, **61**, 462–8.

Islam, S. (1982), 'Monetary and Credit Aggregates and Economic Activity: Evidence from Germany, Japan and the United States', *Research Paper* n° 8203, Federal Reserve Bank of New York.

Jonung, L. (1981), 'An Empirical Identification of the Swedish Money Stock', *Scandinavian Journal of Economics*, **32**, 68–78.

Judd, J.P. and J.L. Scadding (1982), 'The Search for a Stable Money Demand Function: A Survey of the Post-1973 Literature', *Journal of Economic Literature*, **20**, 992–1023.

Keynes, J.M. (1936), *The General Theory of Employment, Interest and Money*, London: Macmillan.

Laidler, D.E.W. (1969), 'The Definition of Money', *Journal of Money, Credit and Banking*, **1**, 508–25.

Laidler, D.E.W. and M.J. Parkin (1970), 'The Demand for Money in the United Kingdom 1956–1967: Preliminary Estimates', *Manchester School*, **38**, 187–208.

McMillin, W.D. and J.S. Fackler (1983), 'Monetary vs Credit Aggregates: An Evaluation of Monetary Policy Targets', *Southern Economic Journal*, **45**, 711–23.

Modigliani, F. and A. Ando (1976), 'Impacts of Fiscal Actions on Aggregate Income and the Monetarist Controversy: Theory and Evidence', in J.S. Stein ed., *Monetarism*, Amsterdam: North Holland, 17–42.

Pautler, P. and R. Richard (1979), 'Choosing a Money Aggregate: Causal Relationships as a Criterion', *Review of Business and Economic Research*, **15**, 1–18.

Sargent, T.J. (1976), 'The Observational Equivalence of Natural and Unnatural Rate Theories of Macroeconomics', *Journal of Political Economy*, **84**, 631–40.

Selody, J. (1978), 'On the Definition of Money: Some Canadian Evidence', *The Canadian Journal of Economics*, **1**, 52-80.

Sims, C.A. (1980), 'Macroeconomics and Reality', *Econometrica*, **35**, 1–45.

Tobin, J. (1963), 'Commercial Banks as Creators of Money' in D. Carson ed., *Banking and Monetary Studies*, Illinois: Irwin Homewood.

Yeager, L.B. (1968), 'The Essential Properties of the Medium of Exchange', *Kyklos*, **21**, 45–68.

7. Precautionary Reserves and Holding Period Certainty

David G. Dickinson

I regard myself as particularly fortunate in having been guided by Jim Ford, both as a PhD student and, later, as a colleague. As every one of his students will testify, he has always been prepared to spend many hours explaining theoretical nuances to eager listeners. In doing so, he has passed on his ability to take a critical but perceptive view of new developments in economic analysis, highlighting both the good and bad points. I hope that I have inherited at least part of that talent and I am happy to contribute a piece to this collection in Jim's honour. In that it is a development of ideas I first had during work on my PhD, I feel it is Jim's work as much as my own, although he is of course, not responsible for any errors or omissions it contains.

1. INTRODUCTION

Since the seminal work of Baumol (1952) and Tobin (1956) on the transactions demand for money, a rather limited amount of work has been devoted to the analysis of individual asset holding behaviour in the face of cash disbursement risk. This has ranged from static, single-period optimization approaches (Whalen, 1966; Gray and Parkin, 1973) to continuous time models (Miller and Orr, 1966; Tsiang, 1972; Frenkel and Jovanovic, 1980). The standard solution technique, following the example of the Baumol/Tobin certainty case, has been the stochastic inventory model, in various guises.

Faced with the choice between alternative models, it is clearly important to select that one which is most appropriate to the case under study. Hence, the continuous time approach has obvious parallels to the situation which faces economic units such as firms whereby continuous income and/or expenditure seems a reasonable approximation. For the individual household, where lumpy payments are common, the continuous time treatment may not be so appropriate. The problem with this division between analytical approaches is that by rejecting one in favour of another, certain desirable elements may be lost, as well as gained. Thus whilst a static, single period, optimization model is simple, and relevant to the case of the household, it suffers from failing to recognize the importance of liquidation timing uncertainty which is the crucial element of the continuous time models. On the other hand, continuous time models are a poor analytical method where discrete, stochastic, cash balance changes are normal and where, at least for the majority of models in this class, planning horizons are limited.

The model presented here will analyse the precautionary demand for reserves by households. It will use a single-period model on the grounds that households only need to plan for a limited period, and will adopt a multi-asset framework (something which the continuous time model cannot handle) since this seems appropriate. However, in order to capture the importance of asset liquidation timing, it will be assumed that the lumpy cash disbursement occurs (if at all) at an unknown point in time in the period. The relevance, to the precautionary demand, of holding period uncertainty has been well-documented in the formal analyses of the individual's demand for precautionary reserves (see, for example, Taylor, 1976; Goldman, 1978; Plessner and Reid, 1980).

The major concern of the model presented here is the pattern of liquid asset holding, which the household adopts so as to minimize the expected case of meeting unexpected positive cash disbursements occurring at an uncertain time. The restriction to positive cash requirement highlights a feature of the analysis that is not dealt with well by a continuous time treatment, that is that normally no distinction is made between costs of unexpected cash inflow or outflow. The reason why this is important is that the precautionary demand is not an analysis of the transactions demand under uncertainty. It is the modelling of additional liquidity requirements, because asset liquidations are unexpected and hence involve a specific liquidation cost in excess of any planned transaction costs. This is a crucial point which has not been recognized by some authors (Frenkel and Jovanovic, 1980), while being given specific attention by others (Tsiang, 1972).

The remainder of this chapter is divided into three parts. In the next section a detailed description of the model is presented with a derivation of the solution equations for optimal asset holdings. Section

3 contains a review of the comparative static properties of the model. The final section is a commentary on some of the implications of the analysis for the precautionary demand for money and also contains concluding comments.

2. A MODEL OF HOUSEHOLDS' PRECAUTIONARY DEMAND FOR RESERVES

The basic structure of the model (which is similar to Gray and Parkin, 1973) can be summarized as follows:

1. The household chooses from n liquid assets with the holding of each asset denoted by X_i ($i = 0 \ldots.(n-1)$). The $(n+1)$th asset is classed as non-liquid and is indexed by n.
2. Households plan the precautionary reserve over a period between income receipts. This planning period, of length T, is determined exogenously. Asset purchases and sales at each income receipt are costless because they are planned.
3. During the planning period, unexpected expenditure may occur. Both the timing and volume of this expenditure is uncertain and represented by probability density functions g(T) and f(x), respectively. Only one occurrence of the unexpected expenditure can take place during the planning period (this rather restrictive assumption can be re-interpreted as that only the first occurrence of unexpected expenditure entails liquidation costs). The distributions of holding period length and volume are defined across the whole range of x (can be negative) and t (can be outside of planning period).
4. Each asset offers a rate of interest (r_i) and incurs a per unit liquidation cost ($b_i(T-t)$) when sold to meet unexpected expenditure before the end of the planning period. Note that the liquidation cost varies according to the time of expenditure. By assumption, $b_n >> b_{n-1}$ so that n is a non-liquid asset.
5. Assets are chosen so as to minimize the expected cost of managing the precautionary reserve.

Hence, the basic decision facing the household is to provide a structure of liquid assets to meet both timing and volume uncertainty. The introduction of a planning period, with costless transactions at the beginning and end of it, relieves the (often unstated) problem that the inherited reserve structure is a constraint on achieving a desired precautionary portfolio. The assumption that unexpected income can be invested at zero cost allows emphasis to be placed on the problem of asset liquidation (effectively transactions costs are very small compared to liquidation costs). The assumption of per unit liquidation costs is made on the basis that it may represent some sort of 'credit-line' cost. This cost might very well be expected to vary with the liquidity of any collateral (asset holding) against which the borrowing is made (see, for example, recent papers on compensating balances such as Clarke and Speaker, 1986). Given this structure, the expected cost function for minimization can be written as:

$$EC = T\sum_{i=0}^{n-1} \{ X_i \, (1-G(T)) \, (r_n - r_i) \}$$

$$+ \int_{X(n-1)}^{\infty} \{ \int_0^T [t \sum_{i=0}^{n-1} X_i \, (r_n - r_i)] \, g(t)dt \} \, f(x)dx$$

$$+ \sum_{k=0}^{n-1} \{ \int_{X(k-1)}^{X(k)} \{ \int_0^T t \, [\sum_{i=0}^{k-1} X_i \, (r_k - r_i) + X(r_n - r_k)]$$

$$+ T \, [(\sum_0^k X_i - X)(r_n - r_i) + \sum_{i=k+1}^{n-1} X_i (r_n - r_i)] \, g(t) \, dt \} \, f(x)dx \}$$

$$+ \sum_{k=0}^{n-1} \{ \int_{X(k-1)}^{X(k)} \{ \int_0^T [b_k (T-t)(X - \sum_0^{k-1} X_i)] \, g(t)dt \} \, f(x)dx \}$$

$$+ b_k \, X_k \int_{X(k)}^{\infty} \{ \int_0^T (T-t) \, g(t)dt \} \, f(x)dx$$

$$+ \int_{X(n-1)}^{\infty} \{ \int_0^T b_n (T-t)(X - \sum_0^{n-1} X_i) \, g(t)dt \} \, f(x)dx, \qquad (1)$$

where:

$$X(M) = \sum_{i=0}^{M} X_i.$$

The derivation of this equation is discussed in the Appendix where it is also shown that the solution to the cost minimization problem generates the expressions:

$$F\left(\sum_{0}^{k-1} X_i\right) = 1 - \frac{\Omega\,(r_k - r_{k-1})}{(r_k - r_{k-1}) + (b_k - b_{k-1})} \tag{2}$$

(k = 0, 1, ..., (n−1))

and

$$\Omega = \frac{T}{\int_0^T (T-t)\; g(t)\; dt},$$

and F(.) is the cumulative density function of the cash requirements distribution.

This expression is consistent with that found by Gray and Parkin (1973) and Sprenkle (1985). Note that Sprenkle analyses the case of a variable, but known, end of holding period which although generating similar results has a substantially different and narrower methodological basis than the one here.

The optimizing expressions demonstrate the conventional separation property that choice of one asset depends only upon the rate of interest and liquidation costs of the asset itself and the two assets which are closest substitutes (in terms of rate of interest and liquidation cost). Furthermore, it is interest rate and liquidation cost differentials which determine asset holding, not the absolute levels of those variables.

Of course, what the expression does contain, which is new, is the term Ω. I shall call this the measure of holding period certainty. Ω must lie in the interval $1 < \Omega < \infty$. As holding period certainty increases then Ω will increase since G(T) for $0<t<T$ will fall, that is, there is a greater chance of surviving to the end of the period. Note that this implies a steady process of excluding liquid assets. In order to see this, it is necessary to spell out in detail the non-dominance requirements for each asset. Given optimizing expression (2) for adjacent assets $(k-1)$ and k we must have:

$$\frac{(r_k - r_{k-1})}{(r_k - r_{k-1}) + (b_k - b_{k-1})} > \frac{(r_{k+1} - r_k)}{(r_{k+1} - r_k) + (b_{k+1} - b_k)},$$

and in addition for assets 0 and $(n-1)$:

$$\frac{(r_1 - r_0)}{(r_n - r_{n-1}) + (b_1 - b_0)} < \frac{1}{\Omega}$$

$$\frac{(r_n - r_0)}{(r_n - r_{n-1}) + (b_n - b_{n-1})} > 0.$$

If these three conditions are satisfied then all assets will be held. Alternatively, once an optimum portfolio is found the assets in it will satisfy these conditions. It is worthwhile noting that as Ω increases the condition on holding asset 0 (and hence all other assets) becomes tighter. This is because there is less incentive to diversify and, in particular, hold very liquid assets as holding period certainty increases. Indeed, at a sufficiently high value of Ω then only the non-liquid asset will be held. This value of Ω, which will be denoted Ω_{max} is given by:

$$\Omega_{max} = 1 + \frac{(b_n - b_{n-1})}{(r_n - r_{n-1})}.$$

Note that this result is independent of consideration of the actual size of expenditure. In other words, as the probability of expenditure occurring within the planning period falls, the individual will have less and less incentive to hold liquidity to protect against its consequences – the holding period risk dominates the size risk. Since the volume density function does not appear in the dominance conditions (except indirectly) it will not have these consequences. It is important to realize that these results are dependent on the assumption of zero transactions costs at planning points.

It is interesting to compare the analysis here with that of Sprenkle (1985) where the holding period is variable but known. The optimizing conditions in this case are:

$$F\left(\sum_{0}^{k-1} X_i\right) = 1 - \frac{\Omega^* (r_k - r_{k-1})}{(r_k - r_{k-1}) + (b_k - b_{k-1})} \tag{3}$$

where $\Omega^* = T/(T-t)$ and t is the incidence of expenditure. (Note that this does not correspond exactly to Sprenkle because of our assumption that liquidation costs are time dependent.)

If we interpret t as the expected time of expenditure then (2) and (3) are identical if t is defined over the range 0 to T. In other words, unexpected expenditure must occur during the planning period. Hence, the known but variable holding period can be viewed as equivalent to a holding period uncertainty model where the expenditure will occur in the planning period and the known holding period is equivalent to the expected holding period under uncertainty.

Finally, it is also worthwhile comparing the holding period uncertainty version with the conventional precautionary demand model where any unexpected expenditure occurs at point in time $T=1$. The optimizing expression in the conventional case is:

$$F\left(\sum_{0}^{k-1} X_i\right) = 1 - \frac{(r_k - r_{k-1})}{(b_k - b_{k-1})}$$

(assume non-dominance conditions hold).

Note, however, that our holding period uncertainty model has defined the liquidation cost proportional to the time when the liquidation occurs. In order for a direct comparison with the conventional approach we must drop this requirement and then the optimizing expression under holding period uncertainty (with $T=1$) is given by:

$$F\left(\sum_{0}^{k-1} X_i\right) = 1 - \frac{(r_k - r_{k-1})}{\theta^*(r_k - r_{k-1}) + (b_k - b_{k-1})},$$

$$\text{where} \quad \theta^* = \int_0^1 (1-t)\ g(t)\ dt$$

Since $\theta^* > 0$ then it is clear that holding period uncertainty will increase the holding of each of the $(n-1)$ liquid assets.

Finally in this detailed analysis of the effects of holding period uncertainty on the precautionary demand for liquidity, it is important to analyse the effect on the structure of liquidity holdings. Note that a required condition for non-dominance is:

$$\frac{(r_k - r_{k-1})}{(r_k - r_{k-1}) + (b_k - b_{k-1})} > \frac{(r_{k+1} - r_k)}{(r_{k+1} - r_k) + (b_{k+1} - b_k)}$$

Hence for any given Ω (holding period certainty) it is clear that there is a larger impact on the more liquid assets. In other words, holding period uncertainty causes a switch towards the more liquid assets.

3. COMPARATIVE STATIC PROPERTIES

The analysis of this section confirms the previous analysis. The results are obtained by totally differentiating solution equations of the form given in (2). For the change in exogenous variable, u_k:

$$\frac{d X_k}{du_k} = \frac{d\left(\sum_{0}^{k} X_i\right)}{du_k} - \frac{d\left(\sum_{0}^{k-1} X_i\right)}{du_k}$$

$$\frac{d\,X_{k-1}}{du_k} = \frac{d(\sum_0^{k-1} X_i)}{du_k}\,; \qquad \frac{d\,X_{k+1}}{du_k} = \frac{-d(\sum_0^{k} X_i)}{du_k}\,.$$

(a) Interest Rate (r_k)

$$\frac{d\,(\sum_0^{k-1} X_i)}{dr_k} = -\frac{\Omega\,(b_k - b_{k-1})}{((r_k - r_{k-1}) + (b_k - b_{k-1}))^2} \cdot \frac{1}{F'(\sum_0^{k-1} X_i)} < 0 \tag{a.1}$$

$$\frac{d\,(\sum_0^{k} X_i)}{dr_k} = \frac{\Omega\,(b_{k+1} - b_k)}{((r_{k+1} - r_k) + (b_{k+1} - b_k))^2} \; \frac{1}{F'(\sum_0^{k} X_i)} > 0. \tag{a.2}$$

(b) Liquidation Cost (b_k)

$$\frac{d\,(\sum_0^{k} X_i)}{db_k} = -\frac{\Omega(r_{k+1} - r_k)}{((r_{k+1} - r_k) + (b_{k+1} - b_k))^2} \; \frac{1}{F'(\sum_0^{k} X_i)} < 0 \tag{b.1}$$

$$\frac{d\,(\sum_0^{k-1} X_i)}{db_k} = \frac{\Omega(r_k - r_{k-1})}{((r_k - r_{k-1}) + (b_k - b_{k-1}))^2} \; \frac{1}{F'(\sum_0^{k-1} X_i)} > 0. \tag{b.2}$$

(c) Planning Period (T)

$$\frac{d\left(\sum_{0}^{k-1} X_i\right)}{dT} = \frac{(r_k - r_{k-1})}{(r_k - r_{k-1}) + (b_k - b_{k-1})} \frac{1}{F'\left(\sum_{0}^{k-1} X\right)} \frac{\Omega}{\theta} > 0 \tag{c.1}$$

and

$$\frac{d\left(\sum_{0}^{k} X_i\right)}{dT} = \frac{(r_{k+1} - r_k)}{(r_{k+1} - r_k) + (b_{k+1} - b_k)} \frac{1}{\left(F' \sum_{0}^{k} X_i\right)} \frac{\Omega}{\theta} > 0, \tag{c.2}$$

where:

$$\theta = \int_{0}^{T} (T-t)\ f(t)\ dt.$$

Note that:

$$\frac{dX_0}{dT} = \frac{(r_1 - r_0)}{(r_1 - r_0) + (b_1 - b_0)} \frac{1}{F'(X_0)} \frac{\Omega}{\theta} > 0 \tag{c.3}$$

$$\frac{d\left(\sum_{0}^{n-1} X_i\right)}{dT} = \frac{(r_n - r_{n-1})}{(r_n - r_{n-1}) + (b_n - b_{n-1})} \frac{1}{F'\left(\sum_{0}^{n-1} X_i\right)} \frac{\Omega}{\theta} > 0. \tag{c.4}$$

(d) Holding Period Certainty (Ω)

$$\frac{d\left(\sum_{0}^{k-1} X_i\right)}{d\Omega} = -\frac{(r_k - r_{k-1})}{(r_k - r_{k-1}) + (b_k - b_{k-1})}\,\frac{1}{F'\left(\sum_{0}^{k-1} X_i\right)} < 0 \qquad \text{(d.1)}$$

$$\frac{d\left(\sum_{0}^{k} X_i\right)}{d\Omega} = -\frac{(r_{k+1} - r_k)}{(r_{k+1} - r_k) + (b_{k+1} - b_k)}\,\frac{1}{F'\left(\sum_{0}^{k} X_i\right)} < 0. \qquad \text{(d.2)}$$

(e) Cash Disbursement Risk (F(.))

$$\frac{d\left(\sum_{0}^{k-1} X_i\right)}{dF(.)} = -\frac{1}{F'\left(\sum_{0}^{k-1} X_i\right)} < 0 \qquad \text{(e.1)}$$

$$\frac{d\left(\sum_{0}^{k} X_i\right)}{dF(.)} = -\frac{1}{F'\left(\sum_{0}^{k} X_i\right)} < 0. \qquad \text{(e.2)}$$

The interpretation of these properties is straightforward. First it may be noted that the response of asset holdings to interest rates and liquidation costs are of the conventional sign and are functions of the holding period certainty parameter. In particular, asset holdings are less responsive as holding period certainty decreases (note that this also implies concentration of precautionary reserves in the more liquid assets). The effects of changes in planning period, holding period certainty and cash disbursement risk are closely connected. By inspection of the relevant derivatives we can observe that $dX_k/dT > 0$ and $dX_k/d\Omega < 0$ (these are intuitively the 'correct' signs) imply that:

$$\frac{(r_{k+1} - r_k)}{(r_{k+1} - r_k) + (b_{k+1} - b_k)} \frac{1}{F'(\sum_0^k X_i)} > \frac{(r_k - r_{k-1})}{(r_k - r_{k-1}) + (b_k - b_{k-1})} \frac{1}{F'(\sum_0^{k-1} X_i)} .$$

From the non-dominance condition then it is sufficient (but not necessary) for the above to hold, that:

$$\frac{1}{F'(\sum_0^k X_i)} > \frac{1}{F'(\sum_0^{k-1} X_i)} ,$$

and this implies that:

$$\frac{dX_k}{dF(.)} < 0,$$

which is intuitively appealing. Hence, we are left to conclude that if the response of asset holdings to cash disbursement risk (probability of liquidation) is negative, this ensures that a planning period increase and holding period certainty decrease have the expected effects on asset holdings. Note, however, that for the most liquid asset and the total level of precautionary reserves, the derivatives unconditionally have the expected sign.

(f) Change in Holding Period and Cash Disbursement Risk with Constant Probability of Liquidation.

A final result which is interesting to investigate concerns the *joint* effects of a change in cash disbursement and holding period risk. In particular, we shall analyse the case where the probability of liquidation of the asset in question stays constant. This allows us to consider the separate effects of holding period and cash disbursement risk. In order to determine behaviour we need to define the effect of holding period risk (G(T)) on the parameter Ω.

Assume that $\int_0^T t\ g(t)\ dt$ is unaffected by the change in G(T) (similar to the idea of a mean-preserving spread). Then it is easy to show that:

$$\frac{d\Omega}{dG(T)} = -\ \Omega^2.$$

Holding the probability of asset k being liquidated, then we require F(X(k−1)) and G(T) to change in such a way that G(T) (1−F(X(k−1))) is constant. This implies that dF(M)/dG(T)=(1−F(X(k-1)))/G(T). Using previously defined results, we have:

$$\frac{d\left(\sum_0^{k-1} X_i\right)}{dG(T)} = \Omega^2 \frac{(r_k - r_{k-1})}{(r_k - r_{k-1}) + (b_k - b_{k-1})} \frac{1}{F'\left(\sum_0^{k-1} X_i\right)} \tag{f.1}$$

and

$$\frac{d\left(\sum_0^{k-1} X_i\right)}{dF(.)} = -\ \frac{1}{F'\left(\sum_0^{k-1} X_i\right)}, \tag{f.2}$$

which with the constant probability condition implies:

$$\frac{d\left(\sum_{0}^{k-1} X_i\right)}{dG(T)} = -\frac{1}{F'\left(\sum_{0}^{k-1} X_i\right)} \frac{\left(1 - F'\left(\sum_{0}^{k-1} X_i\right)\right)}{G(T)} . \tag{f.3}$$

Hence $\dfrac{d\left(\sum_{0}^{k-1} X_i\right)}{dF(T)}$ prob

(where prob means that the probability of liquidation of asset k is constant) will have a sign determined according to the following:

$$\frac{d\left(\sum_{0}^{k-1} X_i\right)}{dG(T)} \text{prob} \gtreqless 0$$

$$\text{as} \quad \frac{\Omega^2 (r_k - r_{k-1})}{(r_k - r_{k-1}) + (b_k - b_{k-1})} \gtreqless \frac{1 - F\left(\sum_{0}^{k-1} X_i\right)}{G(T)} ,$$

and since $\Omega\ G(T) > 1$ then:

$$\frac{d\left(\sum_{0}^{k-1} X_i\right)}{dG(T)} \text{prob} > 0.$$

Since it can also be shown that:

$$\frac{d\left(\sum_{0}^{k-1} X_i\right)}{dG(T)} \text{ prob } < \frac{d\left(\sum_{0}^{k} X_i\right)}{dG(T)}$$

if it is assumed that $dX_k/d\Omega < 0$, then a decrease in holding period certainty, compensated by a reduction in cash disbursement risk, holding probability of liquidation constant, will cause precautionary holdings of the kth asset to rise. Unambiguously the most liquid and total precautionary reserve holdings will increase.

4 IMPLICATIONS OF HOLDING PERIOD RISK FOR MONEY DEMAND

The last two sections have considered the modelling of holding period uncertainty as a motivation for liquidity preference and the implications that it has for the general demand for liquid assets. In this section we shall consider, more specifically, how the results obtained can be applied to the demand for money.

In the context of our model, money can be defined narrowly as the asset 0 (most liquid) or more broadly as a number of highly liquid assets. Attempts to define money as that collection of assets which has a stable demand function therefore rest upon grouping assets which are closely substitutable. In terms of our model this is those with very similar interest rates and liquidation costs. In addition, assets outside the chosen definition will have relatively large gaps between their liquidation costs and interest rates compared with those on assets defined within the monetary sub-set. However, the precision with which this classification can be carried out depends very much upon the holding period certainty. A value of Ω close to one (high probability of early expenditure) will generate a fairly clear differentiation of assets in terms of their moneyness. As holding period certainty increases then the effect of differentials between liquidation costs and interest rates will exert a smaller impact on the individual asset choice (that is the individual will tend to hold smaller amounts of 'money' and more of the less liquid assets). Of course if the probability of expenditure occurring in the period becomes small enough none of the liquid assets are held since $\Omega > \Omega_{max}$ (see earlier discussion of the definition of Ω_{max}). Note that we are looking only at one particular motive for holding liquidity but, within this rather narrow framework, it is interesting to note that the appropriate operational definition of liquidity will vary according to the risk which the individual faces.

Holding period considerations also have implications for the empirical analysis of the demand for money. If the expressions obtained for optimum liquid asset balances are linearized, via some sort of Taylor's series approximation the derivatives which have been found in Section 2 would play a prominent role in interpreting the estimated coefficients. Note the Ω appears as a parameter influencing those derivatives and consequently an appropriate estimation technique for money demand may well involve time-varying coefficients since Ω is likely to vary over time.

A third implication of the model relates to the recent analysis of money market equilibrium via the buffer stock approach (for example Laidler, 1982, 1984; Goodhart, 1984; Milbourne,1987; Cuthbertson and Taylor, 1987). This relies on the precautionary motive to explain the failure of individuals to stay on their long-run demand for money function, where disequilibrium is tolerated because of adjustment costs. The model presented here is not consistent with this representation. The reason is that individuals have a finite planning period, at the end of which adjustment is costless. This was justified on the grounds that receipt of income was fixed by custom and it was this that determined the planning period. Disequilibrium could occur during the planning period as a result of unexpected changes in exogenous variables but not beyond. Given that planning periods are likely to be short, disequilibrium in the aggregate via the 'hot potato' effect (where one person's return to equilibrium is another's disequilibrium) is also unlikely to be even a short-run phenomenon. Hence there is the problem of justifying the presence of a lagged dependent variable in the short-run demand for money function.

Holding period risk may, itself, provide a way of rationalizing the empirical success of money demand functions with lagged endogenous variables. Suppose that Ω falls in the aggregate; then, for all individuals, there is the incentive to shift to less liquid assets and a corresponding effect on interest rates to ensure money market equilibrium (prices and output, short run, exogenous). In addition, the response of money holdings to changes in the exogenous variables are correspondingly increased; hence lower holdings and greater sensitivity. If holding period risk now displays some type of autoregressive structure (quiet and busy periods), then we will have a money demand function which will look like conventional representations with lagged money stock. This has nothing to do with the presence of disequilibrium money phenomena but with the autoregressive behaviour of a stochastic variable which features prominently as a determinant of money demand. (Note that cash disbursements size could follow a similar pattern. See Goodfriend, 1987, who uses similar ideas.)

Finally, we return to the issue which started this analysis, namely whether the separation of holding period and size uncertainty in the modelling of the precautionary demand for liquidity, provides additional insight into individual behaviour in the face of cash disbursement risk. The previous analysis should have demonstrated that this is the case. Under continuous time analysis it is the rate of expenditure which is stochastic. We can represent the implications of a particular rate of expenditure by reference to a size at a particular date. But we are unable to analyse size and timing independently. In other words, by considering size and timing effects separately, we have demonstrated the importance of an additional variable in the precautionary demand for money, namely holding period uncertainty.

In fact, it has been argued that holding period uncertainty is the rationale for the precautionary demand in that it is only when asset transactions are unplanned that liquidation costs are incurred. The conventional analysis of the precautionary demand (Tsiang, 1972, is an exception) does not recognize this element and is really concerned with the transactions demand under uncertainty.

In conclusion, the explicit recognition of holding period uncertainty does provide a new perception of the precautionary demand for liquidity. In terms of the model presented here, it should be noted that it is restrictive in a number of respects:

1. Only liquidation costs appear, with no account taken of transaction costs.

2. The planning period may, to some extent be under the control of the individual (taking into account planning transaction and other costs).

3. The aggregation effects are worth further exploration since the model is only relevant to a particular category of economic unit (the household) and may not be applicable to others (for example, the firm).

Further work on these issues should enhance the model presented here and its implications for the aggregate money demand function.

REFERENCES

Baumol, W.J. (1952), 'The Transactions Demand for Cash: An Inventory Theoretic Approach', *Quarterly Journal of Economics*, **66**, 545–56.

Clarke, J.A. and P.J. Speaker (1986), 'Compensating Balance Requirements and the Firm's Demand for Transactions Balances', *Journal of Banking and Finance*, **10**, 411–29.

Cuthbertson K. and M.P. Taylor (1987), 'Buffer-Stock Money: An Appraisal', in C. Goodhart, D. Currie and D. Llewellyn (eds), *The Operation and Regulation of Financial Markets*, 103–24.

Frenkel, J.A. and B. Jovanovich (1980), 'On Transactions and Precautionary Demand for Money', *Quarterly Journal of Economics*, **94**, 25–43.

Goldman, S.M. (1978), 'Portfolio Choice and Flexibility – The Precautionary Motive', *Journal of Monetary Economics*, **4**, 263–79.

Goodfriend, M. (1987), 'Re-Interpreting Money Demand Regressions', *Carnegie Rochester Conference Series on Public Policy*, **22**, 207–42.

Goodhart, C. (1984), 'Disequilibrium Money', in C. Goodhart, *Monetary Theory and Practice*, 254-76.

Gray, M.R. and M. Parkin (1973), 'Portfolio Diversification as Optimal Precautionary Behaviour', in M. Morishima *et al*, *Theory of Demand – Real and Monetary*, 301–15.

Laidler, D. (1982), 'The Long- and Short- Run Demand for Money', in D. Laidler, *Monetarist Perspectives*, 39–65.

Laidler, D. (1984), 'The Buffer Stock Notion in Monetary Economics', *Economic Journal*, **94**, Supplement, 17–34.

Milbourne, R. (1987), 'Re-Examining the Buffer-Stock Model of Money', *Economic Journal*, **97**, Supplement, 130–42.

Miller, M.H. and D. Orr (1966), 'A Model of the Demand for Money by Firms', *Quarterly Journal of Economics*, **80**, 412–35.

Plessner, Y. and J.D. Reid (1980), 'The Precautionary Demand for Money: A Rigorous Foundation', *Journal of Monetary Economics*, **6**, 419–32.

Sprenkle, C.M. (1985), 'On the Precautionary Demand for Assets', *Journal of Banking and Finance*, **9**, 499–515.

Taylor, C.M. (1976), 'The Precautionary Demand for Money: A Utility Maximisation Approach', *Journal of Economic Theory*, **13**, 67–31.

Tobin, J. (1956), 'The Interest Elasticity of the Transactions Demand for Cash', *Review of Economics and Statistics*, **38**, 241–7.

Tsiang, S.C. (1972), 'The Precautionary Demand for Money: An Inventory Theoretic Analysis', *Journal of Political Economy*, **77**, 99–117.

Whalen, E.L. (1966), 'A Rationalisation of the Precautionary Demand for Cash', *Quarterly Journal of Economics*, **80**, 314–24.

APPENDIX

This Appendix discusses the construction of the expected cost function and the asset holding solution expressions which minimize expected cost. The expected holding cost relates to the differential between the asset interest rate and that on the non-liquid assets, and on the length of time for which the asset is held. Hence with probability $(1-G(T))$ no asset liquidation will occur. In addition the holding costs depend upon how much of the precautionary reserve is liquidated and how far into the planning period this occurs.

In the following we shall use the notation:

$$X(m) = \sum_{i=0}^{m} X_i.$$

For asset k, then, the holding costs will depend on the size of the unexpected cash disbursement (X). If $X<X(k-1)$, then asset balance X_k is held through to the end of the period, whereas if $X>X(k)$, all of asset k is liquidated at the occurrence of expenditure, while if $X(k-1)<X<X(k)$ then $(X-X(k-1))$ of asset holding X_k is held until the occurrence of expenditure while the remainder, $(X(k)-X)$, is held until the end of the planning period. These constraints determine the holding and liquidation costs which are given in equation (1) in the text.

In order to solve for cost-minimizing asset holdings then differentiate (1) with respect to X_k $(k = 0 \ldots (n-1))$. This yields expressions of the form:

$$\sum_{h=k}^{(n-1)} [(r_{h+1} - r_j) + (b_{h+1} - b_j)] \, F(\sum_{i=0}^{h} X_i) = \Omega \, (r_n - r_k)$$

for $k = 0 \ldots (n-1)$

where:

$$\Omega = \frac{T}{\int_0^T (T-t) \, f(t) \, dt}.$$

The solution expressions can be obtained from iterative substitution using expressions of the type above, or alternatively, by expressing the relationships in matrix form and inverting. In either case, the optimizing expression is shown as equation (2) in the main text.

8. The Demand For Policy Loans : An Empirical Analysis With Quarterly Canadian Data

Colin Dodds and Atul A. Dar

A few words of explanation are in order prior to the development of this paper on policy loans. Jim Ford, as Head of the Research Section of the Division of Economic Studies at Sheffield University, was instrumental in spearheading a series of studies into the financial sector of Britain. In those early, heady days of econometric modelling from 1970 through to 1979, Jim Ford, George Clayton and one of the authors of this paper, Colin Dodds, worked on large-scale econometric models of the financial sector. We think it became apparent that computer constraints and data limitations as well as methodological weaknesses in approach, restricted the value of this model. As a result three institutions were selected for study, and Colin Dodds commenced work on the insurance industry. Subsequently, Michael Driscoll joined the team and participated in work on building societies.

It is perhaps not surprising that this present paper still has the insurance sector as its subject matter, albeit in the context now of Canada, given the fact that Colin Dodds relocated here. The paper is still very much rooted in the genre of the heyday of the Sheffield School of that period, examining as it does Canadian data explanations of policy loan behaviour. One of the reasons for choosing this particular topic is that not only does it extend the work on the British experience to Canada (see Dar and Dodds, 1989) but it picks an item in the balance sheets and flows of funds of life insurance companies that is of importance (both in terms of volume and as a proportion of flows) in Canada, but is not particularly relevant in the British case. This, it is hoped, will extend the interest of the reader beyond the confines of a purely UK theme.

1. INTRODUCTION

The flow of investible funds to capital markets via the life insurance sector (an important source of long-term capital), depends primarily upon household decisions regarding the purchase of new policies and/or the continuance of old ones. However, since the life insurance contract permits holders to borrow against the surrender value of their policies, the magnitude of policy loans can significantly affect the availability of funds for investment. The special significance of policy loans arises primarily because their general volatility can lead to considerable uncertainty about the volume of funds life insurers have available for investment. In addition, to the extent that life insurers engage in forward commitments, the uncertainty of cash flow stemming from the volatility can significantly affect the type of activity, and the degree to which that activity can be undertaken. Thus, even though policy loans are a relatively minor liability in the portfolios of households, rapid increases in policy loan demand in certain periods (as experienced in both the United States and Canada) as well as their general volatility can seriously affect the investment activity of life insurers.

There have not been many empirical studies on the determinants of policy loans demand. Those that exist deal with the US experience during the 1960s, during which time there was a rapid increase in policy loans (see Schott, 1971; Pesando, 1974; Cummins, 1975). However, empirical work on the recent behaviour of policy loans in either Canada or the United States, does not appear to have been undertaken. The purpose of this chapter is to examine the short-term behaviour of policy loans in Canada during the 1977–88 span, with the help of a quarterly model of policy loan demand.

During the 1977–88 interval, life insurance reserves and assets in Canada grew at impressive compound annual rates of about 11 and 13 per cent, respectively. In contrast, the stock of policy loans grew at a relatively modest rate of only 7 per cent per annum. However, this masks what appears to be a clear structural shift in policy loan behaviour in the early 1980s. Thus, up to about 1982, the stock of policy loans grew at a rapid annual rate of almost 16 per cent, thereby easily outstripping the growth in reserves (11.2 per cent) and assets (12.9 per cent). Thereafter, the stock of policy loans was more or less flat. At its peak (1982), the policy loan stock amounted to 8.4 per cent of reserves and 4.7 per cent of assets. Thereafter, it fell sharply, and by the end of 1988, it accounted for just 2.3 per cent of assets and 4.5 per cent of reserves.[1]

Data on policy loan flows, the main concern of this chapter, not only display their inherent volatility, but also point to the dramatic swing in policy loan behaviour around 1981–82. Table 8.1 below presents some descriptive statistics derived from quarterly data, which highlight some important aspects of policy loan behaviour over the 1977–88 span.

Table 8.1 : Policy loan and life insurance reserve flows – means and standard deviations

Flows*	1977:1–1988:2		1977:1–1981:4		1982:1–1988:2	
	Mean	SD	Mean	SD	Mean	SD
1. Policy loans	33.2	52.7	66.4	61.0	7.1	24.9
2. Reserves	985.4	385.2	686.6	217.3	1215.3	323.7
3.(1 over 2) %	4.2	6.1	8.7	6.5	0.8	2.6

Note: * in millions of dollars.
SD is the standard deviation.
Data for the calculations were taken from *Financial Institutions: Financial Statistics*, Statistics Canada.

Looking at the flows over the entire 1977–88 interval, it is seen that policy loans depict considerable variability. Thus while the standard deviation of reserves is just 39 per cent of their mean value, the corresponding figure for policy loans is almost 159 per cent. Moreover, it is clear that there is a dramatic decline in the average level of policy loans between the 1977–81 and 1982–88 subintervals. In contrast, average reserves flows almost doubled between these time frames. Thus, while on average, policy loan flows account for some 8 per cent of the flow of reserves in the 1977–81 interval, that average share falls to under 1 per cent during the 1982–88 subinterval. Table 8.1 also shows that the standard deviation of policy loans more than halves (in absolute terms) between the two subperiods. However, in relative terms (that is, relative to the mean), the variability of policy loan flows has increased very sharply between those periods. On the other hand, just the opposite appears to have occurred to the flow of reserves, though the changes involved are much smaller.

Overall, the quarterly data suggest that the relative uncertainty associated with policy loan flows has increased in recent years. There appears to have been a shift in the structure of policy loan demand some time in the early 1980s. The factors explaining the short-run behaviour of policy loans and the question of structural change in policy loan demand relationships form the focus of the rest of this chapter. It is perhaps likely that this structural shift reflects a combination of several developments. First, the pre-1982 and post-1982 periods represent very different economic environments, with sharply rising interest rates and accelerating inflation in the former period culminating in severe recession, and then giving way to a period of relative stability in interest rates and prices. Secondly, there have been changes within the life insurance sector as well. In particular, the growing trend towards term insurance, as well as the sharp increase in surrenders as a means of reducing saving through life insurance, have undoubtedly been partly responsible for the observed shift in the behaviour of policy loans during the post–1982 interval.

The rest of this chapter is organized as follows. In section 2, we outline the model used to estimate the flow demand for policy loans. The estimation approach and the results are discussed in section 3. The major findings and implications are summarized in section 4, while the definitions of variables and data sources are listed in the Appendix.

2. A MODEL OF POLICY LOAN DEMAND

In this section, we discuss the model of policy loan demand estimated in this chapter. While there have been numerous studies on household portfolio choice, their scope has not extended to encompassing policy loans. This is not surprising given that policy loans are a rather small item in household portfolios. On the other hand, some studies that deal with the investment choices of life insurers, have attempted to model policy loan demand. Thus, Cummins (1975) and Pesando (1974) explicitly estimated a policy loan equation within the framework of larger models of the flow of investible funds of the life insurance sector in the United States. Both employed a stock adjustment framework to develop their estimating equations. An earlier study by Schott (1971), also for the United States, however, was not cast in this mould, nor were the estimating equations derived from any explicitly theoretical framework.

The Model

The framework used in this study to estimate policy loan demand is based on the integrated household portfolio model developed by Purvis (1978), and subsequently by Backus and Purvis (1980). While this framework retains the idea of partial adjustment, that adjustment is of a more general nature than that considered by Cummins and Pesando. Backus and Purvis suggest that the long-run demand for an asset/liability by households is proportional to disposable income, the factor of proportionality depending upon a set of variables (typically, own and alternative rates of return on assets/liabilities). This can be stated as:

$$(A_i^*/YE) = f(x), \tag{1}$$

where A_i^* is the desired stock of the ith asset/liability ($i = 1,2, \ldots, k$), YE is expected income, and x is a vector of determining variables. In the short run, however, there is partial adjustment to the optimal stock, reflecting not only the costs of shifting between assets/liabilities, but also departures of income from its expected value. Backus and Purvis, however, consider a multivariate stock adjustment process, where the demand for an asset/liability (in the short run) reflects not only the partial adjustment of the actual stock of that asset/liability to its optimum, but also spillover effects from the discrepancies between desired and actual stocks of all other assets and liabilities. Thus, the short-run demand for the asset/liability can be written as:

$$A_i - A_i(-1) = \theta_{ii} \left[A_i^* - A_i(-1)\right] + \sum_{j \neq i} \theta_{ij} \left[A_j^* - A_j(-1)\right] + \gamma_i(Y - YE) ,$$

where A_i is the actual holding of the asset and Y is actual income. θ_{ii} is the own adjustment parameter, while the θ_{ij} ($i \neq j$) are the adjustment parameters of other assets/liabilities.

Once the determinants x are specified in (1), and substituted in (2), the short-run demand for any asset/liability can be obtained. We assume that the model represented by equations (1) and (2) can be used to represent the long- and short-run demand for the policy loan liability.[2] Our primary task is to specify the determinants x of the desired stock of policy loans in (1) as well as the assets and other liabilities relevant for explaining the short-run demand for policy loans in (2). Starting with the latter question first, we assume that there are only two other liabilities and assets – an aggregate of other loans (total loans less policy loans, mortgages and consumer credit), and an aggregate of all financial assets in the portfolio. With these simplifications, we can rewrite equation (2) using more a convenient notation, to represent the short-run demand for policy loans as follows:

$$SPL - SPL(-1) = \theta_1[SPL^* - SPL(-1)] + \theta_2[SOL^* - SOL(-1)] + \theta_3[SFA^* - SFA(-1)] + \gamma(Y - YE)\ , \tag{3}$$

where SPL is the stock of policy loans, SOL the stock of other loans, and SFA the stock of financial assets. Dividing across by YE, we can rewrite (3) as follows:

$$FPL/YE = \theta_1[SPL^*/YE - SPL(-1)/YE] + \theta_2[SOL^*/YE - SOL(-1)/YE] + \theta_3[SFA^*/YE - SFA(-1)/YE] + \gamma(YT/YE)\ , \tag{4}$$

where FPL = SPL − SPL(−1) is the flow demand for policy loans, and YT = Y−YE is transitory income.

In order to make (4) operational, we need to specify the determinants of the optimal or desired stock of policy loans, other loans and assets. We postulate that the desired stock of policy loans depends primarily upon the (negative) rate of return on policy loans (which is simply the interest rate charged on policy loans), the (negative) rate of return on other loans (the interest rate on other loans), and the rate of return on assets. Thus the desired stock of policy loans is determined as follows:

$$SPL^*/YE = b_o + b_1 RGE + b_2 RPE + b_3 RRE, \tag{5}$$

where RGE is the expected return on assets, RPE is the expected policy loan rate, and RRE is the expected rate on other loans. *A priori*, one would expect the coefficient of RPE to be negative and that of RRE to be positive, reflecting the interest arbitrage discussed by Cummins, Pesando and Schott. On the other hand, the coefficient of RGE can be expected to be negative, since an increase in RGE (for instance) raises the relative cost of holding the policy loan liability.[3] We can similarly specify the determinants of the desired stock of other loans and assets as:

$$SOL^*/YE = d_0 + d_1RGE + d_2RPE + d_3RRE \tag{6}$$

$$SFA^*/YE = e_0 + e_1RGE + e_2RPE + e_3RRE. \tag{7}$$

A priori, the coefficients of RGE, RPE and RRE in (7) and of RPE in (6) would likely be positive (or zero), while the coefficients of RGE and RRE in (6) would likely be negative (or zero). Upon substituting (5), (6) and (7) in (4), and manipulating, equation (4) can be shown to reduce to:

$$\begin{aligned} FPL/YE = {} & \alpha_0 + \alpha_1RGE + \alpha_2RPE + \alpha_3RRE + \alpha_4SPL(-1) \\ & + \alpha_5SOL(-1) + \alpha_6SFA(-1) + \gamma(YT/YE) , \end{aligned} \tag{8}$$

where:

$$\alpha_0 = (\theta_1b_0 + \theta_2d_0 + \theta_3e_0) \;;\; \alpha_1 = (\theta_1b_1 + \theta_2d_1 + \theta_3e_1)$$
$$\alpha_2 = (\theta_1b_2 + \theta_2d_2 + \theta_3e_2) \;;\; \alpha_3 = (\theta_1b_3 + \theta_2d_3 + \theta_3d_3) ,$$

while α_4, α_5, α_6 are the negative of the adjustment parameters θ_1, θ_2, θ_3, respectively.[4]

We assume that each of the expected rates of interest in any given period is simply the most recent (that is, the beginning-of-period) real rate of interest adjusted for the expected rate of inflation (INFE) in that period. That is, letting RE stand for each of the expected rates, we have:

$$RE = r(-1) + INFE \tag{9}$$

where r denotes the real rate of interest.[5]

One of the factors thought to be relevant for explaining the demand for policy loans is the so-called 'emergency fund' hypothesis.

According to this hypothesis, 'depressed economic conditions should be accompanied by increased policy loan demand as policyholders attempt to meet financial emergencies and maintain previous consumption standards' (Cummins, p. 84).[6] It is difficult to examine empirically this hypothesis since it requires finding a measure that captures the behaviour that it implies. Nevertheless, the hypothesis can perhaps be tested within the context of our model, in which YT represents the emergency fund variable. If the hypothesis is valid, one would expect the demand for policy loans and YT to be negatively related ($\gamma < 0$).[7]

While equation (8) represents the basic policy loan model estimated in this chapter, we have considered two additional variables as well. It has been argued above that expectations about inflation affect policy loan demand by altering the expected rates of return. However, inflation might have an additional impact on policy loan demand if, for instance, an increase in the expected rate of inflation boosted consumption and hence led to increased borrowing.[8] We attempted to capture this effect by including INFE as a separate variable in equation (8). A second variable whose separate inclusion was also considered is YE. Equation (8) was obtained under the restriction that the desired stock of policy loans (as well of assets and other loans) is proportional to YE. This assumption can be tested by directly including YE in the equation.

The Estimation Approach

Our discussion of policy loan flows in section 1 raises the question of whether a single regression is valid over the entire sample period.[9] Consequently, we examine this question by estimating the policy loan equation over the entire sample, as well as over two subperiods. The cost of splitting the sample is the loss in degrees of freedom. The potential gain is a more precisely estimated model. Equation (8) is estimated using the ordinary least squares (OLS) method. This method gives consistent estimates of the parameters if the independent variables are not correlated with the disturbance term implicit in equation (8).[10] This condition would not be satisfied in the presence of the lagged dependent variable on the right-hand side if the disturbance term is autocorrelated. In that event, the instrumental variables estimation technique would be required to obtain consistent estimates. As a consequence, we first examine the OLS results and test for autocorrelation.

In order to estimate our equation, explicit measures of YE, INFE and the interest rate variables are required. YE and YT were obtained using the method described in Backus and Purvis (1980), while INFE was measured as the simple average of the inflation rate (of the consumer price index) over the previous three quarters. The yield on government bonds was taken to represent the rate of return on assets, while in the absence of a rate on other loans in general, the prime rate was taken to represent RRE. There are no data on RPE. Consequently, the RPE series was constructed in the manner described in the Appendix from data obtained from a major life insurer. The assumption is that this series reflects the general cost of policy loans in the life insurance sector. All the data are in millions of Canadian dollars, except the rate variables which are in per cent.[11]

3. THE EMPIRICAL RESULTS

The OLS estimates of equation (8) (with and without YE and INFE as distinct independent variables) for the entire sample period are presented in Table 8.2. All equations appear to fit the data well, considering the general volatility of policy loan flows over the period. The inclusion of YE does not appear to matter very much, as its coefficient is not statistically significant at the 5 per cent level. On including INFE, by itself or along with YE, we find that it has a statistically significant positive impact on policy loans, and this is in line with expectations. One consequence of including INFE is that the positive impact of the lagged stock of other loans is rendered insignificant. Since the coefficient of this variable is the negative of adjustment parameter θ_2, its positive value indicates, as expected, that an increase in the desired stock of other loans reduces the flow demand for policy loans. The own partial adjustment coefficient, being the negative of the coefficient of SPL(−1), is positive, and highly significant. However, its size appears to vary substantially across equations. It is clearly unreasonably low in the first equation, implying that only 6 per cent of the gap between desired and actual holdings of the policy loan liability is realized in any period.

On the other hand, an estimate in the 15–20 per cent range implied by the last two equations, while still somewhat low, is consistent with the findings of Backus and Purvis for mortgages and consumer credit (Backus and Purvis, 1980, Table 3). The lagged stock of assets is found to have a statistically significant negative impact on policy loans, and the estimated coefficient is stable across equations. This suggests that an increase in desired stock of assets spills over partly into an increase in policy loan demand.[12] The size of this effect is in the \$1500–\$2200 range for every million dollar increase in the desired stock of assets.

Table 8.2: OLS estimates of equation (8), sample period: 1977:3–1987:4

Independent Variables	(1)	(2)	(3)	(4)
Constant	0.01036 (2.398)	0.015632 (3.012)	0.017053 (4.068)	0.020870 (4.316)
RGE	$-1.1\text{x}10^{-4}$ (1.605)	$-9.5\text{x}10^{-5}$ (1.462)	$-8.6\text{x}10^{-5}$ (1.477)	$-7.9\text{x}10^{-5}$ (1.363)
RPE	$-3.7\text{x}10^{-5}$ (0.968)	$-3.0\text{x}10^{-4}$ (0.799)	$3.8\text{x}10^{-6}$ (0.109)	$-2.6\text{x}10^{-7}$ (0.008)
RRE	$9.6\text{x}10^{-5}$ (2.179)	$1.2\text{x}10^{-4}$ (2.626)	$6.0\text{x}10^{-5}$ (1.510)	$7.8\text{x}10^{-5}$ (1.913)
INFE	–	–	0.000218 (3.444)	0.000205 (3.269)
YE	–	$-1.2\text{x}10^{-8}$ (1.733)	–	$-8.9\text{x}10^{-9}$ (1.503)
SPL(-1)/YE	-0.061063 (1.996)	-0.118283 (2.663)	-0.163082 (4.095)	-0.201038 (4.320)
SOL(-1)/YE	0.002899 (4.890)	0.001971 (2.955)	0.000295 (0.353)	-0.000264 (0.293)
SFA(-1)/YE	-0.002163 (4.890)	-0.002187 (5.085)	-0.001697 (4.157)	-0.001743 (4.339)
YT/YE	0.011317 (2.729)	0.011713 (2.901)	0.014550 (3.900)	0.014662 (4.003)
Summary Statistics				
Rbar^2	0.846	0.854	0.883	0.887
D.W.	0.934	0.893	1.117	1.060

Note: *In all equations, the dependent variable is (FPL/YE).*
The numbers in parentheses are t values, and D.W. is the Durbin–Watson statistic.

Turning to the interest rate effects, we note that they have the correct sign. The negative coefficient of RPE and the positive coefficient of RRE lend support to the view that the two types of loan are substitutes (the interest arbitrage hypothesis). However, the coefficient of RPE is highly insignificant. The coefficient of RRE, on the other hand, is statistically significant in all equations except one. The coefficient of RGE is also not significant, though only barely so in the first equation. It is likely that the collinearity between the rates makes it difficult to estimate their coefficients with precision.[13]

The estimated coefficient of transitory income is not only positive, but highly significant as well in all equations. There is thus no support for the emergency fund hypothesis. However, a positive transitory coefficient is in line with the findings of Backus and Purvis, who obtained a similar result for mortgage loans and for consumer credit.[14] Cummins also obtained a similar result when he used that variable in his policy loan equation to test the emergency fund hypothesis.

In concluding our discussion we note that while these results are, in general, in line with expectations, they are not without problems. In particular, even though the Durbin–Watson statistic in the present context is biased towards 2, it clearly points to the existence of severe autocorrelation in all equations.[15] It is known that in the presence of a lagged dependent variable on the right hand side, OLS estimators are inconsistent, and the resulting estimates need to be interpreted with caution. One approach to the problem is to estimate the equation using instrumental variables. However, before turning to that, it may be noted that the cause for the autocorrelation may be the result of a misspecification stemming from the assumption that the policy loan demand equation has been stable during the 1977–87 interval. However, that assumption is questionable in the light of our earlier discussion on the observed behaviour of policy loans over that period.

We address these issues in two steps. We first consider the application of the instrumental variables estimation method to equation (8). Subsequent to this, we split the sample into two subperiods: 1977:3–1981:4 and 1982:1–1987:4, and obtain estimates of the equation for each sample. A test for structural change is conducted to test the validity of applying a single regression to the entire sample. In the light of the presence of autocorrelation, the instrumental variables method has been used along with an adjustment for autocorrelation.[16] The resulting estimates are reported in Table 8.3. Though there is a considerable improvement in the Durbin–Watson statistic, it is likely that autocorrelation still exists. While the instrumental variable estimates are quite similar to the OLS ones, some major differences stand out.

Table 8.3: Instrumental variables estimates of equation (8), sample period: 1977:3–87:4

Independent Variables	(1)	(2)	(3)	(4)
Constant	0.011962 (1.649)	0.023166 (2.5760)	0.022224 (2.811)	0.025165 (3.166)
RGE	$9.2\text{x}10^{-6}$ (0.132)	$8.6\text{x}10^{-5}$ (0.779)	$-2.6\text{x}10^{-5}$ (0.323)	$-2.3\text{x}10^{-5}$ (0.287)
RPE	$-2.0\text{x}10^{-6}$ (0.031)	$-1.3\text{x}10^{-4}$ (1.512)	$8.1\text{x}10^{-5}$ (1.223)	$5.1\text{x}10^{-5}$ (0.876)
RRE	$5.1\text{x}10^{-5}$ (1.289)	$4.7\text{x}10^{-5}$ (0.837)	$-9.1\text{x}10^{-6}$ (0.156)	$2.0\text{x}10^{-5}$ (0.378)
INFE	–	–	0.000292 (2.611)	0.000257 (2.567)
YE	–	$-2.1\text{x}10^{-8}$ (1.826)	–	$-1.1\text{x}10^{-8}$ (1.123)
$\frac{SPL(-1)}{YE}$	-0.157634 (2.075)	-0.201330 (2.552)	-0.233350 (2.874)	-0.255796 (3.306)
$\frac{SOL(-1)}{YE}$	0.001904 (1.264)	0.001681 (1.543)	-0.000387 (0.253)	-0.000790 (0.553)
$\frac{SFA(-1)}{YE}$	-0.001825 (2.343)	-0.002592 (3.980)	-0.001940 (2.957)	-0.001931 (3.305)
YT/YE	0.008189 (1.896)	0.014192 (2.480)	0.014436 (2.629)	0.015395 (3.029)
Summary Statistics				
D.W.	1.519	1.401	1.56	1.520

See notes at the end of Table 8.2.

First, there is much greater stability in the estimate of the coefficient of SPL(-1), and it continues to be significant. However, the coefficient of SOL(-1) is no longer significant in any equation. This is also true for the coefficient of RRE, which is now insignificant, and the signs of this coefficient are not as expected in all equations. There also appears to be a general increase in standard errors, and this is not unexpected, given that the OLS standard errors obtained earlier could be grossly underestimated in the light of the severe autocorrelation that was found to exist. On balance, while the instrumental variables method overcomes the inconsistency problem associated with OLS, the continued likely presence of autocorrelation in spite of an adjustment for it, suggests that the root of the problem is a misspecification. We suspect that this arises because the policy loan demand equation has not been stable over the entire sample period.

Table 8.4: OLS estimates of equation (8), sample period: 1977:3–1981:4

Independent Variables	(1)	(2)	(3)	(4)
Constant	0.060787 (3.939)	−0.055581 (2.693)	0.057133 (3.443)	0.057414 (2.644)
RGE	$2.2x10^{-5}$ (0.218)	$1.8x10^{-5}$ (0.167)	$8.1x10^{-6}$ (0.077)	$8.1x10^{-6}$ (0.072)
RPE	$-9.6x10^{-5}$ (2.227)	$-9.8x10^{-5}$ (2.166)	$-8.1x10^{-5}$ (1.649)	$-8.0x10^{-5}$ (1.401)
RRE	$-7.4x10^{-6}$ (0.556)	$-2.9x10^{-6}$ (0.058)	$-5.2x10^{-6}$ (0.107)	$-5.5x10^{-6}$ (0.103)
INFE	–	–	$9.2x10^{-5}$ (0.726)	$9.5x10^{-5}$ (0.564)
YE	–	$5.6x10^{-8}$ (0.404)	–	$-4.0x10^{-9}$ (0.022)
$\frac{SPL(-1)}{YE}$	-0.359625 (2.621)	-0.432131 (1.881)	-0.363231 (2.582)	-0.358189 (1.314)
$\frac{SOL(-1)}{YE}$	−0.003632 (1.701)	−0.005408 (1.097)	-0.003734 (1.702)	-0.003611 (0.598)
$\frac{SFA(-1)}{YE}$	-0.00456 (6.298)	-0.002961 (0.785)	-0.004020 (4.242)	-0.004116 (0.930)
YT/YE	0.022541 (3.202)	0.022983 (3.091)	0.020538 (2.659)	0.020459 (2.289)
Summary Statistics				
$Rbar^2$	0.921	0.913	0.917	0.906
D.W.	1.855	1.935	1.882	1.879

See notes at the end of Table 8.2.

We examined the question of stability by estimating equation (8) for each of the subperiods: 1977:3–1981:4 and 1982:1–1987:4. The results are reported in Tables 8.4 and 8.5. We first conducted the Chow test for structural change between the two periods. The test overwhelmingly supported the occurrence of a structural shift in policy loan demand. An examination of Table 8.4 shows that there is a clear improvement in fit. More importantly there is a dramatic improvement in the Durbin–Watson statistic in all equations, and Durbin's h statistic points to the absence of autocorrelation. It also appears that INFE and YE are not significant in terms of their impact on policy loans. In fact, their inclusion, individually or together, appears to destabilize other coefficients. Thus, the inclusion of YE renders the highly significant coefficient of SFA(–1) insignificant, while the significant coefficient of RPE becomes insignificant when INFE is introduced into the regression.[17] Their joint inclusion has the additional effect of rendering the coefficient of SP1(-1) insignificant and reducing the explanatory power of the equation. The coefficient of SOL(-1), on the other hand, is not significant in any of the equations. This is true also for the coefficients of RGE and RRE. Again, there is no support for the emergency fund hypothesis in any of the equations. On balance, the first equation appears to be the best, as it is free of the destabilizing influence of INFE and YE, both of which are highly correlated among themselves and also with SFA(-1). This equation points to a significant negative impact of the policy loan rate and of lagged asset stocks on policy loan demand. The interest rate impact amounts to about $4.5 million in policy loan demand for a one percentage point increase in RPE. However, the elasticity of policy loans with respect to RPE is only -0.77, suggesting that policy loan demand is not very responsive to changes in RPE. Similarly, while YT has a statistically significant effect on policy loans, this is rather weak in that the elasticity is only 0.1. The estimated coefficient of SPL(-1) suggests that about 36 per cent of the discrepancy between the desired stock of policy loans and the actual stock is realized within each quarter.

Turning next to the results from the second subperiod (presented in Table 8.5), it may be noted that in broad terms the results are quite similar to those above. In particular, all equations fit the data rather well, and Durbin's h test again points to the absence of autocorrelation. There are, however, some noteworthy differences.

Table 8.5: OLS estimates of equation (8), sample period: 1982:1–1987:4

Independent Variables	(1)	(2)	(3)	(4)
Constant	−0.006538 (2.541)	−0.018376 (5.441)	−0.007454 (2.552)	−0.020780 (0.136)
RGE	$-3.6\text{x}10^{-5}$ (0.853)	$-3.2\text{x}10^{-5}$ (1.081)	$-3.3\text{x}10^{-5}$ (0.760)	$-2.6\text{x}10^{-5}$ (0.950)
RPE	$-5.5\text{x}10^{-5}$ (1.727)	$-1.7\text{x}10^{-5}$ (0.710)	$-4.7\text{x}10^{-5}$ (1.381)	$-1.2\text{x}10^{-6}$ (0.048)
RRE	. $1.0\text{x}10^{-4}$ (3.546)	$6.9\text{x}10^{-5}$ (3.124)	$9.7\text{x}10^{-5}$ (3.085)	$5.5\text{x}10^{-5}$ (2.495)
INFE	–	–	$2.7\text{x}10^{-5}$ (0.702)	$4.7\text{x}10^{-5}$ (1.860)
YE	–	$-9.8\text{x}10^{-8}$ (4.153)	–	$-1.0\text{x}10^{-7}$ (4.727)
$\frac{SPL(-1)}{YE}$	-0.058595 (2.847)	-0.244866 (5.195)	-0.071259 (2.580)	-0.279689 (5.884)
$\frac{SOL(-1)}{YE}$	0.001297 (4.249)	0.001371 (6.353)	0.000996 (1.878)	0.000855 (2.502)
$\frac{SFA(-1)}{YE}$	-0.001138 (4.519)	-0.000831 (6.353)	-0.001099 (4.198)	-0.000743 (4.033)
YT/YE	0.006098 (3.236)	0.002822 (1.827)	0.006904 (3.092)	0.003983 (2.551)
Summary Statistics				
Rbar	0.921	0.961	0.919	0.967
D.W.	1.733	1.927	1.754	2.078

See notes at end of table 8.2

Among the interest rate variables, all have the anticipated signs. However, only RRE has a coefficient that is significant in all equations. All the adjustment parameters are statistically significant in all equations, and the coefficient of YE has a statistically significant negative impact on policy loans.[18] In fact, the inclusion of YE together with INFE not only increases the explanatory power of the model (as the coefficients of both are significant), but also results in a much more reasonable estimate of the own adjustment parameter.

On balance, the fourth equation appears to provide the best results in the second subperiod. According to this equation, a million dollar increase in the flow demand for policy loans in any quarter would result in a $280,000 dollar decrease in the demand for policy loans in the subsequent quarter (other things being equal). Similarly, a billion dollar increase in the flow demand for assets in any given quarter is predicted to reduce policy loan demand by some $743,000 in the next quarter. The corresponding prediction for the same increase in the stock of other loans is an increase in policy loans in the next quarter of about $885,000.[19] In percentage terms, these impacts amount to a significant response of policy loans to lagged asset and liability stocks.[20] Further, the elasticity of policy loan demand with respect to RRE is 5.6, suggesting that policy loan demand is highly sensitive to interest rates.

In concluding this section, we bring together the salient features of the empirical results. To begin with, there is considerable support for the contention that there was a structural shift in policy loan behaviour in the early 1980s. This probably reflected changes in the economic environment as well as changes in the life insurance sector.[21] While interest rates are found not to have a strong impact on policy loans in the period ending 1981:4, the opposite is seen to hold in the subsequent period, probably reflecting increased consumer sophistication in the management of their portfolios. There does not appear to be any support for the emergency fund hypothesis in either time interval. Existing stocks of policy loans and assets are found to have strong negative impacts on the demand for policy loans in both intervals, while stocks of other loans appear to have a strong positive impact only in the more recent period. Expectations about inflation affect policy loan demand via their impact on interest rates. However, there is little evidence to indicate that expectations about inflation have an independent impact on policy loan demand.

4. CONCLUSION

In this chapter, we examined the short-run behaviour of policy loan demand in Canada during the 1977–87 interval by estimating quarterly policy loan demand equations. The results emphatically support our prior contention that there was a structural shift in policy loan behaviour some time in the early 1980s, reflecting perhaps some of the fundamental changes in the economic climate as well as specific developments within the life insurance sector. While it is likely that because of collinearity problems we were not entirely successful in separating the effects of various interest rates on policy loan demand, the hypothesis that differentials between market rates and the rate on policy loans lead to arbitrage was found to be valid in both periods. However, we found that the interest sensitivity of policy loan demand was found to be high only in the post-1982 period. The rate of return on assets was found to exert a significant influence on the demand for the policy loan liability. Existing stocks of policy loans and assets were found to have a strong negative impact on policy loan demand in both the pre- and post-1982 periods. However, the existing stocks of other loans were found to influence policy loan demand (positively) only in the post-1982 period. Inflation was found to be a relevant factor, but only via its impact on expectations about interest rates. We found little support for an independent inflation impact, but collinearity may have been responsible for this. The data appear to reject categorically the emergency fund hypothesis, and this may reflect the growing importance of surrenders relative to policy loans as a means of reducing saving through life insurance, as well as the general shift in favour of term insurance. In conclusion, it may be noted that while policy loan flows have, on average, diminished in size quite substantially, their sensitivity to interest rates appears to have increased, and they remain highly volatile. Increased volatility in interest rates or inflation rates can only serve to increase this volatility, and thus adversely impact on the investment activities of life insurers, and hence on the orderly functioning of capital markets.

NOTES

1. The growth rates reported in this paragraph were calculated from the data taken from *Financial Statistics*, Statistics Canada.
2. We do not consider demand equations for other assets and liabilities because our primary concern is policy loans, and these are much too small an item in household portfolios to justify a more detailed treatment.
3. That is, other rates held constant, an increase in (say) RGE raises the opportunity cost of holding the policy loan liability.
4. Note that α_1, α_2, α_3, represent the total impact of interest rate changes on FPL. Thus α_1 is the effect of a change in RGE on FPL via its impact on SPL*, SOL* and SFA*. The individual effects as measured by the coefficients in (5), (6) and (7) are not identified in a single equation framework.
5. Note that $r(1) = R(-1) - INF(-1)$, where INF is the inflation rate and R is the nominal interest rate.
6. This hypothesis was first suggested by Linton (1938). It is also examined by Dar and Dodds (1989) in terms of saving through endowment policies and surrenders in the UK.
7. Thus as income falls below YE ($YT < 0$), households increase policy loan demand. When the opposite happens, households pay back past policy loans.

8. Schott argued that increased inflation would induce households to increase policy loans in order to maintain real consumption.
9. This is because of our contention of structural change in policy loan behaviour in the early 1980s.
10. The disturbance term has not been explicitly specified in the equation for convenience.
11. See the Appendix for a more detailed discussion of the variables.
12. In other words, in the short run, households borrow to acquire assets.
13. For example, the simple correlation between RGE and RRE is 0.875.
14 See Backus and Purvis, 1980, Table 3.
15 The bias in the D.W. statistic arises due to the presence of a lagged dependent variable on the right-hand side. See Johnston (1984), pp. 316–8.
16 The method is due to Fair (1979). Fair shows that the lagged values of the dependent and independent variables must be included in the list of instruments in order to get consistent estimates. Other instruments considered are listed in the Appendix.
17. There appears to be fairly high simple correlations between variables in this subsample (particualrly between the lagged assets variables and the others in the equations), and this may be the source of instability in the estimates.
18. This implies that the desired stock of policy loans in not proportional to YE in the subsample.
19. This is simply another way of interpreting the adjustment parameters. Since lagged stocks depend upon the corresponding flow in the previous quarter, any adjustment parameter can be viewed as reflecting the impact on the flow demand for policy loans of changes in any flow (assets, other loans or policy loans) in the previous quarter.
20. This is because the changes considered here are, in fact, very small in percentage terms, given the size of the existing stocks.
21. See the discussion in section 1.

REFERENCES

Backus, D. and D. Purvis (1980), 'An Integrated Model of Household Flow-of-Funds Allocations', *Journal of Money, Credit and Banking*, **12**, 400–21.

Cummins, J.D. (1975), *An Econometric Model of the Life Insurance Sector of the United States Economy*, Lexington: D.C. Heath.

Dar, A. and C. Dodds (1989), 'Interest Rates, the Emergency Fund Hypothesis, and Saving through Endowment Policies: Some Empirical Evidence for the U.K.', *Journal of Risk and Insurance*, **56**, 415–33.

Fair, R.C. (1979), 'The Estimation of Simultaneous Equation Models with Lagged Endogenous Variables and First Order Serially Correlated Errors', *Econometrica*, **38**, 507–16.

Johnston, J. (1984), *Econometric Methods*, New York: McGraw Hill.

Linton, N.A. (1938), 'Panics and Cash Values', *Transitions of the Actuarial Society of America*, **38**, 365–94.

Pesando, J.E. (1974), 'The Interest Sensitivity of the Flow of Funds through Life Insurance Companies: An Econometric Analysis', *Journal of Finance*, **49**, 1105–21.

Purvis, D. (1978), 'Dynamic Models of Portfolio Balance: Specification and Estimation', *American Economic Review*, **68**, 403–9.

Schott, F.M. (1971), 'Disintermediation through Policy Loans at Life Insurance Companies', *Journal of Finance*, **26**, 719–29.

APPENDIX: VARIABLE DEFINITIONS AND SOURCES

(i) Stocks and Flows (millions of dollars)

FPL: net change in policy loan.
SPL: end-of-quarter policy loan stock.
SOL: end-of-quarter stock of other loans.
SFA: end-of-quarter stock of financial assets.

Each stock variable was estimated as the sum of an initial benchmark and the moving sum of the corresponding flow. The flow of other loans was defined as: (loans - policy loans) + mortgages + payables (mainly consumer credit). All these variables were seasonally adjusted by taking a three-quarter moving average.

Sources: *Financial Institutions: Financial Statistics*, Statistics Canada, Catalogue 61–006.
Canadian Socioeconomic Information Management System (CANSIM).

YE: expected disposable income.
(YT: transitory disposable income (YT = Y - YE))

YE was obtained by following the procedure described in Backus and Purvis, 1980, p. 420. In particular, YE is defined as:

$$YE = (Y/C)_E * POP * CPI,$$

where $(Y/C)_E$ is the predicted value of real per capita disposable income, retrieved from a geometric time trend regression, and POP and CPI are population (in millions) and the consumer price index, respectively.

Source: *CANSIM*.

(ii) Inflation and Interest Rates

INFE: expected rate of inflation, defined as:

$$[INF(-1) + INF(-2) + INF(-3)] / 3$$

where INF is the annual rate of inflation as measured by CPI.

Source: *Consumer Prices and Price Indices*, Statistics Canada' Catalogue: 61–010.

RGE: expected rate of return on assets, defined as:

RG(-1) + [INFE - INF(-1)]

where RG is the yield on government bonds with over 10 years to maturity.

RRE: expected rate on other loans, defined as:

RR(-1) + [INFE - INF(-1)]

where RR, the rate on other loans, is measured by chartered banks' prime rate.

Sources: *Bank of Canada Review*, Bank of Canada and *CANSIM*.

RPE: expected rate on policy loans, defined as:

RP(-1) + (INFE - INF(-1)]

where RP is the rate on policy loans, the RP series had to be constructed since no published data are available. Annual data on the policy loan rate were obtained from a major life insurer in Canada. An initial quarterly series was obtained through extra-polation between year-end values. The final quarterly series was arrived at through quadratic minimization. In particular, a penalty function based on the differences between the first differences of the initial and final (adjusted) series was minimized subject to the constraint that the quarterly figures average to the actual annual values.

(iii) Instrumental Variables

Apart from lagged values of the dependent and independent variables in equation (8), the following variables were also included in the list of instruments:

Currency outside banks (relative to YE), lagged one quarter.
Government consumption (relative to YE), lagged one quarter.
Government capital formation (relative to YE), lagged one quarter.
Government debt (relative to YE), lagged one and two quarters.
Expected income per capita, lagged one quarter.
Population.

Source: *International Financial Statistics*, International Monetary Fund.

9. Testing for Market Efficiency in the Exchange Market

David A. Peel

I am delighted and honoured to have been asked to write a contribution to Jim's Festschrift. I have known Jim for many years now. First, as a young lecturer at Liverpool, when Jim was External Examiner, we had many amusing moments, as he arbitrated between the relatively 'headstrong' views at that time of Stan Metcalf, Patrick Minford and myself, on the macroeconomics paper. Subsequently, I met Jim both socially and, of course, professionally. By chance, Jim's father and brother were keen snooker players, and Jim often attended their matches. I was also a keen snooker player in those days (Liverpool Staff Champion 1978), and to my great surprise I once met Jim at a snooker match on the Wirral. A most interesting juxtaposition was endeavouring to discuss the nuances of some aspect of rational expectations whilst watching a player attempt a masse shot.

At a professional level Jim has always been generous in giving me the benefit of his views on aspects of macroeconomics, or economics more generally.

Given his longstanding interests in rational expectations and international economics, for this contribution I have decided to discuss some of the empirical work that I have been conducting, which endeavours to test the efficiency of the forward exchange market. The work reported on, in part reflects some joint contributions with Peter Pope of Strathclyde, and also presents a new empirical test for efficiency using data for the inter-war period.

1. INTRODUCTION

There have been a considerable number of papers over the last decade or so which have investigated the efficiency of the foreign exchange market. One important focus of this work has been to examine the properties of the forward exchange rate as a predictor of the future spot rate. If the forward and spot markets are characterized by the usual conditions that there are no effective barriers to movement of funds and the presence of a large number of investors with ample funds for arbitrage operators,[1] then it is well known that the forward rate for the currency will be equal to the expected future spot rate plus any risk premium. So that:

$$F(1)_t = E_t S_{t+1} + RP(1)_t , \tag{1}$$

where $F(1)_t$ is the forward rate for one period, E_tS_{t+1} is the expected spot rate formed at time t for time t+1, and $RP(1)_t$ is the one-period risk premium.

If, in addition, the market is assumed to be semi-strong efficient, using Fama's terminology (1970), so that all publicly available information is reflected in the expectations formation process, then the forecast error:

$$S_{t+1} - E_t S_{t+1} = e_{t+1} \tag{2}$$

will be white noise (assuming agents have a quadratic cost function) and orthogonal to any information available at the time expectations were formed. In other words, the expectation embodied in the forward rate is assumed to be formed rationally.

We can re-write (1) as:

$$S_{t+1} - F(1)_t = e_{t+1} - RP(1)_t . \tag{3}$$

We note immediately from (3) that the ex-post forecast error for the forward rate is informative concerning the time series properties of the risk premium if expectations are assumed to be formed rationally. In particular, under the stated assumptions, the estimated degree of serial correlation of the one-period risk premium in (3) is the degree of serial correlation of the forecast error assuming zero covariation between the risk premium and the lagged forecast error.

If the spot and forward rate are stationary processes, then a regression of the future spot rate on the forward rate will allow a direct test for bias and efficiency of the forward rate, assuming that if a risk premium exists it is a stationary process. This procedure has been followed by a number of researchers (see, for example, Frenkel, 1980; Macdonald, 1983). In fact, employing appropriate tests for unit roots suggests that the spot and forward rate are invariably integrated

I(1) processes (see, for example, Levy and Nobay, 1986). As a consequence, a regression of the future spot rate on the forward rate is uninformative as to the existence of a stationary risk premium. A coefficient of unity will, in general, be obtained in large samples whether or not a stationary risk premium exists if the series are cointegrated.

However, we can also write (1) as:

$$F(1)_t - S_t = E_t S_{t+1} - S_t + RP(1)_t . \tag{4}$$

It follows that in the regression:

$$S_{t+1} - F(1)_t = a_0 + a_1(F(1)_t - S_t) + \phi_t , \tag{5}$$

where a_0, a_1 are constants, and ϕ_t is the error process; a non-zero estimate of a_1 will, in general, be obtained if a stationary time-varying risk premium exists, since both the dependent and independent variables reflect it. This was the insight of Fama (1984). Fama reports estimates of a_1 which are substantially less than unity. This finding can be attributed to the variance of the risk premium and a negative covariation between the expected depreciation of the currency and the risk premium (see, for example, Hodrick and Srivastava, 1986). Fama's analysis provides one explanation of why the forward exchange rate has been found almost universally in empirical studies to be a biased and inefficient predictor of the future spot rate.

Of course, an alternative hypothesis which will explain these empirical findings is that expectations are not fully rational, so that the forward rate does not fully embody information on the current spot rate. This alternative hypothesis does not, of course, preclude the existence of a time-varying risk premium.

Two mechanisms whereby traders process information in a relatively informed manner, but nevertheless the expectations embodied in the forward rate could be such that the ex-post forecast error is not orthogonal to the current spot rate, are suggested by the work of De Canio (1979), Friedman (1979) and Figlewski and Urich (1978). These mechanisms relate to optimal learning and pooling of heterogeneous expectations of traders to form an aggregate expectation.

Because plausible, 'optimal' mechanisms exist, which are suggestive that expectations in the foreign exchange market may not be fully rational, recently researchers have begun to provide additional evidence which may help to discriminate between the competing hypotheses.

2. SURVEY EVIDENCE

One method of analysis has been to examine the properties of survey data on exchange rate expectations. As pointed out by Blake *et al.* (1986) and Frankel and Froot (1987), survey data expectations will, *a priori*, not contain any risk premium. As a consequence, if the survey data are good proxies for the market expectations, a direct measure of the risk premium can be obtained and its properties examined in conjunction with the spot and forward rate.

To date, relatively few empirical studies have been conducted on the properties of survey data of exchange rate expectations. The few published studies, which employ different survey data, are all suggestive that survey expectations are both biased and inefficient (see, for example, Blake *et al.*, 1986; Frankel and Froot, 1987; MacDonald and Torrance, 1988).

Recently, Pope and I have begun to examine the properties of a new and 'high quality' source of survey expectations. Our survey data were derived from the monthly survey of up to 54 market analysts conducted by the *Euromoney Treasury Report*. Analysts are polled by *Euromoney* at the beginning of each month and asked to forecast the level of the relevant spot exchange rate on the first trading day three months ahead, the base currency being the US dollar. In the analysis we conducted, we employed the survey mean of the respondents though nothing was quantitatively changed by using the median. We examined data for nine currencies over the 52-month period May 1984–August 1988.

An appropriate method of determining whether the survey mean displays constant bias and weak form inefficiency is to estimate the model:

$$S_{t+3} - m_t = a_0 + u_t \, , \tag{6}$$

where S_{t+3} is the natural logarithm of the actual spot rate in period $t+3$, m_t is the natural logarithm of the mean survey expectations of the spot rate in period $t+3$, and a_0 is constant and u_t the error term. Because of the three-period forecast horizon, the error term is expected to follow a moving average error process of up to order 2. In estimates of equation (6), if $a_0 \neq 0$, the survey mean is biased. If the error term is serially correlated to an order greater than 2, the mean expectation is weakly inefficient. Estimates of (6), employing non-linear least squares, are suggestive that for all nine countries we cannot reject the hypothesis that the survey mean is both unbiased and weakly efficient.

We next examine whether the survey mean is strong-form efficient by estimating the relationship between the forecast error and the differences between the survey mean and the forward rate and survey mean and spot rate. It is, of course, critical that the information employed as regressors in these orthogonality tests is actually known to agents at the time expectations are formed. In the process of 'gathering in' a survey, lags could occur. Consequently, as a further potential check on our empirical findings, as well as examining the relationship employing current values of the spot and forward rate (that is, on the survey date) we also examined the values of these variables lagged one and five days. *A priori*, these lags should span any conceivable information lags which could occur in the gathering of the survey expectations data. In fact, the empirical result did not change in any significant manner as a consequence of this change in specification. In Tables 9.1 and 9.2 we report the results. We also report estimates of the form of equation (5), the 'standard' Fama regression, and report both the properties of our direct estimate of the risk premium $(F(1)_t - m_t)$ and its relationship to the ex-post forecast error $(S_{t+3} - F(1)_t)$. The estimates of the coefficients in the regressions are obtained using OLS, which will be a consistent estimator; and, to allow for the biased standard errors due to the overlapping data, we use the method of moments estimator described in Hansen and Hodrick (1980), to compute appropriate standard errors.

From Table 9.1 we observe that, in general, the forecast error for the survey mean is not orthogonal to information embodied in the spot rate (all countries except Switzerland) or the forward rate (all countries except Japan, the UK and Switzerland). We also observe from Table 9.2 that, as with the results reported by Fama (1984), the difference between the forward and spot rate $(F(1)_t - s_t)$ is a significant determinant of the forecast error $(S_{t+3} - F(1)_t)$ for all countries except France. Of course, if our survey measure is a good proxy for market expectations, then these empirical findings could be explained by the inefficiency of expectations. In addition, we can investigate directly the properties of the directly observed measure of the risk premium $(F(1)_t - m_t)$. Also, in estimates of (3) we will obtain a coefficient not significantly different from -1 if our measure of the risk premium is the market one and the theory underlying (3) is correct. The results reported in Table 9.2 show that for five of the

Table 9.1: Orthogonality tests; dependent variable $S_{t+3} - m_t$

Country	Constant	$(m_t - S_t)$	R^2	Constant	$(F_t - m_t)$	R^2
Belgium	0.02 (0.01)	−0.96 (0.35)	0.11	−0.03 (0.15)	1.76 (0.80)	0.11
Canada	−0.005 (0.04)	−1.96 (0.34)	0.34	−0.01 (0.004)	1.67 (0.43)	0.22
France	−0.02 (0.14)	−1.77 (0.82)	0.09	−0.03 (0.02)	1.72 (0.90)	0.09
Italy	−0.02 (0.01)	−2.24 (0.72)	0.20	−0.03 (0.12)	1.76 (0.80)	0.12
Japan	−0.06 (0.02)	−2.30 (0.95)	0.13	−0.02 (0.02)	0.48 (0.73)	0.01
Sweden	−0.023 (0.009)	−1.94 (0.50)	0.24	−0.04 (0.02)	1.76 (0.70)	0.14
Switzerland	−0.03 (0.02)	−1.10 (0.89)	0.03	−0.01 (0.02)	0.22 (0.16)	0.00
UK	0.01 (0.01)	−1.98 (0.74)	0.14	0.015 (0.021)	0.914 (0.85)	0.02
West Germany	−0.05 (0.02)	−2.32 (0.81)	0.16	−0.02 (0.15)	1.81 (0.87)	0.10

R^2 = coefficient of determination; standard errors are computed using the methods of moments estimator.

Table 9.2: Properties of the risk premium: the relationship of $S_{t+3} - F_t$ to $F_t - S_t$ and $F_t - m_t$

	Dependent variable = Risk premium ($F_t - m_t$)				Dependent variable = $S_{t+3} - F_t$			Dependent variable = ($S_{t+3} - F$)		
Country	Mean	Standard deviation	BP_8	ARMA	Constant	($F_t - S_t$)	R^2	Constant	$F_t - m_t$	R^2
Belgium	0.01	0.01	8.40	(0,0)	−0.02 (0.01)	−0.66 (0.16)	0.03	−0.03 (0.01)	−0.77 (0.80)	0.01
Canada	0.006	0.008	4.56	(0,0)	0.01 (0.006)	−5.67 (1.26)	0.25	−0.01 (0.04)	0.67 (0.43)	0.02
France	0.015	0.012	12.54	(0,2)	−0.008 (0.01)	−2.42 (1.91)	0.01	−0.03 (0.02)	0.72 (0.90)	0
Italy	0.028	0.01	15.28	(0,2)	0.027 (0.02)	−4.13 (1.84)	0.07	−0.04 (0.02)	1.22 (0.86)	0.04
Japan	0.02	0.002	7.06	(0,0)	−0.041 (0.01)	−3.1 (1.20)	0.18	−0.018 (0.016)	−0.52 (0.73)	0
Sweden	0.02	0.01	22.21	(0,2)	0.009 (0.01)	−4.13 (1.37)	0.15	−0.04 (0.01)	0.75 (0.58)	0.05
Switz'land	0.019	0.033	36.75	(0,2)	−0.03 (0.01)	−1.09 (0.28)	0.13	−0.01 (0.02)	−0.78 (0.16)	0.08
UK	−0.007	0.002	3.84	(0,0)	−0.047 (0.09)	−10.79 (1.21)	0.53	0.01 (0.16)	−0.08 (0.85)	0
West Germany	0.012	0.002	7.81	(0,0)	−0.092 (0.023)	−9.44 (2.48)	0.21	−0.02 (0.87)	0.81	0

ARMA = autoregressive moving average process; standard errors are computed using the method of moments; critical value for BP_8 = 12.59.

countries the direct measure of the risk premium is white noise, and for the others a second-order moving average error process. The measure of the risk premium has no significant explanatory power for the forecast error except for Switzerland. It is, however, not significantly different from -1 for Belgium, Japan and Switzerland. It would thus appear that on balance the survey measure is either not a good proxy for market expectations (instrumenting the survey mean and in essence taking it as a proxy for the unobserved market expectations made no material difference to the results), or the theory underlying (3) requires modification.

Of course, there are many well-known reasons why survey data may not be an appropriate proxy for market expectations, including factors such as the truthfulness of respondents and whether the weighting of the survey respondents' expectations reflects their weights in the market expectation. Such factors could explain the evidence of ex-post inefficiency we find in our survey data and that other researchers have reported. One difficulty with this view is that survey data derived in a similar manner, in particular the widely employed data on expectations of money supply change produced by Money Market Services Inc. of San Francisco, which reflect the view of 50–60 money market traders and economists, has gained acceptance as reflecting the market expectation because, in part, it has significant explanatory power in explaining changes in asset prices (see, for example, Figlewski, 1983) and gives parameter estimates which are consistent with theory. Nevertheless, many economists remain highly suspicious of the efficacy of survey data, and consequently do not give much weight to rejections of the rationality of market expectations based on empirical evidence which employs it.

Pope and I have recently suggested two alternative methods which might help discriminate between the competing hypotheses.

3. ALTERNATIVE FILTERS

The first method endeavours to exploit the empirical finding that spot and forward rates are non-stationary processes. In particular, the test is based on endeavouring to find a variable, X_t, which has the property that when subtracted from the spot and forward exchange rates makes them difference stationary, but also has the property that $F(1)_t - X_t$ has a variance not much greater than $F(1)_t - S_t$. From equation (1) we have:

$$F(1)_t - X_t = E_t\, S_{t+1} - X_t + RP(1)_t . \tag{7}$$

Consequently, in the regression:

$$S_{t+1} - F(1)_t = g_0 + g_1(F(1)_t - X_t) + Z_t , \tag{8}$$

where g_0 and g_1 are constants and Z_t is the error term.

The estimate of g_1 in the limit is given by :

$$g_1 = \frac{\mathrm{Cov}\ ((S_{t+1} - F(1)_t), (F(1)_t - X_t))}{\mathrm{Var}(F(1) - X_t)} . \tag{9}$$

Assuming rational expectations we can re-write (9) as:

$$g_1 = \frac{a_1 \mathrm{Var}(F(1)_t - St)}{\mathrm{Var}(F(1)_t - X_t)} - \frac{\mathrm{Cov}\ (RP(1)_t \cdot (S_t - X_t))}{\mathrm{Var}\ (F(1)_t - X_t)} \tag{10}$$

where a_1 is the estimate of a_1 in the standard Fama regression.

If the risk premium exists, then we expect to obtain a significant estimate of g_1 in estimates of (8), reflecting the risk premium. The estimate will only be zero if the denominator of (9), that is, $F(1)_t - X_t$ has 'high variance' in relation to the numerator or, conversely, the covariance between any risk premium and $(S_t - X_t)$ is not significantly different from the numerator of the first term in (10).

Pope and I experimented with a number of different variables for X_t – namely, the spot rate lagged one and five days, and the mean survey. The results employing the mean survey are perhaps the most interesting. If the survey mean is a good proxy for market expectations, then g_1 should not differ from -1. We see in Table 9.2 that for the majority of countries it is not different from zero, and has a positive coefficient in five countries. This implies that the covariance term in (10) has to play an important role for the rational expectations hypothesis to be appropriate. However, this term is the covariation between the risk premium and our proxy for the expected depreciation of the currency $(S_t - m_t)$. It is, of course, the postulated negative covariation between the risk premium and the market expectations of depreciation or appreciation of the currency which has to be invoked in order to explain the magnitude of the coefficient of Fama's test. In our estimates the covariance must be non-negligible, but also positive in a number of countries in order to explain the positive point coefficients. This is, a priori, difficult to accept. More work could perhaps usefully be done employing this approach, but at this time the results do not appear supportive of the rational expectations hypothesis.

4. TESTS INVOLVING FORWARD RATES OF DIFFERENT HORIZONS

A second method Pope and I suggest as a potential method for discriminating between the alternative hypotheses involves examining the properties of forward rates of different time horizons.

In particular, consider the three-period forward exchange rate, so that:

$$F(3)_t = E_t S_{t+3} + RP(3)_t . \tag{11}$$

For purposes of later analysis we write (11) in terms of the ex-post forecast error as:

$$S_{t+3} - F(3)_t = e_{t+3} + p_1 e_{t+2} + p_2 e_{t+1} - RP(3)_t , \tag{12}$$

where p_1 and p_2 are the constants in the Wold decomposition of S_{t+3}. If we lead the one-period forward rate two periods and subtract it from (11), we obtain X_t:

$$\begin{aligned} X_t &= F(1)_{t+2} - F(3)_t = E_{t+2}S_{t+3} - E_t S_{t+3} \\ &= p_1 e_{t+2} + p_2 e_{t+1} + RP(1)_{t+2} - RP(3)_t . \end{aligned} \tag{13}$$

Lagging (13) two periods, we obtain:

$$X_{t-2} = p_1 e_t + p_2 e_{t-1} + RP(1)_t - RP(3)_{t-2} . \tag{14}$$

If we examine the covariance of X_t and X_{t-2}, we find that it is non-zero if the covariance between the one- and three-period risk premia determined at time t is non-zero. A non-zero covariance is suggested by theoretical models (see, for example, Mark, 1989). As a consequence, the estimated composite moving average error term in (13), if risk premia exist, can be substantially different in structure from the moving average error process implied solely by expectational errors (see, for example, Harvey, 1981), or that implied by consideration of the properties of the ex-post forecast errors for the horizons defined by the one- and three-period risk premia (equations (3) and (12)) taken in isolation. In addition, if there are no risk premia, the error process (A_t) derived from estimates of (12), namely:

$$A_t = S_{t+3} - F(3)_t - \hat{e}_{t+3} = p_1 e_{t+2} + p_2 e_{t+1} \,, \qquad (15)$$

will not be significantly different from the actual error process (B_t) obtained directly from (13), namely:

$$B_t = F(1)_{t+2} - F(3)_t = p_1 e_{t+2} + p_2 e_{t+1} \,. \qquad (16)$$

A valid method of conducting this test appears to be to examine whether the slope coefficient differs from unity in a regression of A_t on B_t as well as the properties of the residuals from this regression. A significant difference between the error processes A_t and B_t provides evidence of the existence of time-varying risk premia. Moreover, it appears that this result is valid for any process generating expectations which possess the properties of consistency, that is, the forecasts obey the chain rule. Consequently, a significant difference will provide evidence for the existence of a risk premium in some circumstances, even if expectations are formed non-rationally. Alternatively, if the errors A_t and B_t do not differ significantly from each other, and the forward premium is a significant determinant of the forecast errors, we can conclude that there is no significant time-varying risk premium and expectations are formed non-rationally.

In order to provide some empirical evidence on this issue I decided to examine the properties of one- and three-month forward rates for the pound/dollar and pound/franc, using monthly data for the period 1922 to May 1925, which was a period of floating exchange rates. Data spanning this period have previously been investigated by a number of authors, including MacDonald (1983a) and MacDonald and Taylor (1990), though not in the manner suggested above.

Einzig (1937) reports weekly data for each Saturday for the period 1921–36. However, the change in conventions for reporting forward rates on 19 November 1921, whereby rates were quoted for one and three calendar months, dictated our choice of the shorter period. Data were weighted so that observations were centred on the fourth day of each month. Thus, for example, on 2 September 1922, the spot rate for the franc was 57, and the forward rates for one and three calendar months were showing a discount of 11 and 24 cents respectively. The corresponding figures for 9 September were 57.56, 4 and 9. The figures I employ are 37.16, 9 and 18.286. These are obtained by using weights of 5/7 and 2/7 on the raw data. If the data were, for example, for the 3rd and 10th of the month, the weights used are 6/7 and 1/7 respectively. Since the data will clearly include measurement error, we also retained the data for the Saturday preceding the 4th, as a potential instrumental variable.

A battery of different unit root tests, including Dickey–Fuller (1981) and Phillips and Perron (1986), were carried out on the data set. The spot and forward rates were found to be non-stationary I(1) processes at all normal levels of significance. The returns to speculation ($S_{t+1} - F(1)_t$) and ($S_{t+3} - F(3)_t$) and also the differences between the leaded period and three-period forward rates ($F(1)_{t+2} - F(3)_t$), were also found to be stationary. However, the forward premiums ($F(1)_t - S_t$ and $F(3)_t - S_t$) were borderline non-stationary. It seems *a priori* reasonable on balance to accept stationarity of these variables for this sample (though further work may be warranted on the weekly data set).

In Tables 9.3 and 9.4, I report a sample of the more interesting results for the two currencies. Because use of the instrumental variables we created made no material difference to our results, we report results using the current values of the variables. We note from Table 9.3 that the one-period returns to speculation can be described by moving average error processes of the order 1 and 2 respectively for the two currencies. To be consistent with rational expectations, this has to imply that one-period risk premia exist which are respectively described by one and two moving average error processes for the two currencies. For the three-period return to speculation, we find that there is a significant moving average error process of the order of 3 for both currencies. Because the three-month forward rate relates to a 13-week period, the moving average error processes could be greater than the order of 2 without violating efficiency. Alternatively, the three-period risk premium could be described by a moving average process of the order of 3, which will also generate a moving average error process of the order 3 for the ex-post forecast error.

The difference between the forward rate led two periods and the three-period forward rate (X_t) is found to be most parsimoniously described by a moving average error process of the order of 1 for the pound/dollar, and a moving average error process of the order of 2 for the pound/franc. The regressions of the constructed variable A_t on the X_t shows that these variables are significantly different.

Table 9.3: Properties of inter-war spot and forward exchange rates I

Pound/dollar	Dependent variable	Constant	Moving average error process	R^2	BP_8
Pound/dollar	$S_{t+1} - F(1)_t$	0.001 (0.002)	$\Phi_t + 0.35\ \Phi t_{-1}$ (0.16)	0.1	4.9
Pound/dollar	$S_{+3} - F(3)_t$	0.005 (0.002)	$\Phi_t + 1.16\ \Phi_{t-1} + 0.86\ \Phi_{t-2} + 0.27\ \Phi_{t-3}$ (0.16) (0.14) (0.14)	0.73	2.89
Pound/dollar	$F(1)_{t+2} - F(3)_t$	0.004 (0.002)	$\Phi_t + 0.987\Phi_{t-1}$ (0.16)	0.61	7.56
Pound/franc	$S_{t+1} - F(1)_t$	0.02 (0.01)	$\Phi_t - 0.19\ \Phi_t - 0.45\ \Phi_{t-2}$ (0.16) (0.16)	0.19	2.16
Pound/franc	$S_{+3} - F(3)_t$	0.04 (0.02)	$\Phi_t + 0.61\Phi_{t-1} + 0.08\ \Phi_{t-2} - 0.57\ \Phi_{t-3}$ (0.16) (0.17) (0.17)	0.41	2.19
Pound/franc	$F(1)_{t+2} - F(3)_t$	0.02 (0.01)	$\Phi_t + 0.42\ \Phi_{t-1} + 0.061\ \Phi_{t-2}$ (0.17) (0.17)	0.47	3.55
	Dependent variable	Constant	Independent variable	R^2	BP_8
Pound/franc	$S_{+3} - F(3)_t - \Phi_t$	0.002 (0.002)	0.93 (0.07) $(F(1)_{t+2} - F(3)_t)$	0.83	23.3
Pound/franc	$S_{+3} - F(3)_t - \Phi_t$	0.03 (0.007)	0.49 (0.06) $(F(1)_{t+2} - F(3)_t)$	0.62	57.8

Standard errors are in parentheses. Modified to allow for moving average error processes where appropriate. BP = Box–Pierce statistic with eight degrees of freedom.

Table 9.4: Properties of inter-war spot and forward exchange rates II

Currency	Dependent Variable	Constant	Independent variable	R^2
Pound/dollar	$S_{+1} - F(1)_t$	0.005 (0.002)	$-4.80\ (F(1)_t - S_t)$ (2.25)	0.10
Pound/dollar	$S_{+1} - F(1)_t$	0.07 (0.02)	$2.71\ (F(1)_t - F(3)_t)$ (1.43)	0.11
Pound/dollar	$S_{+1} - F(1)_t$	0.065 (0.02)	$-1.77\ (F(3)_t - S_t)$ (0.88)	0.11
Pound/dollar	$S_{+3} - F(3)_t$	0.017 (0.05)	$-5.11\ (F(3)_t - S_t)$ (2.10)	0.22
Pound/dollar	$S_{+3} - F(3)_t$	0.017 (0.06)	$7.41\ (F(1)_t - F(3)_t)$ (3.49)	0.20
Pound/dollar	$S_{+3} - F(3)_t$	0.016 (0.06)	$-15.33\ (F(1)_t - S_t)$ (4.98)	0.25
Pound/franc	$S_{+1} - F(1)_t$	0.048 (0.02)	$-14.14\ (F(1)_t - S_t)$ (6.24)	0.29
Pound/franc	$S_{+1} - F(1)_t$	0.049 (0.014)	$8.47\ (F(1)_t - F(3)_t)$ (1.86)	0.44
Pound/franc	$S_{+1} - F(1)_t$	0.049 (0.016)	$-5.46\ (F(3)_t - S_t)$ (1.51)	0.40
Pound/franc	$S_{+3} - F(3)_t$	0.074 (0.02)	$-4.40\ (F(3)_t - S_t)$ (1.29)	0.13
Pound/franc	$S_{+3} - F(3)_t$	0.072 (0.018)	$6.54\ (F(1)_t - F(3)_t)$ (1.76)	0.13
Pound/franc	$S_{+3} - F(3)_t$	0.075 (0.02)	$-12.61\ (F(1)_t - S_t)$ (4.82)	0.12
Pound/dollar	$F(1)_{t+2} - F(3)_t$	0.011 (0.03)	$-10.58\ (F(1)_t - S_t)$ (3.69)	0.19
Pound/dollar	$F(1)_{t+2} - F(3)_t$	0.012 (0.04)	$-3.58\ (F(3)_t - S_t)$ (1.52)	0.18
Pound/dollar	$F(1)_{t+2} - F(3)_t$	0.077 (0.022)	$-19.58\ (F(1)_t - S_t)$ (8.13)	0.29
Pound/dollar	$F(1)_{t+2} - F(3)_t$	0.074 (0.02)	$-6.86\ (F(3)_t - S_t)$ (2.19)	0.32

Standard errors in parentheses. All standard errors have been modified to make allowance for the moving average error terms as set out in Table 9.4.

In Table 9.4 we report the 'traditional' models of Fama and also results where X_t is regressed on the forward discounts for the two horizons. The standard regressions give significant negative coefficients for both currencies for the one and three months' time horizons, and are consistent with the existence of one- and three-period risk premia. The significance of, respectively, the one- and three-month forward discounts as determinants of the three- and one-month forecast errors is also consistent with the hypothesis of significant positive covariation between the one- and three-month risk premia. Of particular interest is the significant explanatory power of the differences between the one and three month forward rates for X_t. These regressions must of course, given appropriate covariances and variances between risk premia and expected appreciation of the currencies, be consistent with the interpretation involving risk premia and rational expectations. However, they do illustrate that results of this type can be obtained without inclusion of the current spot rate as a regressor. Similarly, the difference between the one-period forward rate led two periods and the three-period forward rate (X_t) is significantly determined by the difference between forward rates and the current spot rate. These results are only consistent with rational expectations if risk premia exist (and the two risk premia have significantly positive covariation).

The difficulty with this explanation is that the moving average representations for X_t are not consistent with the moving average representations of the forecast errors. The one-period forecast errors for the currencies are described by one- and two-period moving average error processes, respectively. This fact alone is sufficient to imply a significantly higher moving average error process for X_t than that actually obtained for the two currencies. If, in addition, it is assumed that the three-period risk premia is described by similar moving average errors, this feature of the data should be even more pronounced. Our results for the inter-war period are thus suggestive of inefficiency of expectations formation. However, the significant difference between A_t and X_t is also consistent with a time-varying risk premium. More analysis, employing this method, and using higher frequency data might be worthwhile.

5. CONCLUSIONS

The purpose of this chapter has been to discuss some methods for testing the efficiency of the forward exchange rates. The new empirical tests we present for two currencies in the inter-war period are suggestive that expectations did not possess the ex-post properties demanded by the rational expectations hypothesis, but that a time-varying risk premium may also exist. Inefficiency of expectations is also strongly supported by all empirical evidence which employs survey data, including our new high quality survey of the UK.

Of course, the finding of ex-post inefficiency of expectations may not violate these definitions of market efficiency which stress the ability to make systematic abnormal profits (see, for example, Jensen, 1978). Abnormal profits will only be systematically made by a traders' rule reflecting ex-post inefficiency in expectations if the departures from rational expectations are predictable.

The 'optimal' methods which suggest departures from rational expectations are also suggestive that such departures will not be mechanistic. However, this issue could be usefully addressed further, employing trading rules based on the methods outlined in the relatively neglected contribution by Jaffe and Winkler (1976).

NOTE

1. Negligable transaction costs is usually cited as an additional requirement. However, the arguments put forward by Ball (1978) suggest this is not a necessary condition.

REFERENCES

Ball, R. (1978), 'What Do We Know About Stock Market Efficiency', in R.M. Guimaraes, B.G. Kingsman and S.J. Taylor (eds), *A Reappraisal of the Efficiency of Financial Markets*.

Blake, D., M. Beenstock and V. Brasse (1986), 'The Performance of U.K. Exchange Rate Forecasters', *The Economic Journal*.

De Canio, S. (1979), 'Rational Expectations and Learning from Experience', *Quarterly Journal of Economics*.

Dickey, D.A. and W.A. Fuller (1981), 'The Likelihood Ratio Statistics for Auto-regressive Time Series with a Unit Root', *Econometrica*.

Einzig, P. (1937), *The Theory of the Forward Exchange*. London: Macmillan.

Fama, E.F. (1970, 'Efficient Capital Markets: A Review of Theory and Empirical Work', *Journal of Finance*.

Fama, E.F. (1984), 'Forward and Spot Exchange Rates', *Journal of Monetary Economics*.

Figlewski, S. (1983), 'Optimal Aggregation of Money Supply Forecasts: Accuracy, Profitability and Market Efficiency', *Journal of Finance*.

Figlewski, S. and T. Urich (1978), 'Market Efficiency in a Market with Heterogeneous Information', *Journal of Political Economy*.

Frankel, J.A. (1980), 'The Forward Exchange Rate, Expectations and the Demand for Money: The German Hyperinflation', *American Economic Review*.

Frankel, J.A. and K. Froot (1987), 'Using Survey Data to Test Some Standard Propositions Regarding Exchange Rate Expectations', *American Economic Review*.

Friedman, B.M. (1979), 'Optimal Expectations and the Extreme Information Assumptions of Rational Expectations Macro Models', *Journal of Monetary Economics*.

Hansen, L.P. and R.J. Hodi (1980), 'Forward Exchange Rates as Optimal Predictors of Future Spot Rates: An Econometric Analysis', *Journal of Political Economy*.

Harvey, A.C. (1981), *Time Series Models*, Deddington: Phillip Allan.

Hodrick, R.J. and S. Srivastava (1986), 'The Covariation of Risk Premiums and Expected Future Spot Exchange Rates', *Journal of International Money and Finance*, Supplement.

Jaffe, J.F. and R.L. Winkler (1976), 'Optimal Speculation Against an Efficient Market', *Journal of Finance*.

Jensen, M.C. (1978), 'Some Anomalous Evidence Regarding Market Efficiency', *Journal of Financial Economics*.

Levy, E. and A.R. Nobay (1986), 'The Speculative Efficiency Hypothesis; A Trivariate Analysis', *Supplement to the Economic Journal*.

MacDonald, R. (1983a), 'Tests of Efficiency of the Impact of News in Three Foreign Exchange Markets: The Experience of the 1920s', *Bulletin of Economic Research*.

MacDonald, R. (1983b), 'Efficient Capital Markets: A Review of Theory and Empirical Work', *Journal of Finance*.

MacDonald, R. and M.P. Taylor (1990), 'The Term Structure of Forward Foreign Exchange Premia: The Inter-war Experience', *The Manchester School*.

MacDonald, R. and T.S. Torrance, (1988), 'On Risk Rationality and Excessive Speculation in the Deutschmark–U.S. Dollar Exchange Market: Some Evidence Using Survey Data', *Oxford Bulletin of Economics and Statistics*.

Mark, N.C. (1989), 'Risk Premiums in the Term Structure: Evidence from Artificial Economies', *Journal of Monetary Economics*.

Phillips, P.C.B. and P. Perron (1986), 'Testing for a Unit Root in Time Series Regression', *Biometrika*.

10. Double Moral Hazard, Buybacks and the Debt Crisis

S. Mansoob Murshed

I first met Jim Ford when I came to Birmingham as a PhD student in 1984. He was later to be the Internal Examiner for my PhD thesis, as well as Head of Department during the first three years of my professional academic career. Jim was, and continues to be, extremely generous with concrete ideas and suggestions, as well as his time. In addition to his mastery in the technical side in economics, he is a wonderful craftsman of the written word; many admire his pithy style.

Jim's perennial interest in risk and uncertainty involved varied theoretical and empirical applications in financial economies and elsewhere. The following essay applies moral hazard theories and the economics of information to a pressing problem of the 1980s, the debt crisis, which continues to be with us even after a decade.

1. INTRODUCTION

Ever since the 'emergence' of the debt crisis in August 1982, a great deal has been published on the subject, both in academic and journalistic outlets. The motivation behind this great interest is the effect of debt repudiation or default on the commercial banks who, as some argue, had over-exposed themselves in some of the most heavily indebted Latin American countries. The emphasis in the earlier years of the debt crisis was on refinancing, which meant it was either regarded as a liquidity problem or a short-run problem. But the crisis has persisted for long enough to make economists and policy-makers realize that there is considerable 'debt overhang' (see, for example, Krugman, 1988; Sachs, 1989). By this, it is meant that the burden of inherited debt is so heavy that future repayments cannot be hoped to be made. This has led to attention being diverted towards debt reduction or debt forgiveness, for example the Brady plan.

Commercial banks, too, can improve their share values and profitability (repayment over contractual debt) by lowering their exposure in heavily indebted countries. It is quite common to lend more to debtors in return for buybacks by debtors, whereby the debtors buy back their own debt at a discount in return for more lending. Other proposals currently gaining favour include debt–equity swaps and the use of an international debt facility to buy back debt at a discount (see the papers by Corden, 1988; Dooley, 1989; Froot, 1989; Helpman, 1989; and in Bird, 1989).

But as Krugman (1988) has indicated, one cannot de-link debt reduction (in whatever form) and repayment from the state of nature. As the states of nature are or could be influenced by both parties, there is a possibility of *double* moral hazard in addition to the externality problem caused by interdependence. Thus there are two sources of market failure. The moral hazard problem arises because of informational imperfections, which also precludes cooperative behaviour, in addition to the usual lowering of the probability of the good state. Moreover, and perhaps more importantly, there could be *equity* considerations which could arise from non-cooperative behaviour. They take the form of a *shift in the burden of doing the preventive activity* from one party (creditor) to another (the debtor).

In Section 2 of this chapter, a state preference approach to the expected profit and utility of the debtor and creditor is outlined. The probability of the good state is increased by actions by creditors and efforts by debtors. Since there is interdependence, a first-best outcome requires co-operation and full information. Non-cooperative (Cournot–Nash) behaviour induced by the inability to monitor the other side results in second-best levels of activity and effort by creditor and debtor. Furthermore, there is the possibility that creditors transfer some of the burden of preventive activity to debtors. Section 3 examines the role of insurance when offered to the creditors. The result is to intensify the efficiency (market failure) problems of section 2, as well as an increase in potential inequity caused by one party (debtor) doing most (or all) of the preventive activity. Finally, section 4 presents some conclusions.

2. DOUBLE MORAL HAZARD AND NON- COOPERATIVE BEHAVIOUR

We assume two states of the world: good (1) and bad (2), which occur with probability π and $1-\pi$, respectively. The probability of the good state, π, is an increasing function of effort (e) by the debtors, and actions (a) undertaken by the creditors (banker). Efforts by debtors, in the main, amount to 'belt-tightening' that is, making more resources available (a larger share of national income) for debt servicing. This would be the case even if more revenues became available from efficiency drives in export promotion, resulting in an increase in trade balance surpluses, as these have an opportunity cost in terms of domestic expenditure. This is the case for many Latin American debtors who run trade balance surpluses, see Pastor Jr. (1989). Actions by the bank include steps to boost overall profitability, reflected in market values; and provisioning for debt, as the examples of Lloyds and National Westminster Banks have indicated (see *Financial Times*, 10 November 1989).

Given this, the expected profits of the creditors or banks, Z, can be denoted as:

$$Z(R,D,B,q,e,a) = \pi(e,a)\, Z_1 + (1-\pi(.))\, Z_2 - C(a)\ . \tag{1}$$

Z_1 and Z_2 are the profits of the banks in the two states:

$$\begin{aligned} Z_1 &= R_1 - qD - B \\ Z_2 &= R_2 - D\ , \end{aligned} \tag{2}$$

where R_1 and R_2 are the repayment of debt in states 1 and 2, respectively; R_1 includes monies used to buy back some of their own debt; B is new lending to the debtors which occurs in state 1 only for the sake of tractability; on the other hand B could reflect public money from creditor nations used to bale out banks which are over-exposed in debtor nations, in which case it would not be deducted from Z_1. This *would not affect the results below.*

The term qD ($q<1$) represents the contractual debt owed to the creditors in the current period, in state 1, and includes discounted debt reduction caused by debt buybacks by the debtors; for the sake of simplicity we assume no debt buybacks take place in the bad state (2); hence in the bad state the contractual debt owed, D, is higher; $R_1 > R_2$ and $qD < D$; C(a) represents the cost of actions undertaken by banks ($C_a > 0$, $C_{aa} > 0$). Thus, our characterization of the creditors captures closely the banks who are trying to reduce their exposure in the area of Third World debt, including those who are willing to lend more to the debtors in return for securing debt reduction. Other banks may take a more long-term view regarding the prospects of

Latin American debtors, wishing to retain exposure so as to be able to be first when the tide turns for these countries. But even these banks' current profitability would benefit from Third World debt reduction, which tends to exert a positive impact on the stock market values of banks.

The expected utility of debtors can be characterized as:

$$U\ (R,B,e,a) = \pi(e,a)U_1 + (1-\pi(.))U_2 - E(e) \quad (3)$$

$$U_1 = M_1 + B - (R_1 + qD); \quad U_2 = M_2 - (R_2 + D)\ , \quad (4)$$

where M_1 and M_2 stand for the incomes of the debtors in the two states, $M_1 > M_2$. E(e) is the disutility debtors obtain from their efforts in improving the probability of the good state, π, $E_e > 0$ and $E_{ee} > 0$.

As far as the effect of effort (e) by debtors and actions (a) by creditors on the probability of the good state, π, is concerned we assume that it increases the probability, but at a diminishing rate. So, $\pi_e > 0$ and $\pi_a > 0$, but $\pi_{ee} < 0$ and $\pi_{aa} < 0$, there is effort and action fatigue as more and more of these are engaged in.

We then move on to analyse the optimum amounts of effort and action when both parties behave in a *cooperative* fashion with full information about each other's actions. In order to proceed we sum the expected profit of the creditors with the expected utility of debtors and obtain total welfare, W, the sum of (1) and (3). Maximizing total welfare:

$$W = \pi(e,a)Z_1 + (1-\pi(.))Z_2 + \pi(e,a)U_1 + (1-\pi(.))U_2 - C(a) - E(e) \quad (5)$$

Taking derivatives with respect to a and e:

$$\delta W/\delta a = \pi_a(Z_1+U_1) - \pi_a\ (Z_2+U_2) - C_a$$

or,

$$\pi_a(Z_1+U_1) - \pi_a(Z_2+U_2) = C_a \quad (6)$$

$$\delta W/\delta e = \pi_e(Z_1+U_1) - \pi_e(Z_2+U_2) - E_e$$

or,

$$\pi_e (Z_1+U_1) - \pi_e(Z_2+U_2) = E_e . \quad (7)$$

Equations (6) and (7) imply that the marginal costs of undertaking a and e, C_a and E_e respectively, to both sides are equal to the *total* marginal benefits to both sides from them. They also allow us to derive the first-best socially optimum quantities of a and e given fixed amounts of the other:

$$a^*(e) \quad (8)$$

and

$$e^*(a) \quad (9)$$

The only manner in which such a first-best optimum can be made enforceable in a contract is if both sides can observe each other's actions and behave in a cooperative fashion. Thus, problems of moral hazard would be precluded with full symmetric information. This would be similar to Raffer's (1990) proposal for applying the US, Chapter 9 insolvency law to Third World debt, as it would lead to a full informational outcome.

If, however, neither party can monitor the other's activities, as is realistic to assume in this case, then outcomes as in (8) and (9) are not possible. What would be the equilibrium quantities of activity and effort by creditors and debtors, and how could it be made enforceable? The answer to the second question is in a Cournot–Nash setting of *non-cooperative* behaviour. The Nash equilibrium would ensure that neither side had incentives to deviate from equilibrium a and e, allowing for non-cooperative behaviour, in the absence of monitoring.

As in Cooper and Ross (1985) the parties play a two-stage game. In the first stage they decide on the levels of new lending (Bs) and debt buybacks (qD). In the second stage they decide on a and e, given some conjecture about the other – the Cournot–Nash game.

Thus the creditors maximize their expected profits, Z in (1) with respect to a. This gives us:

$$\pi_a (Z_1 - Z_2) = C_a . \quad (10)$$

Debtors maximize their expected utility, U, in (3) with respect to e. Thus:

$$\pi_e (U_1 - U_2) = E_e \,. \tag{11}$$

It is apparent from comparing (10) and (11) with (6) and (7) that the equilibrium quantities of a and e, â and ê, will be less than in the cooperative case, as the marginal benefits to both sides of doing a and e are reduced. This is the distortion induced by double moral hazard when parties do not cooperate.

Figure 10.1: Non-cooperative game when a and e are complements

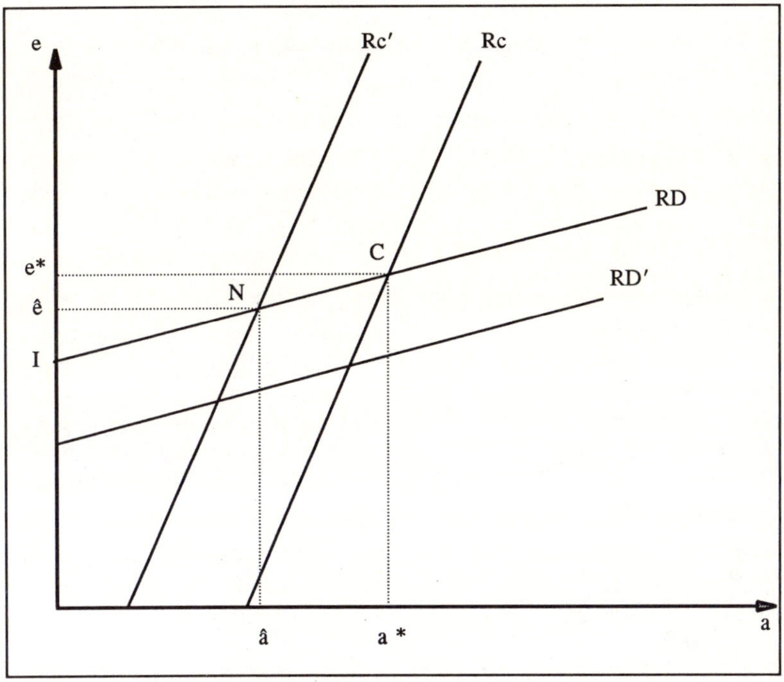

The next step is to set up a reaction function equilibrium for a and e. The reaction functions are subject to profit maximization (10) and utility maximization (11) in a non-cooperative situation with conjectures about e and a by creditors and debtors. Thus for creditors the slope of the reaction function is given by:

$$\frac{de}{da/R_c} = \frac{C_{aa} + \pi_{aa} (Z_2 - Z_1)}{\pi_{ae} (Z_1 - Z_2)} \gtreqless 0 \qquad \text{if } \pi_{ae} \gtreqless 0 \tag{12}$$

and for debtors:

$$\frac{de}{da/R_D} = \frac{\pi_{ae}(U_1 - U_2)}{E_{ee} + \pi_{ee}(U_2 - U_1)} \gtreqless 0 \qquad \text{if } \pi_{ae} \gtreqless 0 \quad (13)$$

Recall that:

$C_{aa} > 0$, $E_{ee} > 0$, $\pi_{aa} < 0$, $\pi_{ee} < 0$, $Z_1 > Z_2$, $U_1 > U_2$ and $\pi_{ae} = \pi_{ea}$.

Thus the reactions functions will be positively sloped if $\pi_{ae} > 0$, that is if the actions by creditors and efforts by debtors are complements. An increase in one leads to a rise in the other along the reaction functions, as in Figure 10.1.

Figure 10.2: Non-cooperative game when a and e are substitutes I

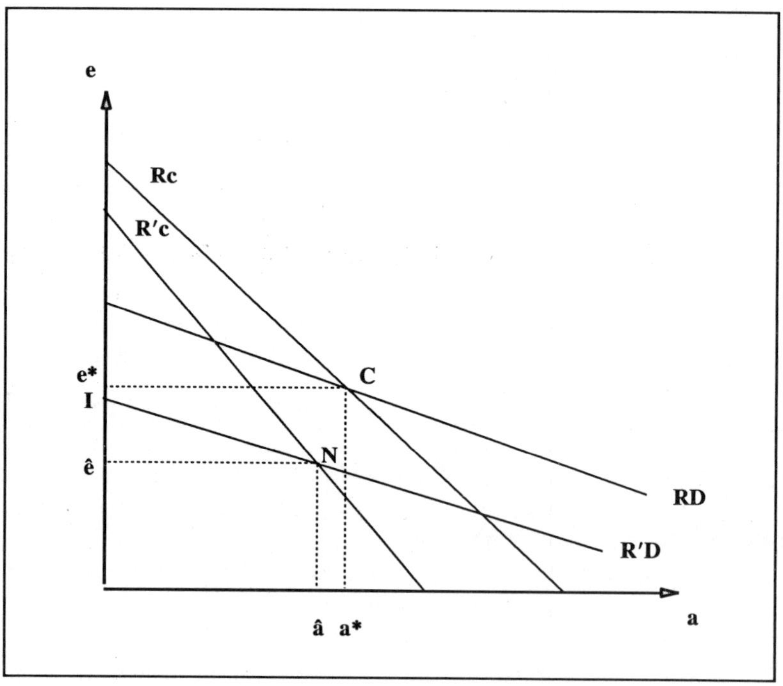

In Figure 10.1 point C shows the cooperative, first-best and full informational outcome, whereas point N indicates the non-cooperative second-best equilibrium. The relative slopes of the reaction functions are dictated by stability. Point C gives a and e indicated by (6) and (7), while N is corresponds to (10) and (11). Clearly both actions by creditors and efforts by debtors are lower in the non-cooperative case.

What if a and e are substitutes for one another, that is, $\pi_{ae} < 0$? Then the reaction functions would be negatively sloped as in Figure 10.2. This implies that as a is increased, e is decreased and vice versa. Once again the relative slopes of the reaction functions are given by stability conditions (the Samuelsonian correspondence principle). The basic message of Figure 10.1 is retained. The cooperative outcome, C, gives more action and effort than its non-cooperative counterpart at N, leading to a sub-optimal second-best outcome. But there is yet another possibility to be considered when actions and efforts are substitutes, $\pi_{ae} < 0$, along the reaction functions. This is the case where, in the non-cooperative equilibrium, one of either e or a is lower than its value in the cooperative case, while the other is higher. This is shown in Figure 10.3.

Figure 10.3: Non-cooperative game when a and e are substitutes II

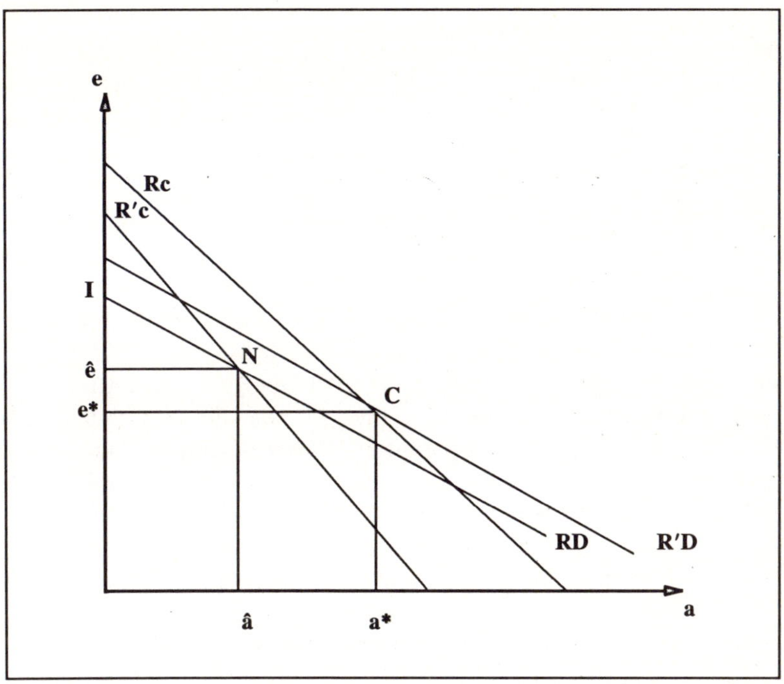

In Figure 10.3 the movement towards lower activities induced by non-cooperation is lesser in the case of the debtors than for creditors. Thus, as a result, at the non-cooperative equilibrium at N, there is higher e but lower a than at the cooperative outcome at C. As we move from cooperation to non-cooperation, both sides would like to reduce e and a. But in this case a reduction of the creditors' actions makes it more 'beneficial' for debtors to raise their efforts. In the context of the current debt crisis this is a clear manner in which the banks can *shift* some of the *burden of adjustment* or the *burden of preventive activity* away from themselves to the debtors. The debtors engage in greater effort to repay than they would have done in the full informational, first best outcome at C. Thus non-cooperative behaviour and the moral hazards associated with it can convey a *negative externality* by the banks towards the debtors. Their utility is further curtailed by the consequent costs (or disutility) of engaging in more effort. These costs could be substantial. Many would maintain that the case presented in Figure 10.3 was the more realistic depiction of the non-cooperative interaction between banks and debtor nations (governments) as far as e and a were concerned, at least until very recently, with the greater emphasis on refinancing. It should be noted that as far as the Cournot–Nash equilibrium in e and a is concerned it would be impossible for both e and a to be higher than in the cooperative outcome. Furthermore, even if $\pi_{ae} = 0$, both a and e would be lower than in the cooperative case, comparing (10) and (11) with (6) and (7).

3. THIRD PARTY INSURANCE

As suggested in Corden (1988), if an international debt facility is brought onto the picture, its role will be to take on the risk of creditors. Thus its role will be to provide insurance to the creditors, through the medium of buying back their debt, at a discount. The reason the insurance principle is pertinent is that the creditors will be risk-averse regarding their international debt exposure, and will be anxious to pass on risk to the international debt facility. The insurance could take the form of the facility buying discounted debt owned by the creditors in the bad state of nature (state 2), in return for a premium that takes the form of a percentage claim on the repayment of debt. This is suggested in Corden (1988), who discusses various numerical examples. Although it could be unrealistic to assume full insurance is offered by the debt facility to the creditors, it is nevertheless instructive to analyse it as a first cut, and this has been proposed by some.

With full insurance offered to the creditors, its actual profits in both states of nature would be some Z_c, the certainty equivalent of the previous expected rate. It is immediately apparent from (10) that if Z_c is offered in both states, the marginal benefit of doing any activity to raise π (the probability of the good state) becomes zero. Hence, with full insurance *no activity*, a (preventive of the bad state), is engaged in by the creditors. In general, insurance will lower their incentives to do a.

As far as the non-cooperative Cournot–Nash game is concerned, (10)–(13) suggests that there is a benefit to either party of doing e or a, even when the other party's a or e is zero, and the reaction functions in Figures 10.1–10.3 do suggest positive inputs of either activity for zero inputs by the other. Thus in Figure 10.1 where a and e are complements, $\pi_{ae} > 0$, it leads to a further *reduction* in e done by the debtor as $a = 0$ at point I. In Figures 10.2 and 10.3, however, $\pi_{ae} < 0$, a and e are substitutes, zero input of a results in *increases* of effort by the debtors at point I. This is greater in figure 10.3. Thus, such behaviour, that is, offering insurance (even partial insurance) could lead to *further shifts in the burden of preventive activity* associated with the debt crisis, *from creditor to debtors*. Be that as it may, offering *insurance to one party alone, leads to third-best outcomes, inferior to the non-cooperative equilibrium without insurance given moral hazard*, as indicated by the I point in Figures 10.1–10.3.

It will also be true, following the analysis of Pauly (1974), that in the presence of moral hazard, excessive and sub-optimal levels of insurance will be purchased from a competitive insurance market. To understand this, let us just consider the optimal insurance supplied by the insurer (debt facility) without moral hazard. Its profits, υ are:

$$\upsilon = P(I) - (1 - \pi)I \,, \tag{14}$$

where P is the premium it receives in the form of a share of R, repayment of debt, and I is the value of insurance in the bad state which takes the form of debt buybacks in state 2. Maximization with respect to I implies:

$$P_I = (1 - \pi) \,, \tag{15}$$

This is the outcome with no moral hazard. With moral hazard and the availability of insurance, the incentive to do the preventive activity, a, is diminished or becomes zero. Thus π, the probability of the good state (1) becomes a function not just of a but diminishes with the value of insurance, I, that is, $\pi_I < 0$; as more insurance reduces the incentive to do a, it *lowers the probability of the good state,* π. The insurer's profit function, υ should become:

$$\upsilon = P(I) - (1 - \pi(I))I , \tag{16}$$

Maximization yields:

$$P_I = (1 - \pi(.)) - \pi_I I > 0 , \tag{17}$$

Comparing (17) with (15) *excessive* or more insurance could be purchased, relative to the optimal level, which the international debt facility would have to take into account. The debtors, too, would purchase excessive insurance, if it were made available to them, in the presence of moral hazard (which eventually raises P as π falls). Furthermore, if the insured parties exhibited good and bad risk types, a pooling equilibrium (one type of insurance contract) would become untenable; it would require a separating equilibrium (separate contracts) as in Rothschild and Stiglitz (1976).

4. CONCLUSIONS

We have attempted to examine the effects of cooperative and non–cooperative behaviour with insurance (to one party) in a state preference framework where the probabilities of the states are affected by the actions of *both* parties in question. This raises the possibility of a double moral hazard. The two sides in question are creditors (banks) and debtors, with the applications to the current debt crisis in mind. We first show the first-best, cooperative and full informational outcome. Each side undertakes the socially optimal level of preventive activity. As action by any one agent benefits the other we have *externality* problems. This is highlighted when the two agents behave in a non-cooperative fashion. The equilibrium levels of preventive activity, actions by creditors and efforts by debtors, are below their social optimum in this second-best Nash equilibrium. Not only is there this sort of market failure, but there are very realistic circumstances when creditors, by reducing their actions, can induce greater effort on the part of debtors, shifting part of the burden of undertaking preventive activity to the debtor. This raises an important issue of equity. Furthermore, if one side, creditors, has access to insurance, in the limit it undertakes absolutely no preventive activity, but in general it will reduce its actions even further. This asymmetric insurance intensifies both the market failure (efficiency) and burden shifting (equity) problems.

What of solutions to the problems raised above? The solutions must lie in the nature of the problems which include efficiency questions of (a) externalities of interdependence and (b) moral hazard, and the equity consideration of the distribution of the burden of adjustments (that is, preventive activity). Some form of public insurance is required and an international debt facility *could* fit the bill, as long as complete insurance is not offered to a single party (creditors) alone.

The problem raised by moral hazard is that imperfect information regarding the undertaking of preventive activity leads to less than optimal amounts of either or both being produced, thus the probability of the good state of nature is lowered, leading to second-best outcomes, including shifts in the burden of preventive activity (from creditor to debtor). These problems are exacerbated when insurance is offered to one party, only the creditor, say, by an international debt facility, as proposed by some. Even less preventive activity is undertaken, and the possibility of larger shifts in the burden of preventive activity from creditor to debtor could occur. If both creditors and debtors are risk-averse, insurance at the socially optimum levels would enhance welfare, but it would be levels of insurance which produced the first best levels of preventive activities (8) and (9), otherwise premiums would keep rising as π fell because less a and e were done. This would raise problems of enforcement of contracts and monitoring of activities by the insurer – but the operational nature of the international debt facility would be different from that currently envisaged, as interests of *both* sides, not just banks, would have to be taken into account.

Some final caveats. Bargaining models rely on the interactive process between representative agents. This might be unsatisfactory but it is common practice to utilize such models to capture the *bargaining process*. But, by their very nature such models cannot capture the origins of the debt crisis which are rooted in the macroeconomic interaction between North and South (on this see Murshed and Sen, 1988 and Murshed, 1990). Nor can the models depict the actual human cost of indebtedness in these countries, which often involves losses in entitlements and the provision of basic needs, in addition to a worsening of the income distribution and increases in the absolute numbers of people below the poverty line. (On this see Bourguignon et al., 1989 and Raffer, 1990, where the impoverishment of entire nations as a consequence of IMF-type structural adjustment programmes has been demonstrated.) Bird (1989) has pointed out the asymmetrical role of organizations like the IMF or the World Bank. While they are able to make developing countries undergo unpleasant and unreasonably harsh adjustments as a precondition for loans, they have no clout in the developed countries, particularly nations with huge current account deficits who swallow up the world savings, refuse to improve their international competitiveness, but threaten to engage in protectionism against developing country exports. Last, but not the least the *public good* aspect of the debt crisis needs to be mentioned and stressed. Without some supra-national intervention, one that has some semblance of fairness to debtors as well as creditors, the debt crisis will lead to aggravated global market failure in international lending.

REFERENCES

Bird, G. (ed.), (1989), *Third World Debt: The Search for a Solution*, Aldershot: Edward Elgar.

Bourguignon, F., W.H. Branson, and J. de Melo (1989), 'Adjustment and Income Distribution: A Counterfactual Analysis', mimeo.

Cooper, R. and T.W. Ross (1985), 'Product Warranties and Double Moral Hazard', *Rand Journal of Economics*, **16**, 103–13.

Corden, W.M. (1988), 'An International Debt Facility', *International Monetary Fund Staff Papers*, **35**, 401–21.

Dooley, M.P. (1989), 'Debt Relief and Leveraged Buy-outs', *International Economic Review*, **30**, 71–5.

Froot, K.A. (1989), 'Buybacks, Exit Bonds and the Optimality of Debt and Liquidity Relief', *International Economic Review*, **30**, 49–70,

Helpman, E. (1989), 'The Simple Analytics of Debt–Equity Swaps', *American Economic Review*, **79**, 440–51.

Krugman, P. (1988), 'Financing Versus Forgiving a Debt Overhang', *Journal of Development Economics*, **29**, 253–68.

Murshed, S.M. (1990), 'Stabilisation Policy, Commercial Policy and Debt in a North–South Framework', in G. Bird, (ed.), *The International Financial Regime*, London: Academic Press.

Murshed, S.M. and S.Sen (1988), 'Northern Monetary Policy and the Southern Debt Crisis', *University of Birmingham Discussion Paper*, No. 284.

Pastor, M. Jr (1989), 'Current Account Deficits and Debt Accumulation in Latin America', *Journal of Development Economics*, **31**, 77–97.

Pauly, M.V. (1974), 'Overinsurance and Public Provision of Insurance: The Roles of Moral Hazard and Adverse Selection', *Quarterly Journal of Economics*, **88**, 44–54.

Raffer, K. (1990), 'Applying Chapter 9 Insolvency to International Debts: An Economically Efficient Solution with a Human Face', *World Development*, **18**, 301–11.

Rothschild, M and J.Stiglitz (1976), 'Equilibrium in Competitive Insurance Markets: An Essay on the Economics of Imperfect Information', *Quarterly Journal of Economics*, **90**, 629–49.

Sachs, J. (1989), 'The Debt Overhang of Developing Countries', in G. Calvo, R. Findlay, P. Kouri, and J.B. de Macedo (eds), *Debt, Stabilization and Development*, Oxford: Blackwell.

11. Forward-Looking Behaviour in the Gilts Market: Some Implications

Marcus Miller

1. INTRODUCTION

In the absence of risk aversion, an efficient capital market will equate the (instantaneous) short-term rate of interest with the sum of the consol rate and the anticipated rate of capital appreciation on consols. If the anticipations held by market participants are correct, and the market is stable, then this 'efficiency condition' implies that the current consol rate will be an average of present *and future* short-term interest rates. In section 2 below (written with Avinash Dixit) we consider a case where the time path of future short rates follows an exponential pattern, and present a simple formula which may be used approximately to determine the price of a consol in that case.

Where future short-term rates of interest differ from the current rate, the rate on consols will tend systematically to differ from the current short rate in the presence of forward-looking behaviour. In such circumstances it will be important to distinguish between short and long rates of interest. In sections 3 to 6 we examine a simple macroeconomic model where the short rate is treated as the opportunity cost of holding money while the long rate is taken as the appropriate measure of the cost of borrowing funds for real investment. Lags in the adjustment of output ensure that short rates take time to reach equilibrium, and so short and long rates of interest do differ. The way monetary and fiscal policy actions and announcements operate in such circumstances is considered (and the contrast with the orthodox IS/LM analysis will be apparent).

2. WHAT PRICE A CONSOL?

In the absence of 'news', an efficient bond market (assuming risk neutrality) would imply:

$$DR = R\,(R - r),$$

where R is the consol rate (coupon divided by price), and r is the (instantaneous) short rate, and D is the differential operation, so $DR=dR(t)/dt$.

Let us also assume that short rates tend towards an equilibrium value as follows:

$$DR=\beta(\hat{R} - r),$$

where

$$\hat{R}$$

(we shall call this Rhat, a convention adopted throughout the text for such equilibrium values of the variables) is the long-run 'normal' rate (to be discussed in Appendix 1). Then, defining variables in terms of deviation from equilibrium:

$$x_1 = r - \hat{R}\ ; \qquad x_2 = R - \hat{R},$$

we have:

$$Dx_1 = -\beta x_1$$

$$Dx_2 = (x_2+\hat{R})(x_2-x_1) = \hat{R}(x_2-x_1)+x_2(x_2-x_1) = -\hat{R}x_1+\hat{R}x_2,$$

to first order, that is:

$$\begin{bmatrix} Dx_1 \\ Dx_2 \end{bmatrix} = \begin{bmatrix} -\beta & 0 \\ -\hat{R} & \hat{R} \end{bmatrix} \begin{bmatrix} x_1 \\ x_2 \end{bmatrix}$$

The phase diagram for this locally linear system is given in Figure

11.1.

Figure 11.1: Phase diagram for bond market equilibrium

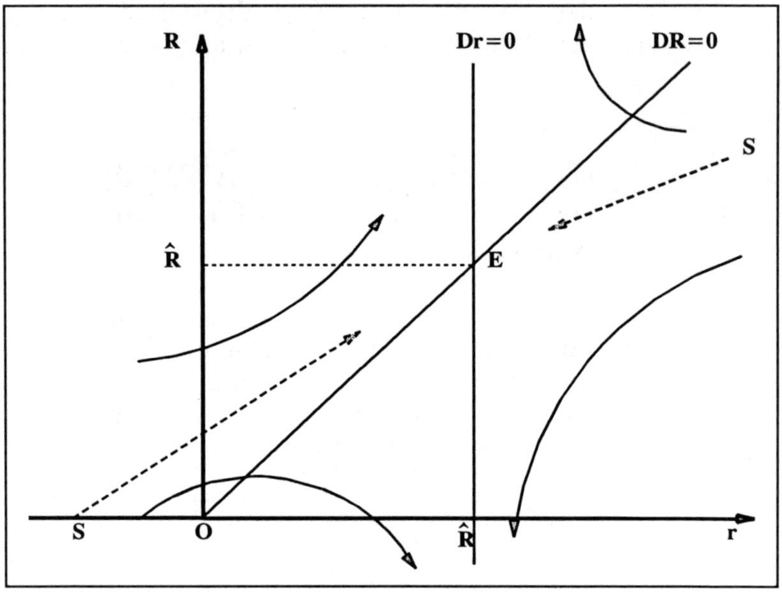

(SO = β)

The slope of the stable locus, SS, can be shown to be

$$\frac{\hat{R}}{\hat{R}+\beta},$$

Since the system will jump onto the locus given r, one can solve for R as:

$$R = \frac{\hat{R}}{\hat{R}+\beta}\,(r+\beta),$$

Hence the price of a consol with a coupon of unity is the reciprocal:

$$P = \frac{1}{R}\left(\frac{\hat{R} + \beta}{r + \beta}\right), \ P \rightarrow \frac{1}{r} \text{ as } \beta \rightarrow 0, \ P \rightarrow \frac{1}{R} \text{ as } \beta \rightarrow \infty.$$

The time path of short rates may explicitly be determined by a model of the economy and of government behaviour, as shown in the next section.

3. THE ANALYSIS OF MONETARY AND FISCAL POLICY WITH RATIONAL EXPECTATIONS IN THE GILTS MARKET

We first set out the equations defining both the equilibrium values of output and interest rates, and the time path taken towards this equilibrium. Then we see how monetary and fiscal policy actions can affect the behaviour of output and interest rates. The equations, and definitions of variables, are as follows:

$$\text{LM: } \zeta = -\lambda r + ky \tag{1}$$

$$\text{IS: } y* = -\gamma R + \alpha y + \delta g \tag{2}$$

$$\text{Lundberg lag: } Dy = \psi (y* - y) \tag{3}$$

$$\text{Efficient markets: } DR = \hat{R}(R - r) \tag{4}$$

Where:

ζ = the level of real balances
y = the actual level of real output
y* = the desired level of real output
r = the instantaneous short rate of interest
R = the consol rate of interest
g = the level of real government expenditure
D = the differential operator, so $Dx = dx(t)/dt$

Equation (1) is the familiar condition for equilibrium in the money market, namely that the demand for money equals the (exogenously determined) supply. The opportunity cost of holding money is measured by the instantaneous short rate; the rate of interest on money itself being taken as fixed. The short rate is assumed to move so as to ensure that money market equilibrium is maintained at all times (so the economy is always 'on the LM curve').

Equation (2) expresses total desired demand for goods as a function of the level of output, the consol rate and government spending. The dependence of demand upon income will certainly be important for consumption spending: for investment it is assumed to be the long rate which affects spending plans; government spending is taken to be exogenous.

Although, as indicated in equation (3), production is adjusted so as to eliminate discrepancies between the supply of output and the demand for it, nevertheless, wherever the speed of adjustment (measured by ψ) is less than infinite, the goods market will typically not be in equilibrium.

Equation (4) describes the equality between the instantaneous short rate of interest, r, and the total yield on consols (R−DR/R). This relationship is linearized, using the equilibrium long rate (Rhat).

Substituting equations (1) and (2) into (3) and (4) gives the following relationships describing the behaviour of output and the consol rate over time:

$$\begin{bmatrix} Dy \\ DR \end{bmatrix} = \begin{bmatrix} \psi(\alpha - 1) & -\psi\gamma \\ \hat{R}k\lambda^{-1} & \hat{R} \end{bmatrix} \begin{bmatrix} y \\ R \end{bmatrix} + \begin{bmatrix} 0 & \psi\delta \\ \hat{R}\lambda^{-1} & 0 \end{bmatrix} \begin{bmatrix} \zeta \\ g \end{bmatrix} \tag{5}$$

In equilibrium y = y* and R = r, and these equilibrium values are given as a function of fiscal and monetary policy as shown:

$$\begin{bmatrix} \hat{y} \\ \hat{R} \end{bmatrix} = \frac{1}{\Delta} \begin{bmatrix} \gamma & -\lambda\delta \\ -(1-\alpha) & k\delta \end{bmatrix} \begin{bmatrix} \zeta \\ g \end{bmatrix} \tag{6}$$

where $\Delta = k\,\gamma + \lambda\,(1-\alpha)$ and Δ is assumed to be positive (see below).

The dynamics of the approach towards this equilibrium are best considered with reference to Figure 11.2. The equilibrium values of R and y define the point E shown. The schedule along which production is stationary, Dy = 0, is labelled IS(R), and results from setting the top row of equation (5) = 0. To the north-east of this schedule, output will be falling, but to the southwest production will be increasing. This is familiar (see Samuelson, 1947, Chapter 9).

Figure 11.2: Dynamics of gilts market with rational expectations

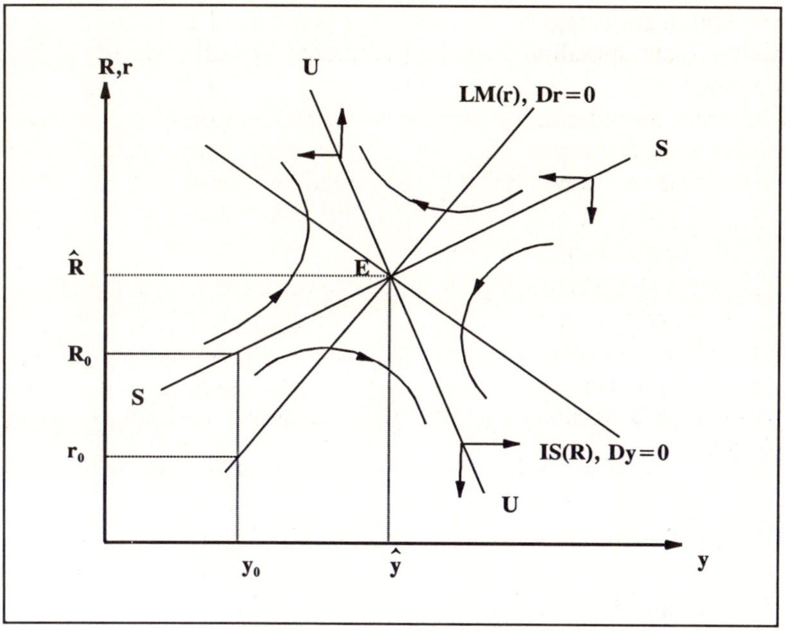

The IS(R) curve is shown sloping downward; the slope is given by

$$\left.\frac{dR}{dy}\right|_{Dy=0} = \frac{\alpha - 1}{\gamma}$$

so clearly this schedule may slope up (if $\alpha > 1$). However, in what follows we assume, as is necessary for stability, that it does not slope up more steeply than the schedule labelled LM(r). This assumption corresponds to the requirement that Δ is positive in equation (6) above. We now discuss the locus of stationary points for the consol rate.

For any given level of real balances there is a one-to-one positive relationship between income and the *short* rate of interest, and this is shown in the Figure by LM(r). This schedule turns out to be the stationary locus for the long rate because, as seen in equation (4), anticipated capital gains must be zero when long rates equal short rates. To the north-west of LM(r), however, long rates stand above short rates, so capital losses must be anticipated, that is, R must be increasing, and vice versa for points to be south-east. Thus the conventional LM curve is a stationary locus for the consol rate so:

$$\frac{dR}{dy}\bigg|_{DR = 0} = k\lambda^{-1},$$

but the consol rate appears to diverge from the LM curve.

Various paths which satisfy the dynamics described in equation (5) are shown in Figure 11.2; and it is evident that equilibrium E is a saddle-point equilibrium. There is only one path which leads ultimately towards E, and this is shown as SS in the Figure. This path is associated only with the stable root of the dynamic system; the path associated only with the unstable root is shown as UU in the Figure. All other paths are associated with both roots.

At any given time the level of output is determined by past history (though its derivative depends on current excess demand), but in this chapter we assume that the price of consols can adjust freely and so will adjust as to place the economy on the stable locus, SS. On the assumption that the economy is characterized by efficient financial markets, which are also stable in this sense, we can analyse the operation of monetary and fiscal policy by manipulating the IS(R), LM(r) and the SS schedules. Equilibrium will be shown by the intersection of IS(R) and LM(r); the SS locus will show the path taken by output and the consol rate towards that equilibrium, while the LM(r) curve will show that path followed by the short rate.

From what has just been said it will be apparent why the SS locus must slope upwards as shown. At any given level of income such as y_0 shown in the Figure, the short rate at r_0 must lie below its long run equilibrium value at E; but as the economy is stable income will be adjusting towards yhat, so short interest rates will rise towards Rhat at E. The consol rate being an average of the currently low short rate and the higher rates to be expected in the future, must currently lie at some point between r_0 and Rhat, as shown by R_0 on the SS locus. (A formal proof that the SS locus slopes upwards is given in Appendix 2).

4. THE RELATIONSHIP BETWEEN SHORT AND LONG INTEREST RATES

The short rate of interest which clears the money market is shown by the LM curve, while the forward-looking long rate lies on the SS curve as has been explained in section 3. The relationship between these two schedules and therefore between the two rates is easy to describe, as it corresponds to what has already been examined in section 2 above.

We see (from Appendix 2) that the slope of the SS curve is:

$$\frac{dr}{dy} |SS \equiv b = (\frac{\hat{R}}{\hat{R}-\rho_s}) k \lambda^{-1},$$

but by replacing ρ_s, the negative stable root, by its absolute value which we denote by β, and noting that the slope of the LM curve is $k\lambda^{-1}$, we can write:

$$\frac{dR}{dy} |SS = (\frac{\hat{R}}{\hat{R}+\beta}) \frac{dr}{dy} |LM ,$$

that is, that the slope of the SS curve is flatter than the slope of the LM curve by the factor relating changes in short and long rates described in section 2. There we found that:

$$\frac{dR}{dr} = \frac{\hat{R}}{\hat{R}+\beta}$$

when both rates were converging towards an equilibrium value of Rhat along exponential paths (with a half-life of $\ln(2/\beta)$). As the macroeconomic model of section 3 is an example of the sort of process described in more general terms in section 2, it is only to be expected that this formula will apply.

Since $\frac{\hat{R}}{\hat{R}+\beta}$ is always less than one, the SS locus must be flatter than the LM curve. How much flatter depends obviously on the speed of adjustment of output ψ. It can be seen from the characteristic equation that the stable root will tend to infinity in absolute value as ψ tends to infinity. So for a given slope of the LM curve, a flat SS locus means that adjustment towards equilibrium is quick, so the long rate principally reflects a future near equilibrium; conversely, when adjustment is slow, the SS locus will lie closer to the LM curve, as much time will be spent away from equilibrium.

5. MONETARY POLICY

Assuming the economy is initially in equilibrium we may analyse the operation of contractionary monetary policy as shown in Figure 11.3. We start with an open market sale of consols which was not anticipated by the market – an unanticipated contraction of the money supply. This will immediately shift the LM(r) curve over to LM′(r) and also shift the SS locus to S′S′. Thus on impact the short rate will rise from E to point C, and the long rate rise to point A. Thereafter, in the absence of any further (unforeseen) events, income and interest rates will contract gradually towards point E′, with short rates following the L curve and the consol rate moving along the SS curve (with the common speed of adjustment given by the stable root).

One would not expect a fully anticipated sale of consols to have the same effect on the price of consols, because the discrete rise in consol rates just described represents a capital loss to consol holders, a loss which they would take steps to avoid if the market is efficient and the information available in advance. To see what happens when an anticipated sale of consols takes place, consider the effects of contractionary monetary policy announced in advance.

Following the principles implicit in the preceding paragraph we want to find a path for consol prices that shows a discrete movement at the time of the announcement but *not* when the anticipated sale of consols takes place. Such a path is shown starting at B in Figure 11.3. What happens is that the economy at the time of the announcement moves away from its stable equilibrium at point E onto one of the 'unstable' paths which satisfy the efficiency conditions of equation (5).

Figure 11.3: Dynamics of adjustment after an announcement of a sale of consols

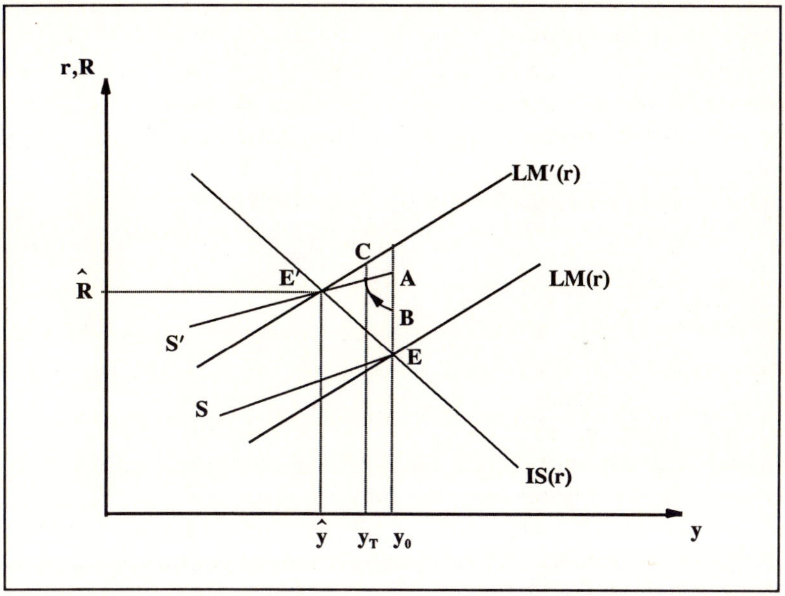

It is assumed to choose that path which, T periods later, will arrive on the stable locus S′S′. From period T onwards the consol rate will then follow S′S′ towards E′. Thus at time T there will be a sharp rise in the short rate of interest, from the lower LM(r) curve to the higher one, and there will be a peak in consol rates, when an announcement precedes the policy action. This is shown separately in Figure 11.4 to make it clearer. What this example illustrates is how anticipated future monetary policy will begin to exert its effects beforehand as the gilt-edged market discounts the future short-term rates.

Figure 11.4: Paths for long and short interest rates after an announcement of a sale of consols

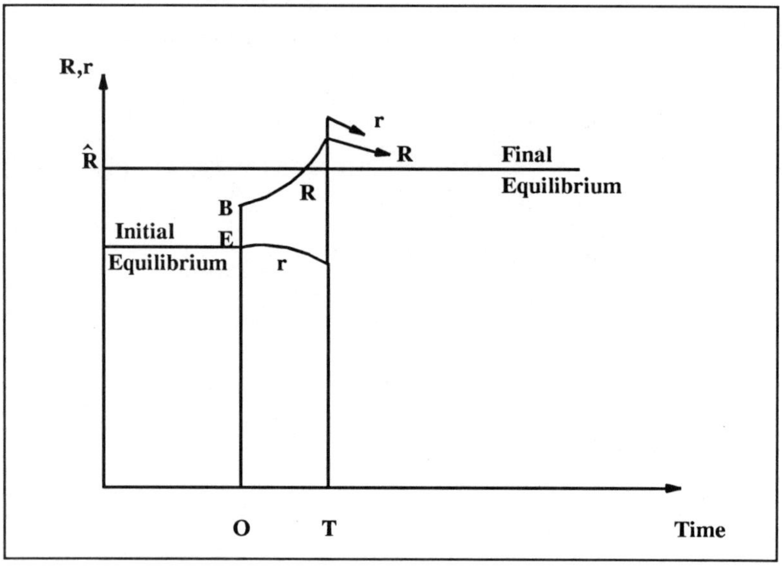

The market, however, may not fully believe an announcement about future policy. In Figure 11.5 we consider the case where the market attaches only a 50 per cent probability to the announcement of an open market sale of a given amount at time T. In this case the economy would pursue the path starting at B′ and ending on S″S″ at time T, where S″S″ corresponds to an open market operation of only *half* the announced magnitude.

At time T itself, the consol price will show a further discrete movement as the market discovers whether its scepticism was justified or not. If the authorities fail to sell any consols then the consol rate will fall back to C on SS and the economy will then approach the initial equilibrium, E, from the south-west along SS. If the authorities do actually carry out their announced policy, then the consol rate will rise further on S′S′ and the economy will proceed towards E′, approaching it from the north-west. If this analysis is correct it implies that a policy of making announcements which are not subsequently fulfilled will, over time, tend literally to discredit itself!

Figure 11.5 : The effect of a not fully credible announcement of a sale of consols.

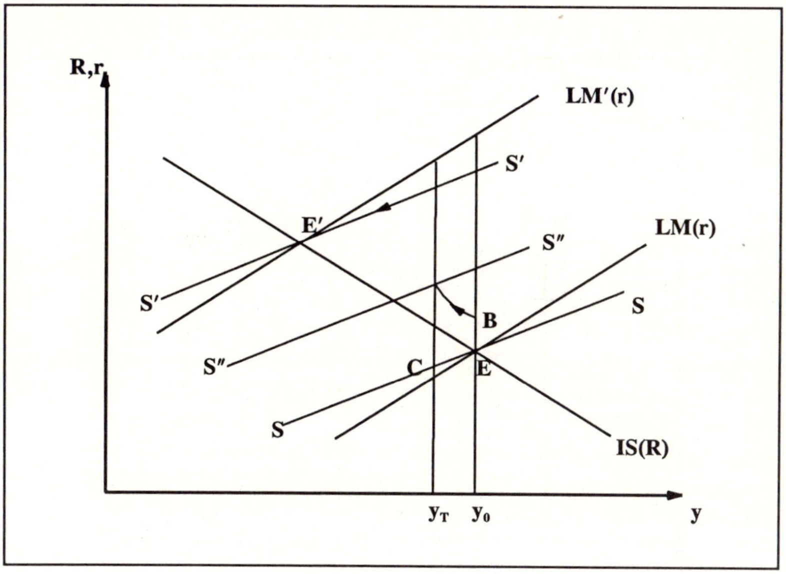

6. FISCAL POLICY

The same principles can now be applied to the analysis of fiscal policy, except in this case it is, of course, the IS curve which moves, or is expected to do so.

Starting with (unanticipated) contractionary fiscal policy, we see from Figure 11.6 that the stable locus falls to S′S′ when the IS curve shifts to IS′. Hence the long rate falls immediately from E to point A. The short rate, however, shows no change on impact, because neither the money stock nor the level of income have shown any change. Once again the long rate is anticipating future shorts, because it forecasts that future short rates will be lower as the short rate proceeds towards E′ along the LM curve. The long rate itself will continue to decline towards the same long-run equilibrium level, but more slowly, as it has jumped part of the way already.

Figure 11.6: The dynamics of contractionary fiscal policy

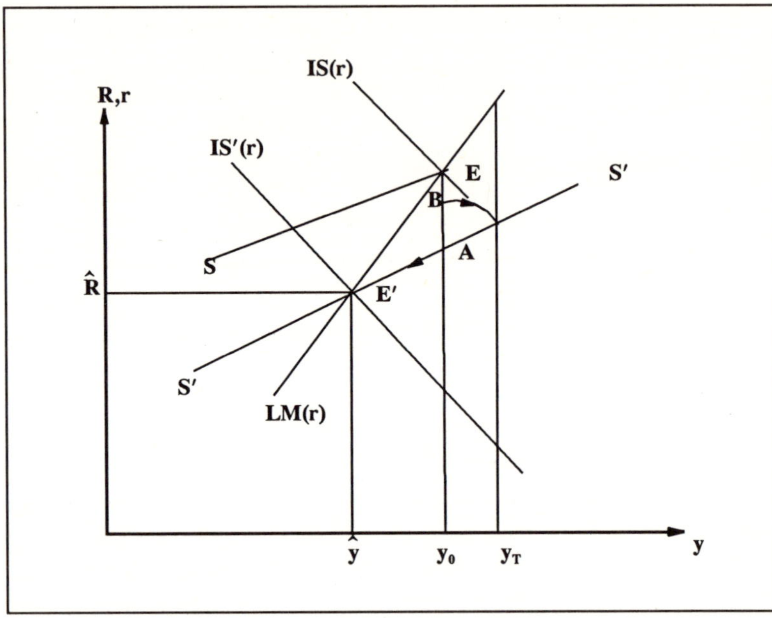

The case of anticipated future contractionary fiscal policy is slightly more tricky. In this case the gilt-edged market anticipates the lower future short rates associated with the fiscal contraction, but this lowers the gilt-edged rate which acts as a stimulating factor in the short run. This is shown in Figure 11.6, where the response to an announcement of fiscal contraction at time T is for the long rate to fall to B and for the economy to proceed in a south-easterly direction towards the S′S′ locus which is reached after T periods.

Once again the time path of interest rates, short and long, is illustrated separately in Figure 11.7 for the case when the announcement precedes the policy action.

Figure 11.7: Paths for long and short interest rates after a fiscal contraction

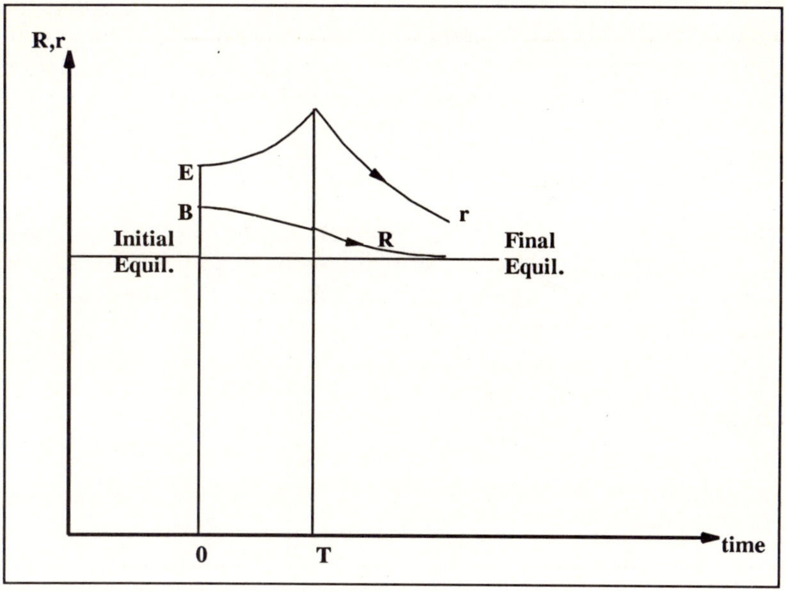

A feature of this example is that financial operators here forecast a recession and their consequent adjustment to gilt prices has led producers to expand investment and output. This may not be judged realistic; however, by allowing businessmen to forecast one could allow their forecasts of future contraction to offset this stimulant. This could be the subject of future research.

7. CONCLUSION

Speaking of the long term-rate of interest in Chapter 15 of the *General Theory* Keynes observed:

> It is evident, then, that the rate of interest is a highly psychological phenomenon ... at a level *above* the rate which corresponds to full employment, the long term market rate will depend, not only on the current policy of the monetary authority, but also on market expectations concerning its future policy. The short term rate of interest is easily controlled by the monetary authority ... but the long term rate may be more recalcitrant when once it has fallen to a level which, on the basis

> of past experience and present expectations of future monetary policy, is considered *unsafe* by representative opinion.

Keynes went on to emphasize the psychological factors which may play an important part in determining the long rate; but in this chapter the part which economic forecasting may play has been emphasized by assuming that market participants will use information about current and future policy, together with their knowledge of how the economy works, to determine the likely path of future interest rates and so the current long rate.

The unsung hero of the story we have told is the bold assumption that all market participants share the same information set, which happens to include a simple and correct account of how the economy works!

REFERENCE

Keynes, J.M. (1936), *The General Theory of Employment, Interest and Money*, London: Macmillan.

APPENDIX 1

To show the slope of the stable locus in Figure 11.1 is $\dfrac{\hat{R}}{(\hat{R}+\beta)}$.

The eigen vector determining the stable locus SS, measured from the point of equilibrium Rhat, rhat, labelled as E, can be written as (1,b), where b will measure the slope of SS. From the equation of motion, it is evident that this eigen vector must satisfy the condition:

$$\begin{bmatrix} -\beta & 0 \\ -\hat{R} & \hat{R} \end{bmatrix} \begin{bmatrix} 1 \\ b \end{bmatrix} = \rho_s \begin{bmatrix} 1 \\ b \end{bmatrix}$$

where ρ_s is the stable root of the left-hand matrix whose characteristic equation is:

$$\rho^2 - (\hat{R} - \beta)\rho - \beta\hat{R} = (\rho - \hat{R})(\rho + \beta) = 0.$$

Using the observation that the stable root is $-\beta$ and substituting this into the second equation above we find:

$$-\hat{R} + \hat{R}\,b = -\beta b \rightarrow b = \frac{\hat{R}}{\hat{R} + \beta}.$$

APPENDIX 2

To show that the stable locus in Figure 11.2 slopes upwards to the right

The eigen vector determining this stable locus, measured from the point of equilibrium yhat, Rhat, labelled as E in the Figure, can be written as (1,b) and b will measure the slope of the locus. From the equations of motion, (5), we see that it must satisfy the condition that:

$$\begin{bmatrix} \psi(\alpha - 1) & -\psi\gamma \\ \hat{R}k\lambda_{-1} & \hat{R} \end{bmatrix} \begin{bmatrix} 1 \\ b \end{bmatrix} = \rho_s \begin{bmatrix} 1 \\ b \end{bmatrix}$$

where ρ_s is the stable root of the left-hand matrix. That there exists a real negative root can be confirmed by observing that the discriminant of the characteristic equation is positive and that the determinant of the matrix is:

$$-\psi\,\hat{R}\,\Delta\,\lambda_{-1},$$

a negative number under the assumption that $\Delta > 0$.

Since ρ_s is real and negative, and we find from the second equation above that:

$$-\hat{R}\,k\,\lambda^{-1} + \hat{R}\,b = \rho_s b \rightarrow b = \frac{\hat{R}\,k\,\lambda^{-1}}{\hat{R} - \rho_s} > 0,$$

the existence of a real negative root is confirmed.

12. Monetary Neutrality and Non-Neutrality in Disequilibrium Models

Somnath Sen

When I first met Professor Jim Ford, around 1979, the so called 'rational expectations revolution in macroeconomics' was at its full height, at least in the UK. After having spent an academic lifetime studying expectations, Jim was understandably sceptical about 'revolutions', particularly in the field of expectations formation theories. Nevertheless, his active mind had immediately mastered the techniques involved in such research, and he quickly began an empirical demolition of the neutrality results. Straddling both theoretical and empirical domains he was quick to spot that rational expectations and structural neutrality (of policy) were conceptually different concepts and that one did not necessarily imply the other. This is all rather well appreciated now; but in the late 1970s the British macroeconomic establishment had yet to digest the implications of a conceptual separability. When I presented my own papers on rational expectations and non-neutrality under disequilibrium (Sen, 1980, 1981), they were well received at meetings of the Econometric Society. But journal referees were rather sceptical since rationality and disequilibrium seemed somewhat inconsistent with each other.

Another perennial interest that Jim had was for dynamic analysis. He was always critical of the standard mathematical treatment of dynamic models where differential (difference) equations with respect to time were used to analyse stability and comparative dynamics. He coined a term, 'pseudo dynamics', to emphasize the fundamental difference with real time analysis. The requirements of tractability forced him to use such models and, as was usual for him, the volume of research output with the use of such techniques was prolific. However, the search for fundamentals, and perfectionism, continued.

Jim was also continuously challenged by the history of economic analysis and the feeling that the great masters had 'said it all'. Having been in such close contact with Professors George Shackle and

John Hicks, it was natural that he would draw inspiration and ideas from the Olympians. Once again, he used classical concepts as catalysts to further his own prolific research without circumscribing the great originality of which he himself was capable.

1. INTRODUCTION

This chapter analyses the impact of monetary policy on real output and discusses the conditions for (non-)neutrality in a disequilibrium dynamic model under rational expectations. The basic model is classical in nature, in that it incorporates the tenants of the old quantity theory as well as that of the theory of loanable funds. However, even within such a classical (and monetarist) framework, it shows that money can be non-neutral. The chapter therefore brings together a number of research issues which enthused Jim for many years. It demonstrates that neutrality of anticipated monetary policy depends crucially on the structure of the underlying economic model, rather than on the assumption of rational expectations. More important, it shows that the impact of real money balance on aggregate demand (Patinkin's real balance effect (1965)) makes monetary policy, even if perfectly anticipated, non-neutral. The structural characteristics of the model exhibit disequilibrium in the sense that markets do not clear continuously and prices adjust in response to such disequilibria.

There are many reasons why markets fail to clear and prices are slow to respond to disequilibrium. Earlier analysis emphasized institutional rigidities brought on by differing transactions costs in setting wages and prices (Fischer, 1977; Begg, 1982). More recent analysis expands the range of costs which are associated with rapid changes, implied by market-clearing models, and hence increase the possibility of rigidities (Greenwald and Stiglitz, 1989). Dixit (1992) evolves an important 'theory of optimal inertia' whereby uncertainty and evolving information (possibly through learning) produces a high value of waiting before investment is undertaken. He summarizes this value of waiting succinctly:

> Three features are common to most investment decisions ... First, ... an investment entails some sunk costs, an expenditure that cannot be recouped if the action is reversed at a later date. Second, the economic environment has ongoing uncertainty, and information arrives gradually. Finally, an investment opportunity does not generally disappear if not taken immediately; the decision is not only whether to invest, but also

> when to invest. ... When these three conditions are present, waiting has positive value. In the evolving environment, time brings more information about the future prospects of the project. As long as the opportunity to invest remains available, a later decision can be a better one. And because there are sunk costs, it does not always pay to take a less perfect action and change it later (Dixit, 1992, p. 108).

As a result, small rigidities and frictions are exacerbated as decisions to invest (thus creating aggregate demand in macroeconomic models) are delayed. Concomitant price adjustments are correspondingly slow and markets fail to clear.

Nothing that has been said in the foregoing statements regarding disequilibrium and rigidities contradicts the essential tenets of the rational expectations hypothesis (REH) as stated by Muth (1961): 'expectations, since they are informed predictions of future events, are essentially the same as the predictions of relevant economic theory, and are therefore based on the structure of the relevant system describing the economy'. If the underlying structure exhibits disequilibrium, then the REH, being an efficient method of expectations formations, should take such disequilibrium features into account. Certainly, the assumption of strong-form efficiency implies the use of the complete model and the full information set which requires accounting for disequilibrium phenomena. It must also be stressed that when prices are sticky, and rationing exists, transactors may also form rational *quantity* expectations in addition to price expectations. Therefore, expectations on output and demand, based on the underlying model itself, will be a prominent characteristic of the formal models that are presented later.

But why, if expectations are formed rationally and agents respond to such expectations optimally, would disequilibrium persist? There are many candidate explanations: transaction costs, informational uncertainty, long-run implicit contracts, overlapping contracts, the gains from waiting when irreversible investment decisions are to be taken, the existence of sunk costs either in physical assets or firm-specific human capital investment, and so forth. Under these and other conditions, not only would disequilibrium be possible, but it even could be optimal given legitimate microtheoretic foundations (Hahn, 1980).

Disequilibrium analysis can be of two types. First, we can assume a tatonnement process by which no transactions take place unless the 'correct' prices have been called by the auctioneer. Alternatively, a better assumption would be to use the 'minimum' condition such that actual transaction is equal to the minimum of effective demand or supply. Coupled with this we need a price adjustment rule (assuming sticky but not fixed prices) which states that the change in prices is a function of excess demand in relevant markets. The speed of adjustment obviously needs to be finite, since infinite speed implies that equilibrium always prevails.

Lucas (1980) objects to the use of so-called 'free parameters'. Speed of adjustment of any variable in response to market disequilibrium is a 'free parameter' in the sense that it is exogenously specified (at a positive finite level) without being optimally derived. Disequilibrium theory postulates speeds of adjustment without saying what its value should be. On the other hand, in defence of such parameters Burmeister (1980a) points out important reasons why they can be utilized to achieve internal consistency of dynamic models. The convergence, stability and uniqueness properties of models using the REH can be strengthened by the judicious use of adjustment parameters and thus are probably essential if we are to get logically satisfactory models. Note also that since the REH depends crucially on model selection, if such models are non-convergent then it is useless to utilize the hypothesis *per se*. Further, there seems to be equal analytical validity in assuming that speeds of adjustment are all equal to infinity (the case of equilibrium) as in assuming that they are constant but less than infinity (as in disequilibrium). Finally, one can ideally construct a model with speeds of adjustment as functions of prices and then study their properties (although such models would generally be intractable without simulation). Overall, there seems to be good reason for the use of dynamic adjustment equations in a disequilibrium framework.

The central purpose of this chapter is to investigate whether perfectly anticipated money supply has real effects (monetary policy effectiveness) under rational expectations within the framework of a disequilibrium model. It is often claimed that when markets fail to clear, the new classical neutrality propositions do not hold generally. In other words, disequilibrium is a sufficient condition for non-neutrality. Honkapohja (1979) comments: 'Some differences of opinion remain, but the results suggest that the neutrality proposition in general fails to hold when markets do not continuously clear'. In like vein, Begg (1982) claims: 'Rational expectations can be applied in models which do not impose continuous market clearing and conventional stabilisation policy will then have conventional Keynesian effects, even though the policy is understood and incorporated into the process of expectations formation'. Even though the first part of the Begg statement is unquestionable, the second part regarding non-neutral monetary policy (the so-called conventional Keynesian effects) is controversial. As I shall show later, money can be neutral even under disequilibrium and simply assuming rigidities and slow price adjustment will not allow policy to be effective. Disequilibrium might be necessary, but it is certainly not sufficient to demonstrate monetary policy effectiveness.

I have repeatedly emphasized that the underlying parameters and structure of the model will determine whether anticipated monetary policy is neutral or not. Even under disequilibrium specifications, it can be shown that the neutrality result holds. Clearly there is a wide choice regarding model selection and how prices adjust when markets do not clear. In this chapter a class of disequilibrium rational expectations models are analysed which may be termed 'classical'. Evidence for the use of such adjustment rules are found in Metzler (1951) and Patinkin (1965).

The two major price variables within the postulated macroeconomic framework, are the aggregate price level and the real rate of interest. We assume that the price level adjusts to disequilibrium in the money market such that excess supply of money raises price. This accords with a monetarist explanation of inflation. We implicitly assume the transmission mechanism between money supply and price level even though there are intermediate steps. On the other hand, the interest rate reacts to conditions prevailing in the bond market. It can be shown that under the *classical* transmission mechanism, the interest rate adjusts positively to the excess demand for output. If aggregate demand for output exceeds supply, then investment is greater than saving. In a classical world, investment can be interpreted as the supply of loanable funds. Given an excess demand for loanable funds, we have an equivalent excess supply of bonds. (Demand for bonds = supply of saved funds. Supply of bonds = demand for investible funds.) Thus the price of bonds falls and the interest rate (inversely related to bond price) rises.

The quantity theory of money and the loanable funds theory of saving and investment can be used to yield the type of adjustment equations we have proposed. These assumptions were commonly used to analyse the behaviour of money, commodity and bond markets in the writings of the old classical school. It is instructive to analyse their behavioural equations in the light of the workings of the new classical macroeconomics.

Essentially, we wish to retain the spirit of classicism even within the disequilibrium framework. Thus our aggregate price and interest rate adjustments follow theories proposed by classical (monetarist) authors (see Patinkin, 1965). Quite often they arrived at conclusions regarding the long-run neutrality of money, even though on the transition path, money could have real effects. Our purpose is to evaluate the conclusions reached by *new* classical macroeconomics (Lucas *et al.*) in the light of some of the assumptions made by *old* classical macroeconomics. The quantity theory of money and loanable fund theory were important contributions made by the latter. How would they affect rational expectations conclusions?

Note that an important underlying proposition of classical theory was that real variables clear real markets while (monetary) variables clear nominal markets. In our model real rate of interest equilibrates the commodity/real bond markets, while the money price level equilibrates the money market.

The purpose of the chapter may therefore be briefly summarized. A disequilibrium model of rational expectations must postulate suitable adjustment rules for price level and interest rate, in the presence of excess demand (or supply). The choice of rule is a matter of judgement. We wish to remain as close as possible to the central tenets of classical macro models, and see whether standard rational expectations conclusions hold or not. We invoke two basic theories – the quantity theory of money and the loanable funds theory of bond financing – to specify the structural characteristics of the disequilibrium model. Given this classical framework we intend to analyse solution paths of models with rational expectations and study the neutrality question.

In the next section, we construct models which have disequilibrium in both commodity and money markets. Adjustment rules follow classical tradition. Three types of model are used. First, anticipatory price-setting is postulated and prices depend on *expected* excess demand. Secondly, we assume that prices change according to *actual* excess demands. In both these models real balance effects are ignored. In the third type we assume that the stock of real balance affects aggregate demand. These three types of model are discussed given a simplifying assumption that expected future price inflation is equal to zero. The results can be extended, and similar conclusions derived, when expected price inflation is non-zero.

Our primary purpose in these models is to study the multiplicity (or uniqueness) of solution paths and then see whether anticipated money is neutral or not for some or all of these paths. It is shown that disequilibrium (of the classical type) *per se* does not necessarily give non-neutrality. Rather, it is the structure of the model which produces relevant policy effectiveness conclusions. Models without real balance effects always show money is neutral. Models with real balance effects invariably give non-neutral results. Thus, neither rational expectations nor disequilibrium determine whether policy is effective or not. It is usually the assumptions of the underlying *model* that produce relevant policy conclusions.

2. THE MODELS

The first model has anticipatory price setting rules. We have the following system of equations:

$$y_t = a_1 (p_t - {}_{t-1}p_t^*) + u_{1t} \tag{1}$$

$$e_t = b_1 r_t + u_2 \tag{2}$$

$$m_t^d = p_t + c_1 r_t + c_2 e_t + u_3 \tag{3}$$

$$p_t - p_{t-1} = \lambda(m_t^s - {}_{t-1}m_t^{d*}) + v_t \tag{4}$$

$$r_t - r_{t-1} = \Omega({}_{t-1}e_t^* - {}_{t-1}y_t^*) + w_t \tag{5}$$

$$m_t^s = m_t + u_{4t} , \tag{6}$$

such that $a_1 > 0$, $b_1 < 0$, $c_1 < 0$, $c_2 > 0$, $\lambda > 0$, $\Omega > 0$ (where y_t, e_t, m^s_t, m^d_t and p_t are logs of output supplied, output demand, money demand, money supply, and price level; r_t is the rate of interest, and no distinction is made between real and nominal rates since expected price inflation is zero. A star (*) indicates an expected value).

Expectations for *all* variables are formally rational. Thus for any variable x_t, its expected value formed at period t−1 is given as ${}_{t-1}x_t^*$ = E[x_t/information available at time t−1] where E is the mathematical expectations operator. In our model rational expectations are assumed for money demand, effective demand (e_t), aggregate demand (y_t) and price level (p_t). To simplify the notation, we shall write from now on, x_t^*, for variables whose expectations are formed in t−1. Care will be taken to state explicitly the date of expectations formation, if it is not t−1.

Equation (1) is the Lucas supply function expressed in *deviation* form from the natural rate. Thus in all subsequent analysis we drop an extra term invoking factors which determine the natural rate of unemployment. Similarly, aggregate demand (in deviation form) is given by equation (2) as a function of the rate of interest (real or nominal). Equation (3) gives the demand function for money. (A model similar to (1) (2) (3), but only for an *equilibrium* situation, has been used by Woglom, 1979. It can be shown that if $y_t = e_t$ and $m_t^d = m_t^s$, money is neutral.) The supply of money in equation (6) is kept arbitrary to make the monetary rule as general as possible. It is easy to use specific rules and conclusions remain invariant. Money supply is perfectly anticipated at level m_t except for white noise terms.

Equation (4) uses the classical monetarist rule that prices respond positively to an increase in the supply of money. If the supply of money (perfectly forecast except for error U_{4t}) is greater than the expected demand for money, the price level will rise from its previous value. Thus inflation depends on the *expected* excess supply of money. Note that price setting is anticipatory in the sense that p_t is fixed at the beginning of period t with information from t-1 used to forecast rationally the expected value of m_t^d. In an exactly analogous fashion, the interest rate is determined at the start of period t and e_t^* and y_t^* are predicted rationally. It is assumed that expected excess demand for output (implying investment greater than saving) will cause an expected excess supply of bonds. This will lower the price of bonds and raise the rate of interest.

The error terms u_{it}, v_t, and w_t are white noise terms, mean zero, constant variance and serially uncorrelated. We may assume without loss of generality that $u_{it} = 0$ and concentrate on the errors v_t and w_t in the price/interest rate formation equation.

The semi-reduced form of the equation with endogenous variables p_t, y_t, e_t, m_t^d and r_t in terms of exogenous and expected variables can be written as:

$$p_t = p_{t-1} + \lambda(m_t - m_t^{d*}) + v_t \tag{7}$$

$$r_t = r_{t-1} + \Omega(e_t^* - y_t^*) + w_t \tag{8}$$

$$y_t = a_1 p_{t-1} + a_1\lambda(m_t - m_t^{d*}) - a_1 p_t^* + U_1 \tag{9}$$

$$m_t^d = p_{t-1} + (m_t - m_t^{d*}) + (c_1 + c_2 b_1)[r_{t-1} + \Omega(e_t^* - y_t^*)] + U_2 \tag{10}$$

$$e_t = b_1 r_{t-1} + b_1\Omega(e_t^* - y_t^*) + U_3 . \tag{11}$$

We now invoke the minimum condition from disequilibrium theory. Assume actual output (y_t^a) is the minimum of supply and demand. Thus:

$$y_t^a = \min(y_t, e_t). \tag{12}$$

Now taking expectations, from (7) we get:

$$p_t^* = p_{t-1} + \lambda[m_t - m_t^{d*}] = p_t . \tag{13}$$

Thus, using (1) it is clear that y_t is unaffected by money supply m_t, since $y_t = u_{1t}$. Similarly from (1) or (9),

$$y_t^* = 0. \tag{14}$$

From (11), taking expectations of e_t we get:

$$e_t^* = b_1 r_{t-1} + b_1 \Omega e_t^* - b_1 \Omega y_t^*$$

or

$$e_t^* = (b_1/1-b_1\Omega) r_{t-1} .$$

Substituting in (8):

$$r_t = r_{t-1} + \Omega[b_1/1-b_1\Omega] r_{t-1} + w_t$$

or

$$r_t = [1/1-b_1\Omega] r_{t-1} + w_t , \tag{15}$$

From (2) therefore:

$$e_t = (b_1/1-b_1\Omega)r_{t-1} + u_{2t}\ . \tag{16}$$

It is clear that r_t is a function of its past values (from (15)) and this is not influenced by money supply, m_t. Therefore, e_t dependent on r_{t-1} is not affected by *any* m_{t-1} (i = 0, 1, 2, ...). We therefore see from (1), (12), (15) and (16) that *both* y_t and e_t cannot be influenced by anticipated monetary policy. Actual output, y_t^a, being independent of m_t, we have neutrality, and anticipated money rules are ineffective in affecting output.

We now turn to the other part of our enquiry – the analysis of solution paths. From (4) take expectations, substitute for e_t* and y_t* and solve for m_t^{d}* to get:

$$m_t^{d*} = \frac{p_{t-1}}{1+\lambda} + \frac{\lambda}{1+\lambda}m_t + \left(\frac{c_1+c_2b_1}{1+\lambda}\right)\left(\frac{1}{1-b_1\Omega}\right)r_{t-1}\ , \tag{17}$$

Given:

$$p_t^* = p_{t-1} + \lambda(m_t - m_t^{d*}) = p_{t-1} + \lambda m_t - \frac{\lambda}{1+\lambda}p_{t-1} - \frac{\lambda^2 m_t}{1+\lambda}$$

$$+ \left(\frac{c_1+c_2b_1}{1+\lambda}\right)\left(\frac{1}{1-b\Omega}\right)r_{t-1}\ . \tag{18}$$

Using (15) and (18) we can express r_t and p_t* as functions of r_{t-1} and p_{t-1} *plus* exogenous and random variables.

$$\begin{bmatrix} r_t \\ p_t^* \end{bmatrix} = \begin{bmatrix} \frac{1}{1-b_1\Omega} & 0 \\ \lambda\left(\frac{c_1+c_2b_1}{1+\lambda}\right)\left(\frac{1}{1-b_1\Omega}\right) & \frac{1}{1+\lambda} \end{bmatrix} \begin{bmatrix} r_{t-1} \\ p_{t-1} \end{bmatrix}$$

$$+ \text{ exogenous and random terms.} \tag{19}$$

The Jacobian matrix A equals

$$\begin{bmatrix} \left(\frac{1}{1-b_1\Omega}\right) & 0 \\ \lambda\frac{(c_1+c_2b_1)}{(1+\lambda)}\frac{1}{(1-b_1\Omega)} & \frac{1}{(1+\lambda)} \end{bmatrix}$$

We may now use a theorem due to Blanchard and Kahn (1980) regarding solution paths of the difference equation system (19). Note that in our model, the rate of interest in any period t, that is r_t, is fully determined by information available at period t−1. Since r_t depends on e_t^* whose expectations are formed in t−1, the interest rate variable r_t is a *predetermined* variable. On the other hand p_t depends on current shocks at period t (through m_t^s and is therefore a 'jump' or *non-predetermined variable*. Therefore in our model, we have one predetermined variable and one jump variable. To analyse the possible solutions to (19) we have to find the number of unstable (or stable) characteristic roots of (19).

Clearly the trace of the matrix is:

$$\left(\frac{1}{1-b_1\Omega}\right) + \left(\frac{1}{1+\lambda}\right),$$

and the determinant of the matrix is:

$$\left(\frac{1}{1-b_1\Omega}\right)\left(\frac{1}{1+\lambda}\right).$$

Therefore it is obvious that the roots are $(1/(1-b_1\Omega))$ and $(1/(1+\lambda))$. Since $\lambda>0$, $b_1<0$, $\Omega>0$, both roots are less than unity. Therefore, the number of unstable roots (zero) is less than the number of jump or non-predetermined variables (one). Under these conditions, there are an infinite number of solution paths to the system.

We may summarize our conclusions in the following proposition:

Proposition 1: There are an infinite number of possible solutions to the model set out in equations (1) to (6). However, all solution paths exhibit neutrality, that is perfectly anticipated monetary policy does not affect either aggregate demand or supply.

We now turn to our next model (within the basic framework) and assume that price-setting is no longer anticipatory. Now price changes depend on actual rather than expected excess demands in respective markets. Once again we wish to analyse the neutrality proposition as well as study the existence (and possible multiplicity) of rational expectation solution paths. We have:

$$y_t = a_1\ (p_t - p_t^*) \tag{20}$$

$$e_t = b_1 r_t \tag{21}$$

$$m_t^d = p_t + c_1 r_t + c_2 e_2 \tag{22}$$

$$m_t^s = m_t \tag{23}$$

$$p_t - p_{t-1} = \lambda(m_t - m_t^d) + v_t \tag{24}$$

$$r_t - r_{t-1} = \Omega(e_t - y_t) + w_t\ . \tag{25}$$

Structurally, this is similar to the first model except that in price and interest adjustment equations (24) and (25), actual variables have replaced anticipated ones. Once again the dynamic adjustments follow classical modes in that the price level responds to excess demand in the money market and interest rate changes are a function of excess demand in the output (bond) market. From (21) and (22):

$$m_t^d = p_t + (c_1 + c_2 b_1) r_t\ . \tag{26}$$

From (24) and (25):

$$p_t = \frac{p_{t-1}}{1+\lambda} + \frac{\lambda}{1+\lambda} m_t - \frac{\lambda}{1+\lambda} (c_1 + c_2 b_1) r_t\ . \tag{27}$$

From (25), (20), (21) and (27) we get:

$$B\,r_t = r_{t-1} - \frac{\Omega a_1}{1+\lambda} p_{t-1} - \frac{\Omega a_1 \lambda}{1+\lambda} m_t + \Omega a_1 p_t^* \tag{28}$$

where

$$B = 1 - \Omega b_1 - \frac{\Omega a_1 \lambda}{1+\lambda}(c_1 + c_2 b_1) > 0$$

and B > 1.

Thus (28) may be rewritten as:

$$r_t = J_1 r_{t-1} + J_2 p_{t-1} + J_3 m_t + J_4 p_t^* \tag{29}$$

where $J_1 = 1/B$, $J_2 = -[\Omega a_1/B(1+\lambda)]$, $J_3 = -[\Omega a_1 \lambda/B(1+\lambda)]$, $J_4 = \Omega a_1/B$ and $J_1 > 0$, $J_2 < 0$, $J_3 < 0$, $J_4 > 0$.

Substituting (29) into (27) we get:

$$p_t = K_1 p_{t-1} + K_2 m_t + K_3 r_{t-1} + K_4 p_t^* \tag{30}$$

where:

$$K_1 = \frac{1}{1+\lambda} - \frac{\lambda}{1+\lambda}(c_1 + c_2 b_1) J_2$$

$$K_2 = \frac{\lambda}{1+\lambda} - \frac{\lambda}{1+\lambda}(c_1 + c_2 b_1) J_3$$

$$K_3 = -\frac{\lambda}{1+\lambda}(c_1 + c_2 b_1) J_1$$

$$K_4 = -\frac{\lambda}{1+\lambda}(c_1 + c_2 b_1) J_4 .$$

Taking expectations of (30) we get:

$$p_t^* = \frac{K_1}{1-K_4} p_{t-1} + \frac{K_2}{1-K_4} m_t + \frac{K_3}{1-K_4} r_{t-1} . \tag{31}$$

Substituting in (29) we get:

$$r_t = (J_1 + \frac{J_4K_3}{1-K_4})r_{t-1} + (J_2 + \frac{J_4K_1}{1-K_4})\ P_{t-1}$$

$$+ (J_3 + \frac{J_4K_2}{1-K_4})\ m_t + \text{ random terms.} \qquad (32)$$

Once again, equations (32) and (31) may be investigated to find the nature of rational expectation solution paths. The relevant Jacobian is now A_2 equals:

$$\begin{bmatrix} J_1 + \dfrac{J_4K_3}{(1-K_4)} & J_2 + \dfrac{J_4K_1}{(1-K_4)} \\ \dfrac{K_3}{(1-K_4)} & \dfrac{K_1}{(1-K_4)} \end{bmatrix} \qquad (33)$$

Observe that the determinant of A_2 (giving the product of the roots) is:

$$\det A_2 = J_1/(1+\lambda)(1-K_4).$$

Since:

$J_1 = 1/B$ and $B > 1$, therefore $J_1 < 1$;

$(1+\lambda) > 1$ since $\lambda > 0$

$(1-K_4) = 1 + \lambda\ (1-(c_1+c_2b_1)J_4/1+\lambda > 1$ since $(c_1+c_2b_1) < 0$.

Therefore det $A_2 < 1$. Thus either both roots are less than unity (both roots stable) or one root is less than unity (one root stable). So the number of unstable roots is either zero or one.

However, note that unlike in the previous case both variables are non-predetermined in this model given by (20) to (25). This is because both p_t and r_t can respond to current shocks and news and are determined on the basis of events in period t. We have therefore the number of non-predetermined variables (2) greater than the number of unstable roots (1). Thus there must be an infinite number of solutions.

To analyse neutrality, observe that e_t is a function of r_t alone. Therefore the effect of money supply increase (m_t) must operate through r_t. We have to evaluate in (32) the coefficients $[J_3+J_4K_2/1-K_4]$ to get the current effect of m_t and the coefficient $[J_2+J_4K_1/1-K_4]$ to get the past effects of m_{t-1} via its influence on price level.

It can be easily calculated that:

$$J_3 + \frac{J_4K_2}{1-K_4} \quad \frac{J_3+\lambda J_3+J_4\lambda}{1-K_4} = 0 \tag{34}$$

and

$$J_2 + \frac{J_4K_1}{1-K_4} = \frac{J_2+J_2\lambda+J_4}{1-K_4} = 0\ . \tag{35}$$

Thus from (32), (34) and (35):

$$r_t = (J_1 + \frac{J_4K_3}{1-K_4})\, r_{t-1} + \text{ random errors}$$

or

$$r_t = (J_1/1-K_4)r_{t-1} + \text{ random errors.} \tag{36}$$

Once again it is clear that r_t depends on its past history and is not influenced by monetary shocks. Since:

$$e_t = (b_1J_1/1-K_4)r_{t-1} + \text{random errors.} \tag{37}$$

aggregate demand is therefore uninfluenced by monetary policy. It is obvious that y_t is also uninfluenced by anticipated money, since $p_t - p_t^*$ is equal to random errors. Thus actual output $y_t^a = \min(y_t, e_t)$ is not affected by systematic monetary rules.

We sum up the results in the proposition:

Proposition 2 Even if price-setting is not anticipatory and all prices adjust to current events, there are an infinite number of rational expectation solution paths in our classical model. However, all these paths exhibit neutrality.

The two disequilibrium models studied until now highlight an important conclusion. Neutrality (or non-neutrality) does not necessarily depend on disequilibrium behaviour. We set classical price adjustment rules and found that given rational expectation (of all price and quantity variables), perfectly anticipated money stock does not affect the structure of output.

We now proceed to a third model which is essentially similar to the first one (given by equations (1) to (6)), except that a real balance effect is introduced. Since our adjustment rules are classical in spirit, it is quite appropriate to assume that the stock of real balance affects aggregate demand (see Patinkin (1965)). The Pigou effect has been used by traditional neutralists to counter Keynesian objections to the existence of full employment equilibrium output. It seems logical and valid therefore to analyse the neutrality proposition within rational expectation assumptions in a model where real balance effects are present.

We therefore have:

$$y_t = a_1 (p_t - p_t^*) \tag{38}$$

$$e_t = b_1 r_t + b_2 m_t - b_2 p_t \tag{39}$$

$$m_t^d = p_t + c_1 r_t + c_2 e_t \tag{40}$$

$$m_t^s = m_t \tag{41}$$

$$p_t - p_{t-1} = \lambda[m_t - m_t^*] + v_t \tag{42}$$

$$r_t - r_{t-1} = \Omega[e_t^* - y_t^*] + w_t \tag{43}$$

$$\text{Actual output} = \text{minimum } (y_t, e_t). \tag{44}$$

Once again, price- and interest rate-setting is anticipatory. The new innovation is that positive real balance effects are assumed given $b_2 > 0$.

From (37) and (38):

$$m_t^d = p_t + c_1 r_t + c_2 b_1 r_t + c_2 b_2 m_t - c_2 b_2 p_t \, . \tag{45}$$

Therefore:

$$p_t = \frac{m_t^d}{1-c_2 b_2} - \frac{c_1 + c_2 b_1}{1-c_2 b_2} r_t - \frac{c_2 b_2}{1-c_2 b_2} m_t \, . \tag{46}$$

From (42):

$$p_t = p_{t-1} + \lambda m_t - \lambda m_t^{d*} + v_t \, . \tag{47}$$

Equating (46) and (47) and using (43) we get:

$$m_t^d = (c_1 + c_2 b_1)(r_{t-1} + e_t^* \Omega - \Omega y_t^*) + m_t(c_2 b_2 + \lambda - \lambda c_2 b_2)$$

$$+ p_{t-1}(1-c_2 b_2) - \lambda(1-c_2 b_2) m_t^{d*}. \tag{48}$$

(For simplicity we drop from now on all terms involving errors v_t and w_t. This does not affect the final conclusions.)

From (39) and (43):

$$e_t = b_1(r_{t-1} + \Omega e_t^* - \Omega y_t^*) + b_2 m_t - b_2 p_{t-1} - b_2 \lambda m_t - b_2 \lambda m_t^{d*}. \tag{49}$$

Taking expectations of (48) and (49) we get two equations for m_t^{d*} and e_t^* which may be written as

$$m_t^{d*}(1 + \lambda(1-c_2 b_2)) - (c_1 + c_2 b_1)\Omega e_t^* = \hat{L}_1 \tag{50}$$

$$m_t^{d*}(\lambda b_2) - (1 - b_1 \Omega) e_t^* = \hat{L}_2 \, , \tag{51}$$

where

$$\hat{L}_1 = m_t(c_2b_2+\lambda c_2b_2) + (c_1+c_2b_1)r_{t-1} + (1-c_2b_2)p_{t-1} \tag{52}$$

and

$$\hat{L}_2 = (b_2\lambda-b_2)m_t - b_1r_{t-1} + b_2P_{t-1} \tag{53}$$

Equations (50) and (51) can be used to solve for m_t^{d*} and e_t^*. When these values are substituted into equation (42) we get the expression for p_t. Taking expectations of p_t we can derive p_t^*. Similarly, substituting the value of e_t^* in equation (43) we get an equation in r_t (note v_t^*). These are extremely tedious to solve, but one can derive in an exactly analogous fashion to the first model, a Jacobian matrix, A_3, such that:

$$\begin{bmatrix} p_t^* \\ r_t \end{bmatrix} = A_3 \begin{bmatrix} p_{t-1} \\ r_{t-1} \end{bmatrix} \quad + \text{ exogenous and random terms.}$$

Unlike the first model, it is not possible to predict the nature of the characteristic roots derived from matrix A_3. However, the roots depend crucially on the values of λ and Ω, the speed of adjustment terms. Thus existence of solution, multiplicity or uniqueness, and convergence depends explicitly on the values of λ and Ω (similar results have been obtained by Burmeister, 1980b).

It is possible however to study the neutrality proposition in some detail. From the values of m_t^{d*} and e_t^* we can get the values of p_t and r_t. Substituting these into the expression for e_t in (39) we can get the value of e_t as a function of r_{t-1}, p_{t-1} and m_t. The *coefficient* of m_t is given by the following:

$$[b_1\Omega+b_1\Omega\lambda(1-c_2b_2) + b_2\lambda(c_1+c_2b_1)\Omega-b_2\lambda]b_2(\lambda-1)$$

$$+ [b_1\Omega\lambda b_2\Omega(c_1+c_2b_1) - b_2\lambda(1-b_1\Omega)][c_2b_2+\lambda-c_2\lambda b_2] = \delta e_t/\delta m_t > 0$$

after suitable substitution.

Thus if the stock of money increases, the aggregate demand increases. If actual output is equal to demand, then it will increase too. Therefore money is *non-neutral* and perfectly anticipated money has real effects. Note that this coefficient is positive given $b_2 > 0$. If $b_2 = 0$, $\delta e_t / \delta m_t = 0$ (b_2 gives the real balance effect).

We have proved:

Proposition 3 If real balance effects are present, then the existence and uniqueness of rational expectation solution paths depends explicitly on the speed of adjustment: nothing specific can be predicted unless the actual values of λ and Ω are known. However, for any solution path, money is non-neutral and anticipated monetary policy is effective.

4. CONCLUSION

Analysis of classical macroeconomic transmission mechanisms has had a long and distinguished history. Policy shocks were transmitted through the economy and affected major macro variables through two fundamental methods, embodied in the quantity theory of money and the theory of loanable funds. One of the major purposes of this chapter was to study the implications of rational expectations in a framework put forward by pre-Keynesian economists. We analysed the conclusions of new classical macroeconomics in the light of the principles of old classical macroeconomics.

The other strand of the chapter was to study alternative adjustment rules under non-clearing market disequilibrium. Since, in general, adjustment rules are *ad hoc* ('free parameters'), it is important to see how sensitive major conclusions are to different specifications. As mentioned earlier, our adjustment rules followed classical postulates, thus integrating disequilibrium methods with traditional concepts.

The general supposition that disequilibrium *per se* leads to non-neutral effects with perfectly anticipated money, is found to be incorrect. The structure of the model determines the nature of solution paths and gives suitable results regarding policy effectiveness (or otherwise). Models with real balance effects show that even under rational expectations, perfectly anticipated stock of money can influence effective demand, and thus under Keynesian unemployment can have real effects in the short run. On the other hand, without real balance effects affecting aggregate demand, money is neutral for all possible solution paths. Assumptions regarding the existence of non-zero expected rate of inflation do not influence the final results. These disequilibrium conclusions agree broadly with those found for equilibrium models.

Neither rational expectations nor disequilibrium by itself is sufficient to give neutral (or non-neutral) monetary policy. The structure of the model and underlying behavioural assumptions are crucial in the debate as to whether anticipated money can influence output and employment, as well as to find out how strong these monetary policy effects will be in practice.

REFERENCES

Begg, D. (1982), *The Rational Expectations Revolution in Macoeconomics*, Oxford: Philip Allan.

Blanchard, O.J. and C.M. Kahn (1980), 'The Solution of Linear Difference Models Under Rational Expectations', *Econometrica.*

Burmeister, E. (1980a), 'On Some Conceptual Issues in Rational Expectations Modelling', *Journal of Money, Credit and Banking.*

Burmeister, E. (1980b), *Capital Theory and Dynamics,* Cambridge: Cambridge University Press

Dixit, A.K. (1992), 'Investment and Hysterisis', *Journal of Economic Perspectives,* Winter

Fischer, S. (1977), 'Long-Term Contracts, Rational Expectations and the Optimal Money Supply Rule', *Journal of Political Economy*

Greenwald, B and J.E. Stiglitz (1989), 'Towards a Theory of Rigidities', *American Economic Review Papers and Proceedings.*

Hahn, F. (1980), 'Monetarism and Economic Theory', *Economica.*

Honkapohja, S. (1979), 'Monetary Non-Neutrality with Anticipatory Price Setting and Rational Expectations', *Economic Letters.*

Lucas, R.E. (1980), 'Methods and Problems in Business Cycle Theory', Paper presented at the American Enterprise Institute Conference on Rational Expectations.

Metzler, L.A. (1951), 'Wealth, Saving and the Rate of Interest' *Journal of Political Economy.*

Muth, J.F. (1961), 'Rational Expectations and the Theory of Price Movements', *Econometrica.*

Patinkin, D. (1965), *Money, Interest and Prices*, London: Harper Row.

Sen, S. (1980), 'Rational Expectations and Monetary Policy in a Disequilibrium Model', Paper presented at the 4th World Congress of the Econometric Society, Aix-en-Provence.

Sen, S. (1981), 'Rational Expectations and Non-Neutrality under Dis-equilibrium', Paper presented to the European Meeting of the Econometric Society, Amsterdam.

Woglom, G. (1979), 'Rational Expectations and Monetary Policy in a Simple Macroeconomic Model', *Quarterly Journal of Economics.*

Bibliography: Professor J.L. Ford

1962

'The Leontief Paradox and the Ohlin–Heckscher Theory of the Basis of Commodity Trade', *Economia Internazionale,* May, pp. 3–25.

'Patinkin on Price Flexibility and Employment', *Indian Economic Journal*, pp. 82–9.

'Two Propositions in Economic Theory and the Gains from the Proposed European Common Market', *Rivista Internazionale di Science Economiche e Commerciali (RISEC)*, December, pp. 3–14.

1963

'General Observations on a 'Dynamic' Theory of Commodity Trade', *Economia Internazionale,* February, pp. 3–15.

'Trade and Factory-Prices: two cases', *Indian Economic Journal,* July, pp. 443– 9.

'The Ohlin–Heckscher Theory of the Basis of Commodity Trade', *Economic Journal*, September, pp. 458–76.

'Flexibility and Employment', *Economia Internazionale,* November, pp. 3–8.

'Measures of Factor-Endowments and of Factor-Intensities', *Oxford Economic Papers,* November, pp. 273–7.

1964

'A Note on the Investment Decision', *Economie Appliquée,* January–February, pp. 113–6.

'The Effects of Commodity Trade on Factor Prices', *Economia Internazionale,* February, pp. 3–34.

1965

The Ohlin–Heckscher Theory of Commodity Trade, London: Asia Publishing House.

'Competition and a Trade Model', *Kyklos*, Fasc. 2, pp. 333–4.

'Some Statistical Analysis of the Long-Term Rate of Interest in the UK 1948–1963', *Oxford Bulletin of Economics and Statistics*, November, pp. 287–97 (with T. Stark).

'On Structure of, and Gains from, International Trade', *Kyklos*, Fasc. 4, pp. 670–84.

1966

'On an Aspect of International Trade Theory', *Manchester School*, January, pp. 81–6.

'More on the Factor-Price Equalisation Theorem', *Kyklos*, Fasc. 2, pp. 260–6.

'On an Aspect of Customs Union's Theory', *Relations Economiques Internationales*, Cahier (Series P) of IESA, Paris, pp. 57–65.

'Protection and the Real Return of the Scarce Factor', *Manchester School*, May, pp. 179–88.

'Measurement of Capital, the Production Function, and Relative Factor Endowments', *Economic Journal*, June, pp. 425–28.

'A Note on a Macroeconomic Model and the Postwar UK Economy', *Kyklos*, Fasc. 4, pp. 719–23 (with T. Stark).

'Measurement of Capital and Neutral and Technical Progress; or the Non-Equivalence of the Hicks and Harrod Definitions', *RISEC*, October, pp. 984–96.

Review of: J.W.F. Rowe, 'Primary Commodities in International Trade', *American Economic Review*, December, pp. 952–4.

1967

Long and Short-Term Interest Rates: An Econometric Study, Oxford: Basil Blackwell; New York: A.M. Kelley (with T. Stark).

'Non-Identity of Production Conditions With and Without Factor-Reversal Points and Patterns of Trade', *Economia Internazionale*, August, pp. 3–13.

'The Average Age of Equipment and the Rate of Return on Capital', *Metroeconomica*, February, pp. 132–5.

'On Factor-Mobility as a Substitute for Commodity Trade', *Kyklos,* Fasc. 2, pp. 767–8.
'The Role and Concept of Capital in the Classical Theory of Comparative Costs', *RISEC,* March, pp. 431–48.

1968

'Notes on the Factor-Proportions Theory of International Trade', *Relations Economiques Internationales,* Cahier (Series P), of IESA, Paris, July, pp. 1015–27.
'On the Equivalence of the Classical and the Factor Proportions Models in Explaining International Trade Patterns: A Rejoinder', *Manchester School,* March, pp. 79–82.
'More on the Equivalence of Trade Models in Explaining Trade Patterns', *Manchester School,* December, pp. 393–5.
Review of: B. Ohlin, 'Interregional and International Trade' (revised edition, 1967), *Economica,* August, pp. 312–13.

1969

'The Heckscher–Ohlin Theory with Three Factors of Production', IESA, Cahier (Series P), July, pp. 1985–2014.
'Variable Returns to Scale and the Factor-Price Equalisation Theorem', *RISEC,* August, pp. 756–80.
'Cost Functions for the Water Supply Industry in the UK', *Journal of Industrial Economics,* November, pp. 53–63 (with J. Warford).
'Specific Factors of Production and the Ricardian and Ohlinian Doctrines', *Yorkshire Bulletin*, November, pp. 119–31.

1972

Editor with C.F. Carter: *Uncertainty and Expectations in Economics,* Oxford: Basil Blackwell; New York: A. M. Kelley.
'Expectations, Uncertainty and the Term-Structure of Interest Rates', essay in C.F Carter and J.L. Ford (eds), *Uncertainty and Expectations in Economics,* pp. 74–121 (with J.C. Dodds).
Review of: B.N.A. Lietaer, 'Financial Management of Foreign Exchange', *Economic Journal*, June, pp. 148–50.
Review of: Harry G. Johnson, 'The Two-Sector Model of General Equilibrium', *Kyklos,* Fasc. 2, pp. 408–10.

1973

The Nature of Economic Thought, University of Sheffield, December (inaugural lecture).

Review of: E. Claassen and P. Salin (eds), 'Stabilisation Policies in Interdependent Economies', *Economic Journal,* March, pp. 277- 80.

Review of: F.Machlup, W.S. Salant and L.Tarshis (eds), 'International Mobility and Movement of Capital', *Economic Journal,* December, pp. 1307–10.

Review of: H.G. Johnson (ed.), 'Readings in British Monetary Economics' (1972), *Kyklos*, Fasc. 1, pp. 197–9.

1974

Expectations, Uncertainty and the Term-Structure of Interest Rates, London: Martin Robertson; New York: Barnes and Noble (with J.C. Dodds).

'An Econometric Model of the UK Financial Sector: Some Preliminary Findings', an essay in H.G. Johnson and A.R. Nobay (eds), *Issues in Monetary Economics,* Oxford: Oxford University Press, February (With G. Clayton, J.C. Dodds and D. Ghosh), pp. 323–61.

Joint review of: R.E. Caves and R.W. Jones, 'World Trade and Payments: An Introduction', and W.M. Scammell, 'International Trade and Payments' (1974), *Economic Journal*, December, pp. 1032–5.

Review of: Raveendra N. Batra, 'Studies in the Price Theory of International Trade', *Journal of the Royal Statistical Society,* Series A, Part 3, pp. 450–52.

1977

Expectations, Uncertainty and the Term–Structure of Interest Rates, London: Martin Robertson; New York: Barnes and Bone (with J.C. Dodds). Paperback edition.

Review of: J. Tobin, 'Essays in Economics, Vol. 2, Consumption and Econometrics', *Kyklos*, Fasc. 3, p. 572.

1978

Review of: M. Parkin and M.T. Sumner (eds), 'Inflation in the United Kingdom', *Manchester School,* December, pp. 408–9.

Review of: W.T. Ziemba and R.G. Vickson (eds), 'Stochastic Optimisation Models in Finance' (1975), *Kyklos*, Fasc. 4, pp. 748–50.

1980

'The Stability of the Demand for Money Function and the Predictability of the Effects of Monetary Policy', *Economic Journal*, December, pp. 867–84 (with M.J. Driscoll).

Review of: J.D. Hey 'Uncertainty in Microeconomics', *Economic Journal*, September, pp. 215–31.

1982

'The Ricardian and Heckscher–Ohlin Explanations of Trade Patters: An Equivalence Theorem and its Empirical Implications', *Oxford Economic Papers,* March, pp. 1–9.

'Protection, the Value of Imports and Optimal Trade-Restricting Policies', *Weltwirtschaftliches Archiv*, Vol. 18, pp. 317–31 (with M.J. Driscoll).

'Rational Expectations, Random Parameters and the Non-Neutrality of Money', *Economica*, Vol. 49, pp. 241–48 (with D.G. Dickinson and M.J. Driscoll).

'The Aggregation Error in Divisia Monetary Aggregates: Some Findings for the UK 1963–1980', *Economics Letters*, Vol. 10, pp. 123–8. (with R.W. Bailey, M.J. Driscoll and A.W. Mullineux).

'Real Sector Parameter Instability and the Optimal Choice of Monetary Policy', *Journal of Macroeconomics,* Vol. 4, pp. 339–48 (with M.J. Driscoll).

Monetary Aggregates and Economic Policy, University of Birmingham, January (inaugural lecture, 1981).

'Monetary Aggregates and Economic Activity: A Reply', *South African Journal of Economics*, December, pp. 378–81 (with M.J. Driscoll and J.J.A du Plessis).

1983

Choice, Expectations and Uncertainty, Oxford: Basil Blackwell (Martin Robertson); New York: Barnes and Noble.

'Money, Output, Rational Expectations and Neutrality: Some Econometric Results for the UK', *Economica*, Vol. 51, pp. 259–68 (with M.J. Driscoll, A.W. Mullineux and S. Sen).

'Protection and Optimal Trade-Restricting Policies Under Uncertainty', *Manchester School*, March, pp. 21–32 (with M.J. Driscoll).

'The Gains and Losses to Predicting Nominal Income by Disaggregating via the New Classical Aggregate Supply and Rational Expectations Hypotheses', *Journal of Empirical Economics*, Vol. 8, pp. 47–58 (with M.J. Driscoll and A.W. Mullineux).

'Monetary Aggregates and Economic Activity: Reply and Rejoinder', *South African Journal of Economics*, June, pp. 318–28 and 329–33 (with M.J. Driscoll and J.J.A. du Plessis).

'Testing the Rational Expectations and Structural Neutrality Hypothesis: Some Econometric Results for Austria, 1965(1)–1974(4)', *Empirica*, No. 1, pp. 3–13 (with M.J. Driscoll, W. Kohler and A.W. Mullineux).

Review of: Robert E. Lucas, 'Studies in Business Cycle Theory', (1981), *Kyklos,* Fasc. 3, pp. 506–7.

1984

'Revenue Raising Trade-Restricting Policies under Uncertainty: The Expected Welfare Criterion and Some Safety-First Results', *Zeitschrift für Nationalökonmie,* Vol. 44, pp. 387–403 (with D.G. Dickinson and M.J. Driscoll).

1985

Protectionism, Exchange Rates and the Macroeconomy, Oxford and New York: Basil Blackwell (with S. Sen).

'The Elasticity of Prices with Respect to Monetary Components: Some Estimates for the UK', *Journal of Applied Economics*, No. 1, pp. 95–106 (with M.J. Driscoll and A.W. Mullineux).

'Monetary Aggregates, their Information Content and Aggregation Error: Some Preliminary Findings for Austria (1965–1989)', *Journal of Empirical Economics*, Vol. 10, pp. 103–25 (with M.J. Driscoll, W. Kohler and A.W. Mullineux).

'G.L.S Shackle: a Brief Bio-Bibliographical Portrait', *Journal of Economic Studies*, Special Issue on G.L.S. Shackle, Vol. 12, pp. 3–12.

'Shackle's Theory of Decision Making under Uncertainty: Synopsis and Brief Appraisal', *Journal of Economic Studies*, Special Issue on G.L.S. Shackle, Vol. 12, pp. 49–69.

Review of: Paul de Grauwe and Theory Peeters, 'Exchange Rates in Multicountry Econometric Models', *Economic Journal,* June, pp. 518–19.

Economic Choice under Uncertainty: A Perspective Theory Approach, Aldershot: Gower Press (Edward Elgar Publishing) and New York: St Martin's Press.

Review of: W.H. Buiter and R.C. Marson (eds), 'International Economic Policy Co-ordination' (1985), *Zeitschrift für Nationalökonomie,* No. 1, pp. 116– 9.

Review of: V. Bergström, S. Honkaphja, and J. Södersten (eds), 'Growth and Distribution: International Problems', *Manchester School*, March, pp. 920–24.

1988

'Money, Output, Rational Expectations and Neutrality: the Evidence for France', *Revue Economique*, May–June, pp. 364–82 (with C. Bordes, M.J. Driscoll and A.W. Mullineux).

'Tariffs, Exchange Rates and Macroeconomic Activity', in Hans Singer (ed.), *World Trade and Development*, New Delhi: A.H. Wheeler and Co., pp. 103–24 (with S. Sen).

1989

'G.L.S Shackle: A Bio–Bibliographical Study', in D. Greenaway and J. Presley (eds), *Pioneers in Modern Economics*, London: Macmillan.

Review of: C.P. Kindberger, 'International Capital Movements' (1987), *Zeitschrift für Nationalökonmie,* No. 3, pp. 320–22.

Review of: Dorian Owen, 'Money, Wealth and Expenditure: Integrated Modelling of Consumption and Portfolio Behaviour', *Economic Journal*, pp. 489–90.

1990

Current Issues on Open-Economy Macroeconomics, Paradoxes, Problems and Policies, Aldershot: Gower Press (Edward Elgar Publishing); New York: Gower Press.

'G.L.S. Shackle's Theory of Expectations: A Critical Overview', Shackle Conference, Guildford 1984, in S. Frowen (ed.), *Conference Volume*, London: Macmillan, pp. 21–46.

Time Expectation and Uncertainty in Economics: Selected Papers of G.L.S. Shackle, edited with an Introduction: Aldershot: Gower Press (Edward Elgar Publishing); and New York: Gower Press.

Review of: John D. Hey (ed.), 'Current Issues in Macroeconomics' (1989), *Manchester School*, pp. 310–11.

1991

'Uncertainty, Liquidity Preference and Portfolio Choice: Aspects of the Hicksian Approach', *Review of Political Economy*, Vol. 3, pp. 320–48, Hicks Festschrift.

1992

'Financial Innovation and Divisia Monetary Aggregates', *Oxford Bulletin of Economics and Statistics*, August (with A .W. Mullineux and W.S. Peng).

'Shackle on Expectation, Investment, the Business Cycle and Economic Development', *Review of Political Economy*, Vol. 4, Shackle Festschrift.

Index